From Grantmaker to Leader

Emerging Strategies for Twenty-First Century Foundations

Edited by
Frank L. Ellsworth
and Joe Lumarda

JOHN WILEY & SONS, INC.

Copyright © 2003 by John Wiley & Sons, Inc., Hoboken, New Jersey. All rights reserved.

Published simultaneously in Canada

For general information on our other products and services, or technical support, please contact our Customer Care Department within the United States at 800-762-2974, outside the United States at 317-572-3993 or fax 317-572-4002.

Wiley also publishes its books in a variety of electronic formats. Some content that appears in print may not be available in electronic books.

Library of Congress Cataloging-in-Publication Data:
From grantmaker to leader : emerging strategies for 21st century foundations / edited by Frank Ellsworth and Joseph Lumarda.
     p. cm.
  Includes bibliographical references.
  ISBN 0-471-38058-X (cloth : alk. paper)
     1. Endowments. 2. Endowments—United States. 3. Charitable uses, trusts, and foundations—United States. I. Ellsworth, Frank L., 1943- II. Lumarda, Joseph.

HV25 .F76 2003
361.7'632—dc21
                                                                          2002031105

Printed in the United States of America

10 9 8 7 6 5 4 3 2 1

About the Editors

Frank L. Ellsworth joined The Capital Group Companies in January 1997 where he works primarily with Capital Research and Management Company (CRMC) and Capital Guardian Trust Company (CGTC). At CRMC he oversees and coordinates CRMC's various programs and services to endowments, foundations, and other non-profit institutions. He is President and CEO of Endowments, a series of mutual funds managed by CRMC that are offered exclusively to non-profits. The American Funds Group, managed by CRMC is the third largest mutual fund complex in the United States. CRMC and its affiliates manage assets in excess of $350 billion.

Prior to joining the Capital Group, Dr. Ellsworth spent his entire career in higher education. Born and raised in the college town of Wooster, Ohio he received his A.B. *cum laude* from Adelbert College, Case Western Reserve University. He received Masters degrees from The Pennsylvania State University and Columbia University in the City of New York. He was awarded his Ph.D. from the University of Chicago. He recently was awarded the honorary degree of Doctor of Laws from Pepperdine University.

For nearly twenty-five years he combined teaching and administration at Penn State, Columbia University, and Sarah Lawrence College. For nine years at The University of Chicago he served as a dean in its law school and taught the "Great Books" course in the College. In 1979 he was hired as President of Pitzer College, the youngest President in the history of the Claremont Colleges. He is an authority in intercultural and interdisciplinary education. After twelve years in the presidency, he became President of the Independent Colleges of Southern California.

He is also active in many community affairs and serves on the Boards of Trustees of the Japanese American National Museum, Southwestern University School of Law, Pitzer College and the

Japanese Foundation for International Education. He is the Chairman of the Board of The American School of International Training in Seattle, the National Center for the Preservation of Democracy, and Global Partners in Canada. He is a member of YPO (Young Presidents' Organization).

His daughter, Kirstin, is a graduate student at Indiana University. Dr. Ellsworth currently resides in Pasadena.

Joe Lumarda has held the position of Executive Vice President for External Affairs at the California Community Foundation for the past five years. He chairs the Foundation's management team and oversees its asset development program and donor-advised fund grant making. He started at the Foundation in 1990 as a program officer in the area of children and youth, was appointed Vice President for Development in 1991, and was named Executive Vice President for External Affairs in 1997.

Joe is a board member of the Saint Joseph Health System Foundation, Southern California Association for Philanthropy, Coro Southern California, the Peter F. Drucker Graduate School of Management, and the Council on Foundation's Community Foundation Leadership Team. He is also a board member of Endowments, Inc., a mutual fund company serving nonprofit organizations nationwide.

Before coming to the Foundation, Joe served three years as an officer in the U.S. Navy, flying in the tactical navigator seat of the P-3 Orion aircraft. Prior to the Navy, he was Associate Director of Government Relations and Campaign Associate for the United Way of Orange County. He is a graduate of the Coro Foundation Orange County Public Affairs Leadership Program.

Joe received his bachelor's degree in philosophy at Saint John's Seminary College in Camarillo, California. In 1999 he attained an executive MBA at the Peter F. Drucker Graduate Management Center at the Claremont Graduate University. In 2000 Joe was named a German Marshall Fund Community Foundation Fellow. This fellowship sent him to Poland, where he studied and consulted with that country's growing community foundation movement.

Joe currently resides in Pasadena with his wife Denise and two sons, Malone and Elias.

Contents

Contents

Contents

Contents

Contents

Corpus Diem

You and Your Foundation: A Plea to "Seize the Day" before it Seizes All of Us.

How should you handle your foundation grantmaking if your investments produce a higher rate of return than you anticipated, thereby boosting your corpus to significantly higher levels? Naturally, you are likely to feel proud, even relieved, but this is the time for strong strategy rather than braggadocio. Let us assume that you favor a strategy of taking a reasonable risk on an ambitious project or two that promises to have significant positive impact on a community, group, or cause. Or perhaps, if being a strong advocate of the great philanthropist Andrew Carnegie, you concentrate on one or two major goals by emulating how Carnegie endeavored to improve the country's literacy through the building of libraries. Granted, Carnegie controlled his foundation, but it was his willingness to focus and spend money on a strong conviction that was responsible for his being revered as a champion, even a half century later.

Unfortunately, too many foundations today carry reputations more for their massive corpus rather than for their abilities to make major, positive impacts on society. Granted, it is a lot tougher for a leader who is more of a public servant or is seriously constricted by rigid rules emanating from a deceased founder of the foundation than it is for the "big boss" who controls the pot of gold; however, a strategy such as Carnegie's for a reasonable portion of corpus (therefore not held to small percentages) presents greater opportunities for creative work than making scores of small commitments that might become merely mediocre impacts at best.

Okay, Carnegie's fortune was the equivalent of multi billions of dollars today, but here is an example of a more common $10 million foundation that broke ground in 1977 with a plan to give money to nonprofit organizations at the (typical) 5 percent of their $10 million corpus, or $500,000 per year. Investing two thirds in common stocks and one third in bonds set their expectations at a 9.2 percent total annual return (a conservative long-term historical average) assuming a 5 percent fixed-income yield. This allowed the foundation to anticipate a corpus by the twentieth year of around $17 million, but which in reality benefited dramatically from unexpectedly stronger stock returns that grew the principal instead to a whopping $44 million!

Naturally, this was cause for some challenging dialogue within the foundation, where the powers that be decided to continue with their 5 percent annual grant making. Here you had assets that had risen by $37 million, yet annual grant making (*the foundation's reason for existence*) rose by only $350,000. Was that generous and effective? Should not the entity have thought bigger? They could have easily looked for a more powerful, "dream investment" and still earmarked, say, a $13.5 million reservoir to fund grants for a "rainy day" environment in which some additional grants would look mighty important (something that less fortunate nonprofits should be able to put to exceptionally good use).

Why do so many shy away from giving while they have so much? To begin with, many people simply procrastinate and/or find multiple excuses about why they are not doing more philanthropically. And many more simply ignore the goals for their special dreams and suddenly realize late into their lifetimes that they lack the energy to realize them. Others simply worry that their finances will fade away and leave them headed for poverty. Or, just the opposite, some prosperous people think that by compounding their annual returns at a very high rate, they will help society most by postponing their giving. Instead, they focus on making even more money—the bulk of which they plan to donate to charity upon their deaths.

I disagree with this, "give much later" strategy, simply because I believe strongly that it is far more effective and rewarding for the wealthy to make the bulk of their charitable donations during the prime of life rather than concentrating on making yet more money for the good of philanthropy. Most important, however, there is a hidden yet strong and compelling reason for so many of us to proceed more quickly with our intelligent grants, due to the following thesis that makes important arithmetic sense:

> Societal ills generally increase at an exponentially greater rate than does return on capital.

Even exceptional capital returns can rarely keep pace with societal problems, which if ignored, cascade through the generations, as more and more disadvantaged descendants come into the world. Even grandiose plans for a future foundation, while well intentioned, have less long-term impact on empty tummies and uneducated minds than far less money invested in charity now. Think of the many youngsters whose major problems stem from neglect, abuse, or the lack of a supportive home life. The probability of a "cure" increases dramatically the earlier they are exposed to positive environments. If not, these troubled youths often become troubled adults, who are ill equipped to provide their own children with a healthy environment, who are in turn ill equipped to help their children, as the cycle continues and expands exponentially, even with normal population growth. So, acting now versus later is a right and prudent thing, as it is a protective effort. Hence, it is important that more philanthropists think in terms of "effects on generations" realizing what is missed if plans are made too far out. We should constantly remind ourselves that our country (and others) cannot afford to neglect those who desperately need near-term, even immediate, attention.

As a philanthropic research organization committed to educating people on how to budget for charity, my firm, NewTithing Group (*http://www.newtithing.org*), estimates that households with adjusted gross incomes of $200,000 or more and assets of $500,000 or more (excluding personal homes and possessions) can comfortably afford to give substantially more to charity, including to their private foundations. In fact, our IRS-based research conservatively estimates that average households with adjusted gross incomes of $1 million or more can indeed give comfortably nearly ten times more each year to charity than they have been giving.

In planning ahead, you should consider what your actuarial lifetime is likely to be; whom you picture running your foundation; and, whether your chosen non-profit recipients will understand the urgencies that "societal ills" demand. By making significant charitable investments now through your foundation, you will be deciding what is most important—whether your legacies and others grow up in an unhealthy, unsafe, and tentative future—or in a society that has a clean, safe, and more fulfilled environment for most everyone. Making substantial charitable investments earlier rather than later can stem many "societal ills" before they have a chance to increase at an exponentially greater rate than typical returns on capital. Thus, investing more of your foundation corpus now embodies the ancient Latin adage, "Carpe Diem," "Seize the Day". . . . before it seizes all of us. Or as foundations might think of it, "Corpus Diem."

CLAUDE ROSENBERG

NewTithing Group
San Francisco
August 15, 2002

Acknowledgments

First, we want to acknowledge our authors. The reader glancing through the table of contents will see that we are fortunate to have the "best of the best" to present their ideas and strategies. Frank Ellsworth wishes to acknowledge the help of his assistant, Christine Imaoka Curry, and the support of Capital Research and Management Company, The Capital Group Companies. Joe Lumarda wishes to acknowledge the support of the California Community Foundation, in particular its president, Jack Shakely. Additionally, Joe wishes to convey his gratitude to fellow staff members at the community foundation who shared their wisdom, discriminating eye, forbearance, and good humor, in particular, Peter Dunn, Robin Kramer, Catherine Stringer, Judy Spiegel, Amy Fackelmann, and Sylvia Moraton. And, finally, a very special thanks to Joe's wife Denise and two boys Malone and Elias for their patience, care, and smiles even when dad was pounding on the computer or dragging in late.

Introduction

Remarkable changes characterized American foundations in the twentieth century. The history of that time reveals the profound impact foundations have had on our society. The history is not without controversy. The issues and themes are diverse and broad ranging. The impact of the sheer growth of the number of foundations and the substantive increase of assets remains undefined and replete with issues. The evolution of conflicting views of the relationship between public policy and attitudes toward social change could fill volumes. The maturation of the control and governance of foundations from founder to family to professionals to institutional has been bumpy and not without consequences. The constant arrival of new foundations, often entrepreneurial in nature, has provided healthy tension between classical and innovative—and occasionally radical—views of the role and influence of foundations in our society. The strong and rapid emergence of community foundations has brought growing strength to building permanent assets, strengthening the relations between philanthropic individuals and families and organizations within their communities. As community foundations strengthen the essential fabric of their communities helping all organizations gain financial foothold, they find themselves at times in conflict with commercial gift funds whose transactional nature between the donor and the organization stimulates philanthropy in a different fashion.

The Tax Reform Act of 1969 provided a huge impetus regarding the shape of philanthropy, providing new structures for the immense transfer of wealth, strengthening organizations and spawning a flood of family foundations. The specialization of foundations focusing on issues and needs has become commonplace. Themes including the reform of public education, medical education, the health sciences, AIDS, libraries, the environment, social services, the arts, and public policy, and many others are now integral to foundation life and the philanthropic dialogue. We are fortunate to have excellent histories to give us perspective on the century past, beginning with Merle Curti and Roderick Nash's *Philanthropy in the Shaping of American Education,* and continuing through the classic work of Barry Karl and Stanley Katz, "The American Private Philanthropic Foundation and the Public Sphere," and other Karl and Katz publications. For readers interested in pursing the wealth of literature available, an outstanding bibliography has been compiled by Susan Kastan, which appears in *Philanthropic Foundations: New Scholarship New Possibilities,* edited by Ellen Condliffe Lagemann.[1]

This book looks to the twenty-first century. The conversations in philanthropy today continue those from the last century while emphasizing emerging themes and issues, including the transfer of wealth, legislative concerns, IRS audits, and the role of foundations in public policy issues previously ignored, like campaign spending, accountability, planned giving, assessment of the effectiveness of giving, social responsible investment and social return on investment. Time will tell whether these issues weather the realities of time and place and translate into major ones with significant consequence for our communities. A great deal has been written on the grantmakers, although the time is here for an analysis of the commercial gift funds. And much continues to be said about the motivation of philanthropy. Mark Dowie, in *American Foundations: An Investigative History,* suggests that organized philanthropy must become more democratic, and that we are at the beginning of a fundamental shift with foundations becoming more transparent.[2] Guidestar is a much-welcomed vehicle that allows the public more scrutiny of the previously undisclosed operations for most foundations. Conversations continue about how influential and powerful foundations really are. Certainly, the assets and gifts of foundations pale in comparison with individual giving or, indeed, the trillions of dollars in government hands. Do they cater to the right? To the left? Numerous books and articles address these issues. Fast emerging into the dialogue on foundations are global foundations. The extensive bibliography of books on foundations covering these and other topics reveals that the common genre is one of narration and description, usually focusing on one aspect or theme. The reader is left with good and often interesting information but rarely with any sense of the practical implications of the information.

The purpose of this book is to move beyond information gathering and present strategies for leadership. Our audience is the practitioner: the trustee, the chief executive officer, the chief financial officer, members of the investment committee, the information and publication relations staff, the program officer, and committee members. Our audience is the people who work with foundations in a variety of roles. Our distinguished authors in this book come to the task of writing with extraordinary experiences and keen analytical abilities. But their assignment was to move to the practical. They are writing for the individual who not only wants to understand an issue, but also wants and needs to gain insight on how to deal with the issues and create strategies, whether they are of leadership or management in nature, or both. This book presents topics and issues that reflect the unspoken and spoken language of the world of foundations today with an eye toward helping the reader address them effectively. Our intent is to be pragmatic and, at times, provocative, as we attempt to provide a comprehensive and "user-friendly" guidebook for Strategy and Leadership.

The book organizes this practicum of information around three themes. We begin with Section One, "From Carnegie to Gates: The Changing Faces and Needs of Philanthropy." First, we look at family philanthropy and foundations, followed by the promise of community foundations. Given the role of the New Economy at the turn of the last century, we then look at the carryover of the impact of that period today.

Continuing themes and history from the last century, the second section addresses "The Foundation's New Reach: The Emerging Role of Leader, Communicator, and Facilitator of Change." The chapters in this section examine the Meta foundation as venture philanthropy takes a stronghold. How can foundations convey the new wealth and purpose through their messages? Is the message of a foundation important, and, if so, how can the message penetrate the media and other communication venues? Finally, we look at a classic example of how one foundation has successfully addressed public policy issues.

The third section addresses a fundamental fiduciary question which influences crucial management and leadership issues: How Do boards of directors direct foundations? What should the foundation board of the twenty-first century look like? Responsibilities? Backgrounds? What is the role of planning, and how is this accomplished through board policies and interaction with the professional staff? Who else needs to be involved? Why?

Are we in a new era where the very nature of foundations will change as a result of the projected huge transfer of wealth? Will foundations emerge as the twenty-first century passes with a stronger, more pervasive role in our societies around the world? Some would argue not, claiming that the role and influence of foundations will always at best be elitist and selective. Peter Frumkin, Harvard Professor of Public Policy, believes we are at the beginning of significant change as a new generation of visionary philanthropists ". . . signal that donors of large amounts are beginning to assert themselves as never before. This new period of personal giving is challenging us to think differently about the meaning and rationale for philanthropy." Although the editors might like to believe that Frumkin is right in his belief that "we should encourage a broad and active market of competing visions of the common good, while celebrating the huge wave of unfiltered pluralism that donor driven philanthropy is beginning to unleash on American Society," neither of us have seen in our experiences immersed in foundation management and leadership, yet more than a mild ripple in this direction.[3] However, we do subscribe to the belief about the mission of foundations articulated by Adele Simmons, Rebecca Rimel, and Peter Goldmark, whose leadership with the MacArthur, Pew, and Rockefeller Foundations give them credibility in stating:

America's independent foundations—their best—can serve four distinct ways: First they can identify nascent dangers and alert the public before such dangers reach a grave level. Second, foundations can spark initiatives to respond to these dangers. This work usually entails an examination of the root causes of problems rather than their symptoms. Third, foundations can support those who are not well represented in the mainstream of political and social discourse, ensuring that their voices are better heard. Finally, foundations can bring together the energies and talents of many diverse—sometimes adversarial—groups to build new solutions to problems.[4]

Our readers will have differing views of the present and future roles for foundations. That is understandable and the way it should be. We hope, however, that these chapters will be useful for all of us playing our respective roles in management and leadership for The Foundation of the Century.

FRANK L. ELLSWORTH
Endowments, Capital Research and Management Company
The Capital Group Companies

JOE LUMARDA
The California Community Foundation
August 15, 2002
Los Angeles, California

NOTES

1. Merle Curti and Roderick Nash, *Philanthropy in the Shaping of American Higher Education.* New Brunswick, NJ: Rutgers University Press, 1965; Barry D. Karl and Stanley N. Katz, "The American Private Philanthropic Foundation and the Public Sphere," *Minerva 19* (1981), pp. 236–70; Karl and Katz, "Foundation and Ruling Class Elites," *Daedalus 116* (Winter 1987), pp. 1–40; see also Barry D. Karl, "Foundations and Public Policy," in *Encyclopedia of the United States in the Twentieth Century,* ed. Stanley I. Kutler, 5 vols. New York: Scribner's, 1996; Susan Kastan, "Bibliography: Recent Writings about Foundations in History," in *Philanthropic Foundations: New Scholarship New Possibilities,* edited by Ellen

Condliffe Lagemann. Bloomington, IN: Indiana University Press, 1999, pp. 377–403.

2. Mark Dowie, *American Foundations: An Investigative History.* Cambridge, MA: MIT Press, 2001.

3. Peter Frumkin, "He Who's Got It Gets to Give It," *Washington Post,* October 3, 1999, p. 5.

4. Adele Simmons, Rebecca Rimel, and Peter Goldmark, *Energy Foundations,* 1991, Annual Report, p. 3.

Section One

From Carnegie to Gates: The Changing Faces and Needs of Philanthropy

CHAPTER 1

Family Philanthropy in Twenty-First Century America

by Virginia M. Esposito and Joseph Foote

PERSPECTIVES

Philanthropy in many ways starts with family. It extends from familial ties to community connections to wider society. It is often said that philanthropy is a learned behavior. The habits of the heart are almost always taught at home.

Family foundations make up almost 80 percent of all the foundations in the country. More often than not, the dynamics around the family business boardroom and the Thanksgiving table are mirrored in the formal representation of the family's philanthropy, the foundation. The individuals around those tables change, yet the vision of the founder endures. The manner in which future board members honor this vision is an ever-present issue.

No one is better suited to address this topic than Virginia Esposito and Joseph Foote. Virginia is the founding president of the National Center on Family Philanthropy. The National Center was founded to encourage families and individuals to create and sustain their philanthropic missions. A 501(c)(3) nonprofit organization, it was established in 1997 by a group of family philanthropists. It is the only national resource center that focuses solely on matters of importance to families engaged in philanthropy and their effective giving. Joe is a professional writer and editor who specializes in philanthropy and social policy.

The bedrock of American philanthropy today is the family. Families create the most giving vehicles and provide the most funding in formal philanthropy. They bring far more than money, however: they bring family resources, energy, passion, and compassion in measures that constantly refresh the field and remind us all of what philanthropy is truly about.

In sheer numbers, family foundations dwarf every other category of foundation. In aggregate assets, grants awarded, and numbers of nonprofit organizations supported, family philanthropy surpasses corporate, community, and operating foundations combined.

The Internal Revenue Service estimates that some 60,000 private foundations exist in the United States; we estimate that more than two-thirds (35,000 to 40,000) have family involvement at some level.[1] Furthermore, we estimate that most of the 30,000 private foundations created over the past 20 years likely have family involvement. Many of these are still relatively small (less than $1 million in assets), but they often grow substantially over time and particularly on the death of the founder. At least several hundred family foundations have assets of $100 million or more, and at least 20 have assets of $1 billion or more.

The story of family philanthropy begins in the earliest years of American history, when families formed the fabric of communities and family philanthropy reached into every corner of American life. From rural villages to the growing cities of the new nation, family philanthropy took shape wherever families lived, worked, and cared about their neighbors and their communities. This remarkable phenomenon became so enmeshed in American life that it hardly warranted notice.

Rather, in the past century, American philanthropy became marked—and largely defined—by the presence of a few great families with names linked to huge fortunes made in the building of American industry. Although family philanthropy involves far more than foundations, today many Americans think of these families— Ford, Rockefeller, and now Packard and Gates—as much for the foundation bearing their name as for their other works. As well known as they are to the public, however, these families represent only a tiny fraction of the number of families who support foundations and other formal giving vehicles.

As the nation enters the twenty-first century, family foundations are attracting much greater attention as one of the most powerful forces in American philanthropy. Family foundations account for much of the stability, tradition, and financial strength of grantmaking in this country. At the same time, these foundations accounts for much of the dynamic of change, the refreshment of values, and the injection of new and energetic leadership into the field of philanthropy.

Yet little attention has been paid to family philanthropy in general or to the unique nature of family foundations in particular. Myth and reality about family foundations diverge. When standard texts describe the typical family foundation, they often portray a group of wealthy but forever disagreeing people who govern erratically, manage foundation affairs haphazardly, and are amateurish in their grantmaking.

Most families in philanthropy are truly two things—they are families, with all their strengths and weakness, and they are deeply committed and passionate philanthropists. The motivation of families to engage in philanthropy is often the desire to "give back" and to continue or initiate a family tradition of formal giving. Many families find guidance in their spiritual faith.[2] Family philanthropy often involves endowing a foundation, but it also includes volunteer service, lending the family name to worthy causes, personal charitable giving, providing community support through a family business, and other expressions. Society benefits from the compassion and commitment of family philanthropy. The family receives something as well: the privilege of giving back and the joy and sense of accomplishment that attend it.

This overview makes family philanthropy sound rosy and easy. It is not, as any family in the field will attest. The founding, governance, and management of a family foundation come with an extra dimension—it's not only philanthropy but also *family* philanthropy. The founder (often a founding couple) usually considers questions such as: How do we provide for our children as we contemplate committing large sums of money to an endowment? Who among our family members, friends, and trusted advisors should be invited to sit on the board? How long should our foundation exist? How tightly should we bind the foundation to a specific mission, or should we empower future boards to modify the mission? What role do we foresee for future generations of the family in assuming responsibility to govern and manage the foundation?

Management of a family foundation is particularly fascinating. Most family foundations rely on family members to govern, manage, and administer. Typically, all board members are family, at least at startup. The founding couple sorts through grant applications and prepares a list for board review. A daughter with an MBA serves as executive director, and a nephew who is a CPA handles the books. A lawyer cousin acts as general counsel; children too young for board duty sit on an advisory committee and suggest grants in areas of concern to them. The enterprise is truly a family undertaking.

FAMILY PHILANTHROPY IS UNIQUE

Family philanthropy consists of any formal charitable activity that a family (however it defines itself) may undertake. Family philanthropy embraces weekly giving at a religious institution, year-end contributions to a public charity, or giving through a formal charitable vehicle. Before turning to the subject of this chapter, which is family foundations, it is useful to keep in mind that many and perhaps most family foundation founders employ various philanthropic vehicles in addition to their foundation.

The Hunt family of Pittsburgh, Pennsylvania, for example, demonstrates how different giving vehicles can be used for different members and generations of a family, and for different purposes. At the hub of the family's philanthropy is the Roy A. Hunt Foundation (2001 assets: $85 million), formed in 1950, located in Pittsburgh, and governed by a board consisting entirely of family members: Richard M. Hunt and his brother, three of their children, and eight nieces and nephews. They employ an executive director (who is a family member) and a program officer (who is not a family member); the family board members oversee grantmaking in education, the arts, religion, international relations, medicine, and large grants in three areas: community development, youth violence, and protection of the environment.

Richard Hunt, who is The University Marshal of Harvard University, and his wife, Priscilla Stevenson Hunt, also make use of other philanthropic vehicles. They operate their own foundation, the Miramar Fund, named after their honeymoon *albergo* in Italy; they formed this family foundation to support educational projects. Miramar is small today, but is expected to grow.

Richard and Priscilla have also set up a charitable lead annuity trust (CLAT), named Cup Clat (so named because "our cup runneth over," Richard says), which is designed to support what the couple hopes are worthy causes in the world. "Its mission is to support selected projects of our three grown children who have become astute and realistic philanthropists," Richard says. He and Priscilla channel $10,000 of the revenue to charities annually, and their three children can direct an additional $10,000 each to charities of their choice.

Two years ago, the Hunts set up the Magic Mountain Fund (named for Richard's favorite German novel, by Thomas Mann), a donor-advised fund in the Scudder Charitable Fund in New York. Starting with a corpus of $1 million, Magic Mountain now holds $2 million. The Hunts make recommendations on charitable distributions of the income and principal for grants in health care and social service. This fund provides solid growth of the corpus, flexibility in changing grantees, and a steady flow of family charitable gifts to established nonprofit organizations. Management fees are modest, Scudder performs all due diligence on prospective grantees, Scudder also satisfies all the required tax reporting obligations, and the family finds the arrangement virtually hassle-free.

"We give these highly personal and eccentric names to the funds in order to keep them straight and to be able to refer to them in a quick way," Richard Hunt observes.

Richard and Priscilla have also established two charitable remainder unitrusts that provide income to members of the family

7

during their lifetimes, with the corpus reverting to the remainder-man charities on the deaths of the donors. The donors designate where the residual funds will go.

Finally, members of the Hunt family maintain a long tradition of personal gifts to the United Way and certain nonprofit organizations, quite apart from these formal giving vehicles. "For example, my wife and I don't have time to investigate inner-city conditions in Boston," Richard Hunt says, "and United Way does. It's one-stop giving, and they can direct our gifts to our interests, which are inner-city development." The Hunts also have estate-designated gifts. And then they also each make substantial gifts by check each year to a variety of organizations, all tax exempt.

This array of giving vehicles (there are at least seven different vehicles), Richard Hunt says, offers the family many advantages: security of holdings, flexibility of grantmaking or grant recommendations, swiftness of decision making and granting, and ensured due diligence. "It's a layered approach," Hunt says. "It accommodates geographic, lifestyle, generational, and philosophical differences. Some branches of our family are committed to community development, while others are more conservative and want to support museums and established institutions. This way, we can support the full range."

"And these various giving vehicles," he adds, "help keep the family together because of the constant need to consult with each other and decide on the gifts to be made."

WHAT IS A FAMILY FOUNDATION?

A family foundation is a private foundation founded and funded by a donor or donors, in which family members—however they may define family members—play a role in governance. Trustees (by which we also mean directors of corporate-form foundations) often include nonfamily trustees, but family representation on the board is usually designed to pass into the hands of succeeding generations of that family.

This chapter focuses on the characteristics that define a family foundation and make it a special and fascinating member of the philanthropic universe. Understanding its unique characteristics is essential for anyone who is considering starting a family foundation or who would hope to obtain grants from, enter collaborations with, recruit as a member, or otherwise interact effectively with a family foundation.

DONOR AND FAMILY LEGACY ARE DEFINING FACTORS

All family foundations take their initial form from their founder's values and vision. As long as the founder remains at the helm of the foundation, he or she charts its course, decides the size of the endowment that powers grantmaking, and sets the schedule for attempting to achieve grantmaking goals. Over time, as the founder's influence wanes or ends—through retirement or death—succeeding generations take their watch over the foundation. In many cases, the family foundation becomes a family legacy—a means for giving back to society while honoring and remembering the original donor and defining the donor family.

Over the years, adherence to the goals of a family foundation's founder—even when those goals seem less important or lack popular interest—has sometimes led to dramatic changes in society's knowledge and ability to address a specific issue. Consider, for instance, what the Kennedy Foundation has accomplished in its 50-year fight to reduce the incidence of and help those diagnosed with mental retardation.

The Joseph P. Kennedy, Jr. Foundation in Washington, D.C. (2000 assets: $30 million) was established by Ambassador Joseph P. Kennedy, Sr., as a memorial to his eldest son, who was killed in action in World War II while flying a dangerous, volunteer mission in the European Theater.[3]

As a prelude to establishing the foundation, Ambassador Kennedy asked his daughter, Eunice, where she thought the foundation should concentrate its work. She asked for a year to find the appropriate field, and after extensive research, determined that mental retardation was one of the most serious unaddressed problems of American youth. Ambassador Kennedy agreed and in 1946 established the foundation and commissioned her to head it. In the half-century that followed, the Kennedy Foundation became a leader of a national and then international crusade on behalf of persons with mental retardation—first children, then adults, and now the elderly. The Special Olympics, Mental Retardation Research Centers, the National Institute of Child Health and Human Development, the University Affiliated Programs, and Head Start all owe their existence to the Kennedy Foundation.

Many foundations would have difficulty maintaining the singular focus that has defined the Kennedy Foundation. Its strength of leadership and creative decision making have maintained family interest and efforts in helping persons with mental retardation. For instance, all family members and their spouses are permitted to serve as associate trustees of the foundation and as such are able to express their philanthropic impulses and develop grantmaking skills through discretionary grants. As a result, third-generation family members have established programs such as Best Buddies, the Day Care Resource Project for Children with Special Needs, a relocation and treatment center for lead-poisoned children and their families, and a curriculum to provide physicians in training and nursing students with core knowledge of fetal alcohol syndrome and other alcohol-related birth defects.

In addition, the Foundation recently conducted a self-evaluation to determine how effective it has been in achieving its goals, what directions it might take in the future, and whether it should maintain its singular focus on issues related to mental retardation. When results of that evaluation were presented to the board and members were asked to determine future directions for the foundation, the decision was to stay the course.

The RGK Foundation chose a different course. George Kozmetsky and his wife Ronya, both Russian immigrants, were richly rewarded for George's brilliant mind and keen sense of business. After beginning his career teaching at Harvard, George joined Hughes

Aircraft, moved to start the computer wing of Litton, and later became one of the founders of Teledyne. In 1966, the Kozmetskys' daughter was diagnosed with scleroderma, a progressive disease for which there is no cure. Although that diagnosis proved wrong, it led the family to create the RGK Foundation (1999 assets: $116 million) in Austin, Texas, to support basic medical research on the disease.

Today, more than 30 years later, the RGK Foundation has broadened its focus to include innovative projects, without geographic limitations, in the areas of health, education, human services, and community affairs.

Yet another example is the Edna McConnell Clark Foundation (2000 assets: $713 million). This foundation is the product of a door-to-door book salesman, David Hall McConnell, who, in the 1880s, offered potential customers a vial of homemade perfume to encourage sales. When the perfume proved more popular than the books, McConnell formed a company, recruiting housewives as salespersons. That company eventually became Avon and was, for many years, run by Van Alan Clark, the husband of David McConnell's daughter Edna. The Clarks took some of their Avon profits and placed them into a small family foundation run by themselves and their three sons. Most early grants went to favorite charities: universities and hospitals.

In 1969, the Clarks decided to enlarge the foundation, doubling its assets through the donation of Avon stock. Their sons were charged with overseeing foundation staffing and development.

Despite the size of the foundation, the Clarks wanted to maintain their family style of a no-nonsense, no-frills approach to philanthropy. After carefully considering a wide range of possible grant-making opportunities, foundation trustees decided to concentrate grants on specific goals in four areas: the poor, children, the elderly, and the developing world.

In the past 30-some years, the foundation has made grants of more than half a billion dollars, while still maintaining the family's down-to-earth approach to philanthropy. The family still maintains a low profile, but its concern for helping the poor get a break, as Edna would put it, is translated into action daily by foundation grantees. Over the years, succeeding generations of the family have taken their places on the foundation board to continue the work and the family tradition.

Donor Goals Provide a Framework for Grantmaking

A donor's values, as imbedded in the foundation's charter and transmitted to family members, provide the framework for a family foundation's philanthropy. Trustees of many private independent foundations endeavor to interpret and apply the donor's purpose to current grantmaking, of course, but a family foundation donor's values have a direct, personal tie to family-member trustees that gives added meaning.

Upholding the Donor's Philosophy

Established in 1917, the Bothin Foundation (2000 assets: $42 million) was easily run by its founder Henry Bothin, his wife, and his daughter, all of whom lived in San Francisco. Today, four generations later, the family is much larger and no longer fully based in the city of its founder. The founder left no specific vision for the foundation, except the record of his grantmaking and his personal values.

Three Bothin descendants still reside in San Francisco but the others now live in New York and New Mexico. Henry Bothin's great grandson believes that the foundation helps his family bridge the geographic and generational distances. In his words, "One benefit of the foundation is that it keeps the family together. It gives us a reason to meet and brings us into the same room to discuss the same causes. Our family is very proud of the legacy of our foundation and what it has done for the community. At nearly every meeting a family member will say, 'Henry Bothin would have liked this grant,' or 'What would Henry have done in a case like this?'"

George Gund provided a clearer vision. He spent most of his adult life in Cleveland, Ohio. It was there that he became president and later chairman of the board of The Cleveland Trust Company. It was there that he raised his family. It was there that he began to devote his time and some of his wealth to philanthropy. And, it was there that in 1952 he created the George Gund Foundation (2000 assets: $447 million).

When the Gund Foundation was established, the donor's four sons and two daughters were too young to take trustee positions; thus, Gund asked several close associates to serve on his foundation board. Since that time, family members have taken their places as trustees and today lead one of the largest family foundations in the country.

From its inception, the Gund Foundation limited funding to grantees in the northeastern Ohio and greater Cleveland area. Although none of the Gund family trustees now resides in Cleveland, the foundation has not moved. To keep family members apprised of the needs of the city, all trustee meetings are held in Cleveland, and each meeting includes broad discussions of Cleveland matters. In addition, trustees are expected to take an extra day for a more intensive regimen of meetings and site visits to projects that have been funded.

Founders Often Address Philanthropic and Family Goals Simultaneously

Part of the balance involved in managing a family foundation is that the donor often brings two goals to the enterprise: to do something good for the family (create a formal giving vehicle) and to do something good for the community (however the donor chooses to define that term). The donor-founder of a private independent foundation is typically concerned only with the latter goal. For a family foundation, this duality of goals sets up a creative tension that may cause problems for some families and become the source of enormous energy in others.

The Stoneman Family Foundation, formerly the Anne and David Stoneman Charitable Foundation, in Boston is a prime example of this duality. Established in 1957 by Sidney Stoneman, cofounder of the General Cinema movie chain and an honorary director of Harcourt General, this foundation (1999 assets: $26 million) initially provided support for organizations selected by the founder.

For more than 30 years, it supported institutions such as the Boston Symphony Orchestra, hospitals, and Jewish organizations in the founder's home city.

When Mr. Stoneman decided to bring his daughters and grandchildren into the foundation, however, he discovered that they had very different philosophies about grantmaking. The children and grandchildren wanted a nontraditional approach, preferring to fund grassroots organizations that serve impoverished populations in the South—the home of both daughters and most of their children. To address his philanthropic goals and his desire to bring his family into the organization, Mr. Stoneman and the foundation board worked out a power-sharing arrangement that reserved half the foundation's annual giving exclusively for organizations chosen by him and his wife and the remainder for competitive grant proposals for fledgling health, education, and social service organizations in the communities where his children and grandchildren reside.

The Stackpole-Hall Foundation was formed in 1951, with its original donors, Lyle G. Hall, Sr., and two cousins, J. Hall Stackpole and Harrison C. Stackpole, as trustees. The founders saw their foundation both as a means for returning some of what their community had given them and as a way to ensure that they and their descendents would remain active participants in community life. Over the years, fewer and fewer descendants of the Stackpoles and Halls remained in Elk County, Pennsylvania, which had produced their family fortune. Still, their foundation and family responsibility for its stewardship remained.

By the early 1990s, foundation trustees were looking for ways to interest the 19 members of the extended family in both the concerns of northwestern Pennsylvania and the foundation. To surmount the problem of geographic connection, trustees added an adjunct board of six young family members and enlarged the foundation's planning committee by adding four community representatives. To increase family interest, the board designated 10 percent of annual distributable funds (after expenses) for matching grants to be made by trustees and family members to organizations in their own communities. By giving family members new eyes and ears in the foundation's community and by offering them the opportunity to help organizations in their own communities, the Stackpole-Hall Foundation bridged both geographic and generational issues. The foundation (1999 assets: $29 million) makes grants for local projects, but some also go for educational, healthcare, cultural, youth development, social welfare, and community development needs in the areas where branches of the family now reside.

CREATING A COMMUNITY OF CONCERN: REFLECTIONS OF A FAMILY FOUNDATION TRUSTEE

David Dodson, a trustee of the Mary Reynolds Babcock Foundation, a family foundation in North Carolina, and a close observer of the Irwin-Sweeney-Miller family giving programs in Indiana, observes that a family's values and motivations are critical to the family foundation. But, he continues, the great purpose of a family foundation should not be the perpetuation of family interests but the impulse to be of value to something beyond the family circle.

Dodson believes that what characterizes the two family foundations he knows best are the curiosity and compassion with which they approach their foundation work. What families choose to commit to and support should reflect their passions, he advises. But it doesn't end there. Dodson encourages creative family foundations to ask themselves how they can take what they care about and use it to build a community of concern that is alert and responsive to changing circumstances. What the family knows and loves is the logical place to begin a rich process of philanthropic inquiry into what the community needs and how they can serve it.

Dodson notes that the Miller and Babcock families don't seek to perpetuate old ways of doing things but strive in each generation to understand the needs and opportunities facing their communities of interest. The issues may change or they may stay the same, but what a family foundation perpetuates is their posture of caring and compassion.

Dodson observes that the family foundation that is able to construct a view of their giving with the community to be served firmly in the center is able to surround that core with an even more vibrant family circle. He says that such families are motivated to be of service outside the family and are likely to be both curious and compassionate in identifying ways to use the assets they have.

Those assets may even include advisors and networks outside the immediate family. He cites his fellow Babcock trustee, Carol Zippert, and her assertion that family foundations can include those who are members of the "family of blood" and those who are members of the "family of the heart"—related by interests and values but not genealogy. But, he cautions, if families think a foundation may be the instrument to save a troubled family, this is not it.

Family Values Shine through Their Philanthropy

Family foundations significantly define the landscape of American philanthropy at the local level. Most are small, family managed, and very close to their grantees.

The residents of Greenwood, South Carolina, know about family foundations. In 1942, James C. Self established the Self Family Foundation for the sole purpose of building and administering a hospital for the area. At the time, Mr. Self was the founder and president of Greenwood Mills, a corporation with plants in South Carolina, Georgia, Tennessee, and other parts of the world. When Mr. Self died in 1954, his son, Jim, took over the foundation. Ten years later, the foundation gave the hospital to the county and focused on support of health care and education.

In 1995, when Jim Self decided it was time for the next generation to take over the foundation, he sent members of that generation on a retreat—which he did not attend—to begin to find their own way. The result was a new, more proactive and more strategic stance toward grantmaking. The foundation (2000 assets: $53 million) shifted its focus more to primary prevention and community wellness and early childhood development and elementary education. Still, the new board decided to stick with the original donor's intent of supporting health care and education, encouraging self-sufficiency, and helping people help themselves.

The foundation now states its belief that a family foundation serves as a vehicle to strengthen family identity and cooperation, promote importance of working together to continue the family heritage of service to the community, and provide an opportunity to practice democracy within the family that cuts across family branches. With this belief in mind, the trustees established an Adjunct Board composed of members of the fourth generation of the Self family over 18 years of age. The Adjunct Board is developing its own funding guidelines consistent with those of the foundation, and will consider proposals and receive grants up to 5 percent of annual payout requirements.

While the Selfs are working in a small rural area, the family of Hattie Strong is making small steps toward educating Americans through the Hattie M. Strong Foundation (2000 assets: $32 million) in Washington, D.C. Hattie Strong's story is the American dream. A well-educated woman with a failed marriage moves her young son to Alaska to make her fortune in the Gold Rush. Five years later, they return to New York where she marries a buggy whip manufacturer in Rochester. Hattie Strong's new husband, one of the founders of Strong & Eastman (the forerunner to Eastman Kodak) dies within eight years, leaving her with a stake in the company. She does something that was likely unheard of at that time. In 1928, Hattie Strong established a foundation to help people less fortunate—a foundation she continued to run for the remainder of her life.

For more than 70 years now, the Strong Foundation has provided interest-free loans to students in their final year of college. To date, the foundation has given out thousands of loans, and 96 percent have been repaid in full.

Hattie Strong's son and grandson have led the foundation with help first from Hattie Strong's secretary, then the secretary's daughter and granddaughter. These two families continue to follow the foundation guidelines established by Hattie Strong, serving their community and their founders' needs and vision.

Styles of Giving Often Evolve over Time

Families in philanthropy today typically select carefully from among available giving vehicles. Donors typically start by writing checks to favorite charities from their own funds or through the family business. They later add more formal structures, perhaps setting up an endowment at a school or forming a donor-advised fund. They may form a private foundation. Ultimately, as the example of Richard and Priscilla Stevenson Hunt demonstrated earlier in this chapter, a family may operate multiple philanthropic vehicles, depending on the donor's goals and the family's circumstances.

Rockefeller Generations Use Own Vehicles

The Rockefeller family had shown remarkable ingenuity and flexibility in choosing giving vehicles to suite the needs of successive generations.

This world-famous philanthropic dynasty was founded by John D. Rockefeller Sr., who established the Rockefeller Foundation in 1913 and set the style of family giving by specifying that grants—through a written foundation mission—would be used "for the well-being of people throughout the world." Under a board made up predominantly of family members, the foundation set its sights high; in the 1920s, for example, it funded research that won a Nobel Prize in Medicine for developing preventive measures that virtually eradicated yellow fever from the face of the earth.

John D. Rockefeller, Jr., followed in his father's footsteps, overseeing management of the foundation for many years. In 1940, he formed the Rockefeller Brothers Fund to enable his five sons and daughter—the grandchildren of John D. Sr.—to share a source of philanthropic advice and research on charitable activities and combine some of their philanthropic efforts to better effect.

To accommodate a more specialized set of issue interests among some of the 54 "cousins" of the fourth generation, the family founded the Rockefeller Family Fund in 1952, to support a wide range of environmental, political participation and reform, women's rights, and other domestic activist-oriented nonprofit groups, to help nonprofits operate more effectively, and to enable them to gain greater financial self-sufficiency.

In 1986, when the cousins expressed the need for advice on individual giving, the family formed the Philanthropic Department of the Rockefeller Family Office. That organization consolidates expertise in advising the cousins, their offspring (the fifth generation), and other family members in their individual giving. In 1991, a public charity, The Philanthropic Collaborative (TPC), was formed to enable family members to use the flexible giving options created by donor-advised funds. Collaborative projects were an especially important goal that TPC facilitated. TPC's donor advised funds also have been used for international donations, and for special projects such as supporting incubator efforts (the Earth Fund is an example). TPC became an integral part of the services offered by the Philanthropy Department, whose staff managed it. (As a public charity, TPC had its own board.) Some cousins and other family members also retain their own philanthropic advisors.

Around the same period, the Philanthropy Department began offering its services to other families—including management of family foundations and trusts, management of donor-advised funds, advice on individual donor programs, and management of special projects. By 2001, 35 percent of its clients were from outside the Rockefeller family members

In January of 2002, the Philanthropy Department and TPC merged into the newest Rockefeller philanthropic entity—an independent nonprofit called Rockefeller Philanthropy Advisors that combines the practical services of the philanthropy department and TPC with the strong Rockefeller family commitment to improving philanthropy.

For five generations, and now into the sixth, the Rockefeller Family has shown remarkable broadness of thinking, over-the-horizon vision, and the ability to deal with internal cross-currents of family concerns and beliefs.

They have moved forward, generation after generation, on the solid ground of values that are universal, offer broad latitude for freedom of activity and expression, encourage diversity, are nonjudgmental, and focus on the family as the primary concern. The generation in power understands the learning process: it allows the next generation to make mistakes as well as achieve successes. The family encourages risk and accepts what risk may bring.

Foundations Sometimes Find New Life as Donor-Advised Funds

Joseph and Mary Nord Ignat were long-time residents of Oberlin, Ohio. "They died at a young age, but had they lived, they would have done something like this in their later years," says their daughter-in-law Eleanor Ignat. Eleanor Ignat and her husband David established the Joseph and Mary Nord Ignat Fund in memory of his parents, deciding on a donor-advised fund in the Community Foundation of Greater Lorain County, Ohio, as their host organization, even though they live in Vermont.

"We feel we are giving something to the area where the family started," Eleanor Ignat says. "My husband's grandfather was founder of the Nordson Corporation in Amherst, Ohio, and he always set aside profits to give to the local community. As years went on, he established the Nord Family Foundation (2000 assets: $90 million). The family has a long tradition of being very active in Northern Ohio philanthropy and, through the Nord Family Foundation, throughout the country. Now we can continue the tradition ourselves."

More and more host organizations of advised funds now provide special services to families in hopes of attracting their "philanthropic dollars"—some of which came from family foundations. One example is the New World Foundation, an endowed public charity (2000 assets: $41 million). It began life as a private family foundation, but converted about 5 years ago when the family decided they could accomplish foundation goals better in the public charity format. The Foundation is committed to social justice and an environmentally sensitive agenda, and its staff has significant expertise in these areas of grantmaking.

Currently, the Foundation manages several large donor-advised funds and pooled donor-advised funds (referred to as "donor circles") with 10 to 15 donors in each pooled fund. The Foundation advises large donors on grantmaking without charging a fee. According to Foundation president Colin Greer, the reason for no-fee advice is, "Our concern is to maximize the money that goes to specific concerns."

In 1953, Frederick Henry Leonhardt founded the Leonhardt Foundation, a private family foundation incorporated in the state of New York. The history of the Leonhardt Foundation stands as an example of how the philanthropic vehicles of a private family foundation, and of a donor-advised fund within a community foundation, can both be utilized when second- and third-generation family members find themselves in an environment of differing geographic and philanthropic interests.

In 1987, the board of the Leonhardt Foundation decided to allow a third-generation family member to establish a separate private family foundation. This process can be arduous and often requires the help of an attorney to create the new private family foundation vehicle. As a result of this division process, the Dorothea L. Leonhardt Foundation was established and the name of the Leonhardt Foundation was changed to the Frederick H. Leonhardt Foundation (aka, the FHL Foundation). In 1997, the board of the FHL Foundation decided to allow second- and third-generation family members to establish their own donor-advised funds within the Fairfield County Foundation in Connecticut. In comparison to the complexity often associated with creating a new private family foundation, a donor-advised fund within a community foundation can often be setup by simply establishing and entering into a fund agreement,and then making a grant to the managing agency of the donor-advised fund.

Regardless of the vehicle used—private family foundation or donor-advised fund—the granting organization must take the usual and necessary steps to determine that the distribution qualifies under IRS guidelines governing such charitable gifts. An attorney or accountant familiar with the operation of private foundations may be called upon to help with these determinations. Frederick H. Leonhardt, grandson of the founder of the Leonhardt Foundation and now president of the FHL Foundation, cautions, "In either case, these are not decisions that should be taken lightly." Mr. Leonhardt continues by pointing out that, in the case of donor-advised funds, "a philanthropist gives up a certain amount of philanthropic freedom and control." Mr. Leonhardt also suggests that these types of decisions be made in the light of the original donor's vision of philanthropy.

Next Generation of Governance Is a Major Concern

Boards of private independent foundations typically become self-perpetuating, with a board committee assuming charge of recruiting new members. Family foundation boards usually recruit new members from within the family. The new generation is often devotedly committed to the family charitable legacy begun by the donor. The new generation may revisit the question of why the foundation exists, and in so doing may revitalize it for contemporary times. Some may assert new values and interpret the donor's purpose in a new light. The new generation may face formidable challenges resulting from geographic dispersion or diverging interests of its members or from a rising number of family members eligible for a limited number of trustee positions.

Also, the architecture of a family's philanthropy often changes as members pass on, move to distant places, or lose interest. Most families undertake their charitable giving with a powerful understanding of the role of philanthropy in American society, and with a keen appreciation of the stewardship they exercise over the foundation and its assets. For many families, the architecture may change but that understanding and appreciation remain. In some cases, however, the family may split the foundation into one or more pieces, or dissolve it and form several donor-advised funds. New generations with new ideas inevitably assume governance responsibilities.

Finding Common Ground Can Be Rewarding

Although some families have no difficulties agreeing on what issues or causes their foundation should support, instances arise where generational differences are significant. This was the case with the Gilbert and Jaylee Mead Family Foundation of Washington, D.C. (1999 assets: $11 million). When the Foundation was established in 1989, the founders, Gilbert and Jaylee Mead, were interested mainly in supporting nonprofit organizations involved in the performing arts. When the couple's three children became active foundation board members, however, it soon became apparent that their interests centered more on social issues such as education, parenting, and poverty. In addition, individuals within the family often held different views. For instance, two family members proved to be strongly pro-choice, while one was pro-life. As a result, although individual family members are always free to support issues in which family views are split, the Foundation never funds programs on either side of a contentious issue.

It is because of this type of generational accommodation that all members of the Mead family have remained active in the Foundation for the past decade, including one branch of the family that must travel from France to attend meetings twice a year. As Jaylee Mead reports, "The simple process of working with each other, reviewing and writing letters, evaluating proposals, and discussing issues, has taught us so much about each other. We have gotten to know our children much better than we ever would have without the foundation. We now understand the way they think and their interests. The foundation has provided a common bond for our family."

Bringing a New Generation Onboard and Revisiting Roots

In the late 1980s, the Meadows Foundation of Texas (1999 assets: $901 million) identified succession as an issue that needed to be addressed. At the time, a number of Meadows Foundation board members that had received lifetime appointments from the Foundation founders Algur Hurtle and Virginia Meadows, who were over 75 years of age. With nearly 65 living members of the family's first, second, third, and fourth generations, the foundation's board recognized the need to prepare family members, over the age of 21, for the leadership roles they might potentially play on the board in the near future.

The Meadows Foundation addressed the issue of succession planning by first taking family members back to their roots at the gravesite of the founder's parents in Vidalia, Georgia. There, they talked about family traditions, identified the values that led the founder to create a foundation to dedicate his wealth to benefit others and entrust that responsibility to the members of his family. Next, the family traveled to Savannah for a three-day retreat that included discussions of the work of the foundation, exercises designed to enable different generations to share their perceptions of the world and the needs of others, and engaged in efforts to prioritize areas for future funding.

When this and other initial training sessions were completed, family members were given three-year appointments to foundation committees created to look at issues affecting the main areas of the foundation's giving interests. Different committees examined the current and future challenges facing the arts, social services, health, education and other civic and societal concerns. The committees were generally headed by a board members, met at least once a year, received reports, and heard from leading authorities on issues affecting their field of interest. At the end of three years, the trainees were rotated to new committees, where they began the process again. When foundation leaders sensed that trainees were ready, they were placed on board policy committees that were charged with recommending foundation policy positions and actions to the board.

The final phase of the effort was to move some of the individuals onto the board as older members retired. Over the course of this process about one-half of the board membership changed. These changes, which eventually included the selection of a new foundation president, were handled objectively and thoughtfully throughout. As retired president Curtis W. Meadows, Jr., recalls: "The process we went through served as a reminder of the tremendous trust that had been given to us. We honored that trust through performance, understanding that it involved a blending of business as well as family needs and capacities. We addressed succession issues recognizing our duty to family, the donor, and the public trust placed in the board. Succession isn't just a matter of a family resolving power-sharing and leadership selection issues, it is a matter of a family looking at its responsibilities to the public as well."

The Generational Divide Cannot Always Be Crossed

Regardless of whether a family foundation is involved, many siblings go their own ways once parents die—even when no money is involved. The situation is no different in the family foundation arena. Sometimes a family simply cannot come together under a common mission. This was the situation within the Kerr Foundation, Inc. Two problems arose when foundation governance passed to the four children of the donors. First, some of the children no longer lived in Oklahoma City, Oklahoma, where they were raised. Second, opinions were divided about investing and grantmaking. For example, one sibling had reservations about investing in defense industry stocks and wanted grantmaking to focus on sustainable agriculture. Unable to come to agreement, the four siblings resolved that the best solution was to break the foundation into four separate foundations, each located in the community of one of the siblings. (At the time of the split in 1985, assets were $77 million.) The four foundations now operate alone and in collaboration with each other, and, according to Sheryl V. Kerr, president of one of the resulting funds, the Grayce B. Kerr Fund (1998 assets: $35 million) in Easton, Maryland, the division of the foundation "actually resulted in greater unity within the family, not in separation."

THE NATURE OF THE FAMILY ENTERPRISE

Foundations Get Their Start in Many Ways

A family foundation is a dynamic, changing organism that reflects highly individualistic goals, values, and assets—both in terms of family members and investment portfolio. During their early life, most family foundations are an extension of the founder's philanthropy, often run as a family enterprise, staffed by the donor and family members, and encouraged by trusted friends or associates people who care passionately about foundation purposes.

Much like the Gilbert and Jaylee Mead Family Foundation, which is operated informally by the donors and their children from the donors' home, the first-generation, donor-run family foundation is not likely to be a formal bureaucratic organization, staffed by professionals who process grant applications and write checks to grantees. In general, it is not until a family foundation has an asset base of more than $10 million that it begins to employ staff.[4] At that point, the smallest family foundations employ one or two staff members: Foundations with assets of between $50 million and $100 million tend to employ three or more staff members.

There are even examples, such as the McKay Foundation in San Francisco, in which the dynamics of family philanthropy operate in reverse. The McKay Foundation owes its existence not to its "founder" Robert L. McKay, Sr., but to his son Rob. Robert McKay founded the Taco Bell restaurant chain, which, in the late 1970s he sold to PepsiCo. Rob McKay found his calling in the nonprofit world, cutting his teeth in nonprofit organizations in California and Chicago area while earning a master's degree in urban policy.

When Rob McKay approached his father about establishing a foundation, his father agreed to back him and serve on the board if Rob did all of the work of setting up and running the foundation. The foundation (1999 assets: $7.8 million) makes grants to organizations that work for social justice and equality in urban and rural areas of California. Robert McKay and his wife sit on the foundation board, and Rob runs the foundation while also serving in a leadership position at the Vanguard Foundation—a public foundation in San Francisco.

The experiences of George N. Boone and his family foundation are more typical. In 1983, on the advice of his lawyer, George Boone established the Boone Foundation (1999 assets: $2.3 million) in San Marino, California. Neither he nor the other foundation trustees—his wife, his three children, and six legal and financial advisors—knew how to run a foundation or where to learn the skills needed to operate in the philanthropic world. Boone recalls: "For the first two years we sat around the table not knowing what to do. We wrote checks to well-known organizations and found that it was neither satisfying nor different from what we had done on our own." Six years later, Boone had a chance meeting with the trustee of another foundation, who in turn, introduced him to the philanthropic community. Shortly thereafter, the family began to educate itself about grantmaking, honed a mission statement, and pared down its board to include family members only (a five-trustee advisory committee was created to accommodate nonfamily trustees).

In the early years, George Boone ran the foundation, but eventually he turned that over to a son, Nick, who was already experienced in nonprofit work. Today, George Boone reports: "We don't just give money, we provide technical assistance. Our enjoyment comes from conducting site visits and getting to know the people in our community. For us, that's one of the biggest rewards of our grantmaking."

Grantmakers such as Robert McKay and George Boone view grantseekers with special concern, for they are carrying out the donor's purposes. Because of this dynamic, service organizations and support groups often make special efforts to recognize family foundations for what they are. Membership organizations, regional associations of grantmakers, affinity groups, and other service and support groups frequently go out of their way to understand and accommodate family foundations.

Associations of Grantmakers Provide Resources

Throughout the country, family foundations are looking to associations of grantmakers for assistance with their philanthropic enterprises. The Donors Forum of Chicago is one of them. The Forum is dedicated to encouraging philanthropy guided by the values of openness, accessibility, ethical conduct, and sensitivity to the diverse population of the community. About a third of the Forum's members are family foundations, and family foundations are the fastest growing, most active membership category of the organization.

One reason why family foundations turn to the Forum is that it offers resources specifically geared to helping families who are establishing their mission, writing grantmaking guidelines, setting program priorities, and attending to other aspects in foundation operations. Foundations can attend Forum educational programs, conduct research at its extensive library, seek assistance from staff, or obtain referrals to persons at other foundations who can help with a particular issue.

Families receive the Forum's members and partners directory; a directory of Illinois foundations; a biannual survey of nonprofit organizations that are conducting capital and endowment fundraising campaigns; a newsletter; and a philanthropic database of members' grantmaking activities.

Families can also participate with other families in such Forum activities as small breakfasts, peer network discussions on collaborations, and grantmaking challenges, as well as more formal half-day workshops for family foundation donors and trustees.

Northern New Mexico Grantmakers Provides an Informal Network

Fully half of the members of Northern New Mexico Grantmakers are family foundations. Membership is open to most types of grantmaking institutions, with one caveat: Every member foundation is encouraged to make some grants in New Mexico. Family members have access to: roundtable discussions on subjects of grantmaking such as the environment, public schools, or social services, etc.; opportunities for professional development; and a resource center that includes models for grant guidelines, management policies, governance documents, grantmaking evaluation materials, and other related materials.

Because a growing number of families with foundations come to Santa Fe seasonally, the RAG provides a private setting to meet peers and discuss issues in grantmaking. Moreover, it offers an opportunity to learn about and participate in the betterment of the local community and New Mexico as a whole.

Privacy Is Sometimes an Issue

Like other people who are (or are perceived to be) wealthy, families with philanthropies are sometimes concerned about their privacy and safety. They share general concerns with others who are associated with grantmaking: concern about being besieged with requests for grants, about the impact on their personal lives of being known as a foundation person, and about unwarranted scrutiny of foundation affairs.[5]

Families with philanthropies must cope with two additional concerns that arise from their identification with philanthropy and, by extension, with perceived wealth. First, they worry that family matters, often mingled with foundation matters, will become public knowledge. They fear that family confidences, aired in board discussions and among family members, will be disclosed.

Second, they fear for their personal safety and security. Such fears lead some donors not to name the foundation after the family, and others to take measures to stay out of the limelight.

Current literature, which sometimes portrays donor families as aloof from or dismissive of the public, misconstrues families that are secretive or operate in semi-anonymity. These families care just as much as other people in philanthropy; they may even pay an extra price for their generosity, and it seems reasonable for them to try to keep that price as low as possible. While accepting the consequences of stewardship, they still seek to be free to operate privately in the public interest. After all, the donor's goals and money, which have always been extremely personal within the family, are now matters of public scrutiny because the law requires it. Many families find this dimension of foundation life very stressful. Thus, some families limit communication to the required minimum.

This preoccupation with privacy can, of course, guide how a family philanthropy conducts trustees' relations with the community, with foundation colleagues, and even with each other.

Some Families Are Public About Their Philanthropy

All that said, a significant number of family philanthropies make no bones about taking a decidedly public stance. Some are passionate about their mission and want to broadcast their passion to the community as a whole. Others understand that they may be role models and accept that responsibility; a number of women in family philanthropy have been very public about their work in hopes of inspiring other women to do the same. Indeed, some family philanthropists simply desire recognition.

Even families that are public about their philanthropy may limit intrusions by using a post office box, a business telephone, and perhaps a personal assistant to screen calls and keep boundaries between private and public life in good repair.

When Family and Foundation Interests Differ

Trustees of all family foundations are prohibited by federal law from engaging in certain activities, even when those activities might benefit the foundation. For instance, federal law on self-dealing prevents family members from becoming involved in certain foundation business. In addition state fiduciary law holds trustees to strict adherence to rules of prudent care of assets. This legal regulation seems restrictive to some families who operate foundations, but on balance most families are able to use their own members as foundation resources within the federal rules.

To preserve the integrity of private foundations and to minimize the possibility of private abuse, federal tax laws impose on private foundations a number of operational restrictions that do not apply to public charities.[6] For the most part, these restrictions do not involve the application of subjective arm's-length standards and are not a function of fairness, equity, or reasonableness. Indeed, these restrictions involve inflexible rules and absolute prohibitions. Applied automatically, without regard to benefit or detriment to the private foundation, they afford little or no opportunity for the Internal Revenue Service (IRS) or a private foundation to exercise judgment or discretion.

A prohibition against *self-dealing* is among the restrictions that apply to private foundations. Under these rules, certain transactions are absolutely prohibited, even if the foundation will benefit from the transaction. These stringent rules reflect Congress' concerns that certain private foundations had been operated for personal gain and that the IRS had difficulties in determining whether transactions between foundations and their donors, directors, or managers truly occurred at arm's length.

What Is Self-Dealing?

Self-dealing is defined as almost all business and financial transactions between a private foundation and its "disqualified persons"—a broad category of foundation "insiders" that includes contributors to the foundation, its trustees and managers, and certain public officials. In general, rules against self-dealing prohibit the following transactions between private foundations and disqualified persons:

- The sale, exchange, or lease of property;
- The loan of money or extension of credit;
- The furnishing of goods, services, or facilities;
- Compensation or payment of expenses by the private foundation to a disqualified person;
- The transfer to, or use by or for the benefit of, a disqualified person, of foundation income or assets; and
- Payments to government officials.

Penalty for Self-Dealing

Self-dealing restrictions are enforced through the imposition of penalty taxes on disqualified persons and foundation managers who participate in acts of self-dealing. In general, a penalty tax of 5 percent of the amount involved in each act of self-dealing is imposed for each year or partial year until the self-dealing is corrected in accordance with IRS requirements.

Correcting an act of self-dealing involves undoing the transaction—to the extent possible—and placing the foundation in a financial position that is no worse than it would have been in if the disqualified person had been dealing under the highest fiduciary standards. An additional penalty tax of 2.5 percent of the amount involved is imposed on any foundation manager—officer, director, or trustee—who knowingly, willfully, and without reasonable cause, participates in an act of self-dealing.

Families Work to Avoid Self-Dealing

Foundation managers, officers, directors, and trustees take federal and state mandates against self-dealing seriously. Some, such as the Surdna Foundation, give trustees written statements of foundation values and work as well as a description of how board members are expected to behave with regard to the foundation. Many family foundation boards adopt self-dealing and conflict-of-interest statements.

FOUNDATION OPERATIONS VARY WIDELY

How, by whom, and from what location a family foundation conducts its philanthropy are features that often set it apart from other private giving entities. Many family foundations operate without formal bureaucracy, paid staff, or dedicated office space. Family members may conduct foundation functions in different parts of the country—and sometimes the world—from other family members and the populations they serve while also attending to their own professional and family responsibilities. Thus, for family foundations, administration and grantmaking processes sometimes require solutions that are specifically tailored to the needs and traditions of donor families and the distances they must cross to accomplish their foundation mission and goals.

Operating At a Distance Requires Ingenuity

Most of today's baby boomers grew up with family down the street, across town, or maybe in the next county or in an adjoining state. Their children are now lucky if family is within a few hours on the highway or by air. Families have gone the way of the economy—global.

When it comes to philanthropic work, private foundations can select board members who live conveniently near a foundation office, but family foundations often want to include trustees because they are family members, regardless of where they live. Family foundations deal with geography in a number of ways. Some, like the Laird Norton Endowment Foundation (1999 assets: $5.5 million) in Seattle change their mission.

Board members of Laird Norton live in Maine, Michigan, Utah, and Washington State. Originally, the foundation funded religious and educational institutions, primarily in Minnesota where the family had a lumber business. Over time, that mission was widened to include grantmaking in other states where the family had forestry interests and then changed to support forestry education and conservation programs. In 1994, feeling that foundation grantmaking had become "drive-by philanthropy," Patrick de Freitas, a family member, became board president. Over the next three years, he helped the family focus its mission more narrowly on standards for sustainable forestry. De Freitas says that foundation board members "now know more about sustainable forestry than half the foresters in the country, and that makes us feel good." As an added plus, board members are better informed, board debates are more stimulating, and members are more interested in attending board meetings.

Increasingly, telecommunications technology is being used to bridge the distance between geographically separated families. Trustees of many private foundations now communicate by e-mail as well as telephone and fax, but family foundations often find the new technologies have special relevance when frequent in-person gatherings are impossible. For instance, a few years ago sending board members information on management and grants was a time-consuming, paper-heavy process. Today, it is both faster and cheaper—when someone like de Freitas is at the helm.

De Freitas remembers the amount of time he once spent duplicating packets to mail to his nine-member board. Now, his principal means of shipping information is e-mail over the Internet. He uses e-mail to send reports of foundation activities and assets, share his ideas on such topics as board development, and keep the board informed on foundation areas of interest.

Family foundations are also using their Web sites both to inform and help prospective donors determine if their projects might be considered for funding. The technologically sophisticated Beveridge Foundation created a website that guides grantseekers through a series of screens to determine whether they fit the foundation's guidelines. Every proposal received must have a board member serve as its sponsor, and grantseekers who are eligible fill out a preliminary grant proposal on the Web site—preliminary proposals are automatically forwarded to the trustee in the grantseeker's geographic area. The trustee logs onto the website, reviews the preliminary grant proposal, and indicates on the website whether the grantseeker should receive a formal grant proposal package to submit and whether the trustee will serves as an advisor or sponsor. The Beveridge Foundation office is automatically notified by e-mail of all grantseekers who have passed the preliminary grant proposal phase. The office sends out formal proposal packages by regular mail. All remaining grantmaking processes—site evaluations, etc.—are conducted in the usual way.

The Beveridge Foundation also uses instant messenger services to conduct multi-person discussions online and maintains a secure, private website where board members can keep appraised of internal affairs, rejected proposals, foundation assets, and other foundation news.

Streamlining Grantmaking Is a Goal

Imagine family members sitting around at home or in the family business office screening grant applications. Perhaps one member is tasked with preparing packets of potential grantees and sending them by mail or electronically to all trustees. Perhaps the family has adopted a policy of reading every grant application carefully and responding in writing. Maybe the family uses sophisticated grants management techniques and technologies, but maybe it doesn't. If grant applications rise in number, the family may decide against receiving unsolicited proposals altogether. Geographically dispersed board members who are charged with administering a family foundation use a variety of methods to inform, improve, and simplify their grantmaking.

Rotating Board Meetings Help Inform Trustees

Family foundations sometimes tackle issues of geography by divvying up grants to the various locations where family board members reside. Although this means that at least one board member knows the grantseekers in a particular community, others likely do not. To ensure that trustees have knowledge of one another's communities, The Leighty Foundation often rotates board meetings among the three states where board members reside. The trustee-host sets up site visits with select grantees and, time permitting, organizes gatherings at which grantees and out-of-state trustees can get to know one another.

Fewer Meetings, Better Preparation, and Community Involvement Can Improve the Process

R. Stanton Avery launched Kum-Kleen Adhesive Product, later Avery International and Avery Dennison, with a $50 bank loan that his wife, Dorothy Durfee Avery, secured using their Model A Ford as collateral. Established in 1960, their Durfee Foundation (2000 assets: $29 million) focuses on grants to support talented individuals and reward creative, imaginative leaders, teachers, and students in the arts and other areas.

Almost from the beginning, the Durfee Foundation had an executive director. Still, as the foundation created new programs and expanded existing ones, trustee responsibilities mounted. By the 1990s, the board was beginning to burn out. With one member traveling from the east coast and one from northern California, it was becoming difficult to prepare for and maintain a four-meetings per year schedule. To solve the problem, one meeting was eliminated, trustees agreed to complete as much work as possible in committees and to handle small items of business through business calls, and trustees were required to submit agenda items at least 10 days in advance of meetings. To organize and improve the grantmaking process, trustees were given responsibility for shepherding the programs they initiated from start to finish, using a team or panel of knowledgeable people from the community to assist in the process.

This system proved well suited to the trustees' temperaments and schedules. Because programs require extensive staff and trustee time, funding cycles are staggered throughout the year. As a result, trustees have periods of intense participation lasting several months, followed by stretches of rest and recuperation when they are largely free of board responsibilities.

LOOKING AHEAD

The essence of family philanthropy is the personal involvement of the donor, immediate family members, and a widening circle of relatives and trusted friends and associates. This personal involvement of the donor carries enormous potential consequences for American philanthropy. Four of these consequences come to mind.

First, as more and more donors choose to be personally engaged and to involve their families in their charitable giving, they will likely extend and expand the range of philanthropic options. As wealth extends throughout American society, family philanthropy is becoming more diverse. More women and members of minority groups are earning significant wealth and are starting family foundations; often they fashion their giving around gender issues or draw on ethnic traditions for guidance.

Second, many families are making use of multiple giving vehicles in new and innovative ways, sometimes using them individually and sometimes in collaboration. Then, too, many families (and individuals, for that matter) are ratcheting up the levels of funding for donor-advised funds; what used to be a vehicle funded in the thousands of dollars is now increasingly funded in the millions. Families are finding ways to form foundations, dissolve and reshape them as separate foundations or advised funds, use community foundations, and turn to other techniques to give flexibility and elasticity to their giving.

Third, families are by necessity extending the use of new communications technologies in governance and management of philanthropies. Often living in widely dispersed locations, families use telecommunications for governance, management, and grantmaking purposes. They also use telecommunications to coordinate activities of their multiple giving vehicles. Families are likely to continue to seek advances in technologies and software for foundation management.

Finally, families will be the major players in the much-anticipated intergenerational transfer of wealth, estimated by the Social Welfare Research Institute to be at least $40 trillion. Inheritors are typically less generous than the entrepreneurs who amassed the wealth. The future of philanthropy will be shaped as this transfer takes place. An important influence will be today's donors and older family members who train, encourage, and inspire younger family members to become part of the family tradition of giving.

NOTES

1. Our estimates are based in part on original research commissioned by the National Center for Family Philanthropy. See: The Foundation Center, in cooperation with the National Center for Family Philanthropy. *Family Foundations: A Profile of Funders and Trends.* (New York: The Foundation Center, 2000).
2. For a useful introduction to this subject, see *Faith and Family Philanthropy: Grace, Gratitude, and Generosity.* (Washington, DC: National Center for Family Philanthropy, 2001).
3. Family experiences are drawn from source materials published by the National Center for Family Philanthropy; from the four-volume Family Foundation Library, published by the Council on Foundations; other published materials; authors' interviews with family members or foundation staff; The Foundation Center database; and websites. Sources are documented in the References section at the end of this chapter.
4. *See* Council on Foundations, *Foundation Management Reports,* published annually by the Council. *See also,* Association of Small Foundations, *2001 Member Survey: Selected Results.* (Bethesda, MD: Association of Small Foundations, 2001).
5. This section is based on the excellent monograph by Deanne Stone, *Privacy and the Family Foundation: The Impact on Grantmaking.* (Berkeley, CA: Deanne Stone Publications, 1998).
6. Excerpted from Benjamin T. White, "Avoiding Conflicts of Interest and Self-Dealing," *Investment Issues for Family Foundations: Managing and Monitoring*

Your Philanthropic Assets. (Washington, DC: National Center for Family Philanthropy, 1999).

FURTHER INFORMATION

For further information on family philanthropy, please contact the National Center for Family Philanthropy, 1818 N St., N.W., Suite 300, Washington, DC 20036. Tel: 202-293-3424; fax: 202-293-3395; e-mail: *ginny@ncfp.org*; or visit the NCFP website at *www.ncfp.org*.

REFERENCES

Association of Small Foundations. *2001 Member Survey: Selected Results.* (Bethesda, MD: Association of Small Foundations, 2001).

Cooley, Martha, and the Council on Foundations. *Management.* Family Foundation Library. (Washington, DC: Council on Foundations, 1997).

Council on Foundations. *Management Surveys.* (Washington, DC: Council on Foundations, published annually).

Emmons, Winston. *What Needs to Be Done: The History of the Ellis L. Phillips Foundation.* Available from the National Center for Family Philanthropy.

Flather, Newell, Mary Phillips, and Jean Whitney. *Governance.* Family Foundation Library. (Washington, DC: Council on Foundations, 1997).

Foote, Joseph. *Family Philanthropy and Donor-Advised Funds.* Practices in Family Philanthropy. (Washington, DC: National Center for Family Philanthropy, 2000).

Foote, Joseph, and Louis Knowles. *Grantmaking.* Family Foundation Library. (Washington, DC: Council on Foundations, 1997).

Foundation Center, The, in collaboration with the National Center for Family Philanthropy. *Family Foundations: A Profile of Funders and Trends.* (Washington, DC: National Center for Family Philanthropy, 2000).

National Center for Family Philanthropy. *Faith and Family Philanthropy: Grace, Gratitude, and Generosity.* (Washington, DC: National Center for Family Philanthropy, 2001).

References

National Center for Family Philanthropy. *Investment Issues for Family Funds: Managing and Maximizing Your Philanthropic Dollars.* (Washington, DC: National Center for Family Philanthropy, 1999).

National Center for Family Philanthropy. *Living the Legacy: The Values of a Family's Philanthropy Across Generations.* Charles H. Hamilton, ed. (Washington, DC: National Center for Family Philanthropy, 2001).

National Center for Family Philanthropy. *Resources for Family Philanthropy: Finding the Best People, Advice, and Support.* (Washington, DC: National Center for Family Philanthropy, 1999).

Peckham, Virginia. *Grantmaking With a Purpose: Mission and Guidelines.* Practices in Family Philanthropy. (Washington, DC: National Center for Family Philanthropy, 2000).

Robbins, Carol. *Community Kinship: The Story of the Springs Foundation.* Profiles in Family Philanthropy. (Washington, DC: National Center for Family Philanthropy, 2000).

Robinson, Kim. *Collaborative Grantmaking: Lessons Learned from the Rockefeller Family's Experiences.* Practices in Family Philanthropy. (Washington, DC: National Center for Family Philanthropy, 2001).

Rockefeller Foundation, The. The Rockefeller family philanthropy is reported in the following excellent websites: The Rockefeller Foundation (*www.rockfound.org*); The Rockefeller Brothers Fund (*www.rbf.org*); and Rockefeller Family Fund (*www.rffund.org*). The family's work with other grantmakers and organizations is described in Kim Robinson, *Collaborative Grantmaking: Lessons Learned from the Rockefeller Family's Experiences.* Practices in Family Philanthropy. (Washington, DC: National Center for Family Philanthropy, 2001).

Stone, Deanne. *Creative Family Grantmaking: The Story of the Durfee Foundation.* Profiles in Family Philanthropy. (Washington, DC: National Center for Family Philanthropy, 1999).

Stone, Deanne. *Grantmaking With a Compass: The Challenges of Geography.* Practices in Family Philanthropy. (Washington, DC: National Center for Family Philanthropy, 1999).

Stone, Deanne. *Privacy and the Family Foundation: The Impact on Grantmaking.* (Berkeley, CA: Deanne Stone Publications, 1998).

Stone, Deanne. *Sustaining Tradition: The Andrus Family Philanthropy Program.* Practices in Family Philanthropy. (Washington, DC: National Center for Family Philanthropy, 2001).

Stone, Deanne, and Virginia Esposito. *Family Issues.* Family Foundation Library. (Washington, DC: Council on Foundations, 1997).

CHAPTER 2

Philanthropy, Self-Fulfillment, and the Leadership of Community Foundations

by Joe Lumarda

PERSPECTIVES

What is the role of philanthropy in the life of the donor—the originating founder of the foundation? The impulse to give varies from person to person. Seeking a tax deduction, social prestige, community acceptance, even a ticket to heaven, can all be motivation for an individual to become charitably active. Are there ways in which philanthropy satisfies deeper psychological needs?

This chapter explores this question in the context of one of the fastest-growing segments of philanthropy: community foundations. In 1980, national community foundation assets were at a little over $2 billion. Currently, assets are more than $30 billion and growing. How does the rapid growth of community foundations reflect the evolution of donor services within these organizations, and what are the implications for management and leadership?

Joe Lumarda has spent 12 years with the California Community Foundation in various roles, from program officer to vice president of development, to his current position as executive vice president.

From the Psychology 101 college course to marketing discussions in the corporate world, Abraham Maslow's "Hierarchy of Needs" is a concept that resonates. Precise and accessible, it makes sense:

> Its central thesis is that human needs are organized in a hierarchy, with needs for survival, food, and shelter, for example, as its base. At progressively higher levels in Maslow's hierarchy are needs for security and social interaction, with the highest being the need to learn, grow, and reach one's potential. As lower needs become reasonably satisfied, successively higher needs become influential in motivating human behavior. When a lower needs remain unsatisfied, factors such as learning, creativity, innovation, or self-esteem remain stagnant, never rising to the surface.[1]

This hierarchy is most easily distinguished by the pyramid graphic (see Exhibit 2.1).

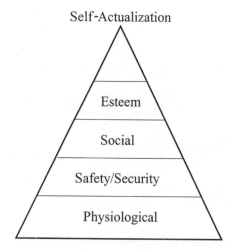

Exhibit 2.1   Maslow's Hierarchy of Needs.

While the concept is crisp, the difficulty that most people have with this model is grasping the tip of the pyramid: self-actualization. When I first encountered Maslow's theory, I didn't know that my work at the California Community Foundation would lead me to understand and also experience this elusive concept. This revelation was a result of my relationship with a very special donor who used a very special turn of phrase.

Several years ago, I was sitting across a kitchen table with a future donor to the California Community Foundation. We were going over the details of his testementary philanthropic plan. Barney (a pseudonym; all donor names and identifying details have been changed) was a self-described small businessman, inventor, tinkerer and "string collector." This was a modest self-description for someone who built up an estate of more than $10 million.

Barney also liked to tinker with his arrangement with the community foundation. After our initial meeting, he would call me up almost monthly to see if we could "go over this thing one more time." At this meeting (the last one we would have in person) we sat across from each other at his kitchen table surrounded by open books, half-done sculptures and sketches, and other projects "in process." His breathing was labored and assisted by a stream of pure oxygen fed to him by nose-tube and tank.

We'd been here before, but this time it was different. He usually leaned over our papers, fiddling with words or asking for my definition (and the community foundation's) of a particular concept. On this morning, he sat back and asked me to talk about what would happen, "When I kick off and this thing kicks in." This was the first time he wanted a presentation without interaction. I calmly covered all the points, emphasizing both concepts and details that we had struggled with over the past several months. His eyes, though almost closed, held me throughout. I finished and sat back in my chair. I gazed at him and noticed that he closed his eyes and leaned his head back for what seemed to be a very long time. I hoped he wasn't falling asleep.

As my anxiety began to mount, his head snapped forward. We stared at each other for a moment. "Thank you, Joe," he said. I nodded my head and gave a slightly nervous grin. He then said, "I guess you'll be me—when I'm no more." When a donor says something like this I can often come back with a quip that dispels the specter of death. Not this time. Instead, I responded, "Yes sir, we will." Not much more was said. We finished our tea and I left.

Barney died about a month later. His estate created a fund at the community foundation that will provide scholarships to vocational schools. He never went to college and wished to support folks who "liked to work with their hands." He chose the community foundation because his fund would not be tied to any one institution and would be free to support the best program to meet his philanthropic vision.

"I guess you'll be me—when I'm no more." This statement (and the way it was said) caused me to reexamine the business of a community foundation: satisfying needs for donors like Barney who want the community foundation to facilitate, or even create, their philanthropic objectives. And this statement prompted a raft of questions that challenged the philosophical underpinnings of my work. *"I guess you'll be me."* What does this becoming—this transfer of actual and philanthropic persona—mean? What is it about community foundations that attract thousands of individuals to utilize their services to fulfill charitable needs? How does fulfilling these needs translate into community foundation operational excellence now and in the future?

PURPOSE

The purpose of this chapter is to examine the services provided, and thus the social and psychological needs satisfied, for donors who choose the community foundation to meet their charitable goals. Setting a historical, theoretical, and managerial context for these complex relationships furthers that examination.

First, a brief historical overview of the community foundation movement in this country—why the need for community foundations arose at the turn of the century—will be provided, along with discussion of the evolutionary and reactionary effects of changes in tax law and the growing and changing needs of the donor.

Next, I will borrow from the theoretical framework of Maslow's Hierarchy of Needs—transposing the five-step pyramid into a hierarchy of donor needs. Since the experience with Barney, I have formulated a parallel hierarchy about the different ways that community foundations fulfill the needs of our past, present, and future donors. I will give a brief explanation of each of Maslow's needs, then offer the donor/community foundation parallel. These counterparts are explained in philosophical, psychosocial, and practical (sometimes even anecdotal) terms.

My corresponding theory offers a different perspective of the heirarchy. Maslow first offered the construct as a tool to explain human motivation and development. He and others then introduced it to the business world as a more humanistic view of management theory. I view the hierarchy as a model of customer needs, with corresponding strategic and management implications for community foundations. With this in mind (and in harmony with the purpose of this book), I will offer several management and leadership challenges and questions along with each donor need.

Most helpful to the development of this theory was the opportunity to give an impromptu presentation of an early rendition of this "theory" to my Development and Donor Services colleagues at the Community Foundation Advancement Network National Conference in the spring of 2000. There was overwhelming affirmation of its validity from the professionals who deal with current and potential donors every day. I would like to thank the participants of this conference and the continual flow of positive comments from my colleagues who confirm this concept resonates keenly with the experience of most of the community foundation world.

COMMUNITY FOUNDATIONS—A BRIEF HISTORY

Community foundations began as a brainchild of banks in 1914. The visionary Cleveland banker Frederick Goff looked into his traditional, staid trust department and saw many languishing charitable trusts with various broadly defined beneficiaries. One would be named for "the health of Cleveland's children," or "the needy and homeless in the City of Cleveland," or "to eradicate tuberculosis." Trust officers would stand around scratching their heads in a quandary—or worse, make grants to their favorite charities, whether or not they were deserving. These trusts would be created with general charitable instructions with or without a particular named agency. Goff came up with the idea of creating a community advisory board to oversee the grantmaking while the bank took care of the trust administration and investments. In a time when the huge multimillion-dollar private foundations were being established (Carnegie, Rockefeller, Ford, etc.), Goff conceived an innovative nonprofit institution in trust form to be the charitable endowment for the little guy. *Little*, of course, was a relative term—it usually meant the philanthropist of moderate wealth.

For years, community foundations were attached at the hip with their founding banking institutions. In Los Angeles, the California Community Foundation was created by Joseph Sartori, one of the founders of Farmers and Merchants Bank, which became Security Pacific, which became Bank of America, later to merge with NationsBank. There was no development person or fund raiser; trust officers would use the community foundation if and as they saw fit. If there were any staff at all, he or she would likely be an executive secretary who would take minutes for the volunteer grantmaking board. And, as one might imagine, that board consisted mainly of bank vice presidents and other community leaders.

It was not until the Tax Reform Act of 1969 and its rather harsh restrictions on private foundations that community foundations began to grow at a rapid pace. The community foundation offered a permanent, accountable, and flexible alternative to the private foundation with a greater tax deduction. Suddenly this philanthropic vehicle was being taken out of the broom closet of bank trust departments to address/fulfill new donors' needs. When discovered by the growing practices of estate, tax, and probate attorneys; accountants; and financial planners, the 75-year-old concept finally took off.

In terms of organizational development, the community foundation began hiring staff in the mid-1970s, beginning with an executive director to manage the bookkeeping and organize the grant-making of the board. The next hire would usually be a more experienced bookkeeper, maybe even a CPA, to handle the increasing number of charitable funds. Next would be a program officer, who would assist the board in proposal analysis for grant distributions. Additions to staff during the 1970s and early to mid-1980s were usually to support Finance/Administrative and Program functions. Any staff interaction with donors were most often handled by the executive director or bank trust officers.

It was not until 1985 that the first asset development professional was hired at a community foundation. Since then, every major community foundation has hired at least one development professional; now most have full departments. In 1990, the California Community Foundation hired its first director of development. At that time (and for several years), my assistant and I were the entire asset development division. In 2002, the development staff had eight members.

Another significant development among community foundations has been the introduction and growth of donor-advised fund services. Before 1969, much of the service provided by community foundations was to manage donors' charitable assets and fulfill their intentions after they died. (Community foundations were once described as the United Way for the dead.) Donor-advised funds allow living donors to make a donation to the community foundation and receive all the tax benefits of making a donation to a public charity. The donor can be the advisor to the fund, making regular grant recommendations to other nonprofit organizations. The significance of this development is that it allows community foundations to serve donors during their lifetimes, not solely after death. The development of the donor-advised fund opened up a world of current donor service and growth of a constituency that had thus far not existed, as it was the first viable alternative to the private foundation. Interestingly, it also created the commercially sponsored gift funds (see Sidebar, "A Philanthropic Line in the Sand: Who Can Serve the Higher Needs of Donors?").

To provide current context, community foundations are one of the fastest growing sectors of American philanthropy. Nationwide, there are more than 500 community foundations serving every major metropolitan area, with total charitable assets at approximately $1 billion in 1980 ballooning to more than $31.5 billion in 2000. The California Community Foundation grew from just less than $20 million in 1980 to more than $550 million in 2002. The October 31, 1996, "Philanthropy 400" edition of the *Chronicle of Philanthropy* stated, "Community Foundations, that raise money and make grants in a single geographic area, saw the biggest increase. Gifts to those foundations nearly doubled, rising by more than 93 percent."[3] Even with the recent economic downturn, community foundations have experienced considerable growth, "Gifts to *community foundations* rose 13 percent, or $466-million, to $4.1-billion. The foundations paid out $2.2-billion in grants, up 12 percent from 1999."[4]

For basic information on community foundations, such as types of charitable funds and grant guidelines, consult your local community foundation. To find your local community foundation, use the Community Foundation Locator at *www.communityfoundationlocator.org* on the Council on Foundations' Web site at *www.cof.org*. For publications discussing community foundation legal and administrative issues, see the Council's publication catalogue at *www.cof.org/applications/publications/index.cfm*.

If you wish to review information on the growth of community foundations, the Columbus Foundation conducts an annual national survey of all community foundations. The survey provides information regarding assets, grants and donations. This information may be obtained on the Columbus Foundation's Web site at *www.columbusfoundation.org*.

To compare the benefits of a community foundation with a private foundation, consult your local community foundation. On the California Community Foundation Web site (*www.calfund.org*) you will also find a community/private foundation comparison.

MASLOW'S HIERARCHY AND LEADERSHIP CHALLENGES

In the 1960s, the renowned father of humanistic psychology, Abraham Maslow, lent his knowledge and insight to the world of business management. He made the connection from his work in psychology and human behavior to professional environments. Maslow published *Eupsychian Management* with the primary aim of examining and creating a workplace that could both be more productive and meet the higher needs of social, self-esteem, and self-actualization. Maybe it was the arcane title (Eupsychian?), but the business community ignored it. According to the reviews of the time and the introduction in its current edition (under the title *Maslow on Management*), this book and its application of humanistic behavior theories were too soft for the then myopic and authoritarian business world at that time.

Building on my experience with Barney and other donors, I clearly could draw a parallel from Maslow's Hierarchy of Needs to those needs fulfilled by the community foundation. Yet, I become aware of a disconnect between the fulfillment of personal needs and the satisfying potentially self-actualizing workplace. A full examination of the needs of the customer must be done in order to provide a truly satisfying donor experience. This examination does not happen in the corporate world because corporations (through their products or services) cannot come close to providing an avenue to self-actualization. General Motors, Microsoft, and Procter & Gamble may like to think that they get close to the top of the pyramid, but they don't. My car, software, and toothpaste can only do so much.

By doing our work well, community foundations have the potential to lead donors through fulfilling basic donor needs to something close to self-actualization. Many nonprofit organizations have the opportunity to aid their clients on the journey up the hierarchy of needs—most notably, churches, educational institutions, and counseling organizations. Nevertheless, community foundations are particularly well positioned to provide a flexible and freely chosen means to satisfy a donor's needs, dreams and desire for self-actualization (see Exhibit 2.2).

PHYSIOLOGICAL TO OPERATIONAL EFFECTIVENESS

The first and most basic needs noted by Maslow are the physiological. These needs are "the most prepotent of all needs." If these needs

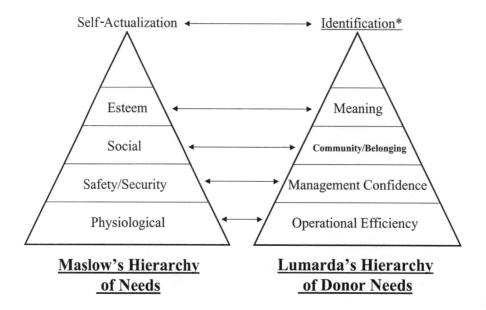

Exhibit 2.2 Maslow-Lumarda comparison chart.

are not being met—Maslow lists air, water, and food as the most fundamental—the other needs will not be attained, if even desired. He dramatizes this point by asserting that "Obviously, a good way to obscure the 'higher' motivations, and to get a lop-sided view of human capacities and human nature is to make the organism extremely and chronically hungry or thirsty."[5] But what are the equivalent of this base and extreme need in a donative context? What is the air, water, and food of the community foundation? I propose that they are: (1) ability to receive dollars, (2) proficient grantmaking administration, and (3) the regular conveyance of information.

According to Webster's Dictionary, a *gift* means, "Something given to show friendship, affection, support, etc."[6] A look at the Treasury Regulations defines a *charitable gift* as, ". . . a contribution or gift to or for the use of . . ." certain types of qualifying organizations[7]—a simple statement with complicating details. When a donor first comes to the community foundation, the donor must feel complete trust in the ability of the organization to initially receive the asset. Cash is one thing. Publicly traded stock is fairly straightforward. Donors come to the community foundations with real estate (both residential and commercial), restricted stock, closely held stock, small business interests, retirement plans, intellectual property, tangible personal property—the list could go on and on. The very basic need of the donor at the point of first contact with the community foundation is the satisfactory completion of this first transaction.

The development/donor service and finance functions of community foundations have grown steadily in the capacity to handle complicated assets. The need for this was even greater in the past when charitable giving was not a specialty of the professional advisor community (this has since changed). Given that tax law is in a constant state of flux, it is more important than ever to fulfill the needs of donors and their advisors by having philanthropic planning expertise at the ready. The following questions come to mind at this first point of transactional contact:

- *Are you available?* The primary complaint that I have heard from donors is that gift planners do not have the same drive for customer service as other professional advisors (lawyers, accountants, financial planners, etc.). This point is reflected most often by the question, *how long does it take for you to get back to me?*
- *Are you competent?* Can you keep up with or even be a charitable giving resource to me and my advisors?
- *Are you honest?* Will you tell me you don't know when you don't?
- *Are you ethical?* This question does not come from every donor or their advisor, but originates from the growing number of charitable tax scams disguised as legitimate techniques. An adjunct question to this is, *Can you say no?* For community foundations are judged as often by the gifts they reject as much as those they accept.

The next basic need of donors is grantmaking administration. When a donor first comes to the community foundation, she sees her asset going into a segregated fund, typically with her name on it. From this fund she will make grants to her favorite charities. She sees the word *foundation* and at that moment, quite naturally, simply ignores the word *community*. She focuses on the word *foundation* as it pertains to her first, immediate, and familiar grantmaking needs.

The donor's needs evolve as the service provided moves from gift completion to grant administration. The donor needs a sufficient level of confidence that her funds are handled well as they come into the community foundation; she needs to know there is commensurate efficiency as her funds are granted. These needs are most apparent with donors and their advised funds. I call them the three A's: Accuracy, Alacrity and Acumen. More and more, community foundations are customizing service for donors. *Accuracy* ensures that all the grantmaking i's are dotted and t's are crossed for each donor and their recommended grantee: Did we get their name correct? Did we send it to the right branch of the Salvation Army (mundane but important)? Though a community foundation is in control of the donor advised grantmaking process, *alacrity,* or promptness, should be expected from a professional grantmaking organization. We should recognize that Length of process may denote the due diligence process, but it can also signify inefficiency. Finally, *acumen,* which stands for the value-added insight that a community foundation provides to a donor advised grant: The donor may ask, "Is there anything I should know about this organization?"

This last point underscores another very basic need of the donor: information. The donor and the community foundation live in the midst of the Information Revolution. Information is available through the Internet and other vehicles of contemporary media dissemination. A stock quotes, bank balances, credit card statements, and children's homework assignments are instantly obtainable at the click of a mouse. This immediacy of information has not spared the community foundation–donor relationship. Donors desire more and more information, more and more quickly. As Jack Shakely, the president of my foundation, jests, "What are they becoming? Day philanthropists?" This has required community foundations to add staff to support the needs of donor advisors as they pursue their charitable objectives—whether those charitable objectives include a simple grant or full analysis of their favorite issue (children's health, the environment, education, etc.).

Leadership Challenge 1: How Do We Build a Workforce of Community Foundation Knowledge Workers?

One of the first rules of management is that a great deal of the success of a manager is hiring the right person. As we bear in mind the work of community foundations, the workforce must embody, as management guru Peter Drucker defined the term, *knowledge workers:* "It demands for the first time in history that people with knowledge take responsibility for making themselves understood (to those) who do not have the same knowledge base. It requires that people learn—and preferably early—how to assimilate into their own work-specialized knowledge from other areas and other disciplines."[8] This does not mean these workers should be without appropriate technical skills or experience. It does mean that attitude and appropriate fit with corporate culture are just as important. One example that Drucker frequently cites is the work of the hospital nurse. He argues that if you feel that the technical expertise of a nurse is the only requirement for the job, then you've never been taken care of by a nurse. According to Drucker, the most important job of the hospital is to exercise compassion, to be fully present for the patient, and to be willing to go the extra mile.

The following are characteristics needed for the community foundation knowledge worker: a compassionate nature, communicative style, intellectual curiosity, and a passion to serve donors and the community. The last aspect is important for our customer— the donor typically comes to the community foundation table with passion for a cause. That enthusiasm and commitment must be met in kind. In the movie *The Color of Money* with Paul Newman and Tom Cruise, there is a scene accurately depicting this intangible attribute of the community foundation knowledge worker. Newman's character is explaining that skill with the cue stick around the pool table is secondary to "the art of human moves." It's the art of human moves that is essential when dealing with donors and their advisors, nonprofit organizations, and our fellow employees.

Leadership Challenge 2: How Will Technology Help Community Foundations be More Transactionally Efficient?

Several years ago, Peter Drucker addressed our Board of Governors for a long-range planning session. He began his remarks with the statement, "After studying your history, documents, and publications it is obvious, you are a financial institution." He went on to touch upon all the other competencies that make community foundations distinctive institutions but his opening remark—joining to us—made a point. Community foundations must take their role as a fiscal fund manager very seriously. This requires a great deal of emphasis on fiscal controls, accounting and information management. In this way, community foundations should look at all the lessons learned by the banking industry in order to manage knowledge—and the most efficient and effective way to manage this information is through state of the art technology. But as most industries have experienced, this is easier said than done.

Like many institutions with a heavy financial emphasis, community foundations are grappling with issues related to the most effective use of technology. Key questions include:

- What are the common internal administrative needs of community foundations nationwide?
- What vendors have provided the best service to community foundations? Is the field growing too dependent on a few vendors? Are there others that need to be explored?
- How do we efficiently disseminate the technological best practices and operational options?
- Many community foundations are the size of small banking/financial institutions with similar needs and fund/ac-

count structure. What are some lessons we can learn from their growth, development and operational technology infrastructure?

Thankfully, the community foundation trade group of fiscal and administrative officers is addressing several of these questions on behalf of the field.

It is obvious to all of us that the community foundation field must have state of the art systems in order to handle both the operational flow of the business and the expected wave of new donors and estates resulting from the coming intergenerational wealth transfer. When struggling with operational issues, the California Community Foundation's Chief Financial Officer, Steve Cobb, often comments, "That's fine while we have 500 donor advised funds and 1,000 total funds. But I see very shortly, 1,000 and 2,000 or 2,500 and 5,000. We must build for then."

SECURITY TO MANAGEMENT CONFIDENCE

I received a call from a donor (let's call him Harry) who will leave the community foundation most of his estate through his trust. He called to set a meeting our office. This request to visit us was rather odd, considering the many times we met in his study on the second floor of his house (Harry's having a little trouble seeing and getting around). He arrived at our offices with his attorney. When I came to the lobby to greet them, they were both surveying the art, the government proclamations, and one framed article from *Forbes* magazine naming our community foundation one of "Peter Drucker's Picks" as one of the 10 best nonprofit organizations in the nation.[9] He then asked for a tour of our offices. Our community foundation is on the thirty-fourth floor of a high-rise in downtown Los Angeles. I showed them our state-of-the-art computer system. I showed our files of thousands of nonprofit organizations. I introduced him to our program staff, who collectively hold more than a century of nonprofit experience. When we ended our tour, we took our seats in a conference room. Oddly, he seemed to be checking the quality of our chairs and tables. Before I could ask him what he wished to discuss, he disclosed one primary goal of the meeting: "Well, Joe, you answered my first question: 'Can you handle my money?'" I had a hunch, but I still was not sure of his comment, so I responded with a puzzled glance. He added, "I will be giving you a lot of money when all is said and done. I wanted to know if you had the people, the facility, and the wherewithal to make sure it was secure. Now, we can talk about what we will ultimately do for the community." We then talked for an hour and a half about how the fund to be created from his estate will support a variety of issues from education to domestic violence to children's health. But before we could do this, he needed the assurance of the safety of his dollars—his trust that we "can handle it."

Maslow describes the need for safety from the perspective of a child, where there is more dependence on the guardian. In order for children to live without undue anxiety or fear, they need to know that their well-being is by and large secure. This means that what is being fed to them daily is hazard free and good, that there is a relative order and predictability to their days, and that they are protected in times of emergency or chaos.

In many ways, donors are in a position analogous to the dependent child Maslow describes. When a gift is given to the community foundation, whether created immediately or through an estate, the donor loses control of those dollars. The Tax Code requires the loss of control to receive the corresponding tax benefit. This leaves the donor in a position of total trust and dependence on the community foundation. Testamentary gifts add an even greater level of faith in the institution's future. The person making a charitable bequest will not be around to make sure their wishes are being honored.

There are three areas in which donors require confidence in the security and management of the community foundation: (1) fiscal security of the dollars, (2) trust in the culture and people, and (3) confidence that charitable wishes will be honored faithfully, within reason.

Now more than ever, donors have the stock market and investment expertise at their fingertips. Because of the availability of investment information, donors and their advisors put community foundation personnel through the paces when it comes to an explanation of investment policy and manager selections. Historical returns, asset allocation, expense ratios, and risk tolerance are the inquisitional hoops that we must jump through in order to satisfy a donor's need to assure fiscal competency.

These questions or challenges take different forms for various generations. Broadly categorizing, the World War II generation, those who lived through the Great Depression, seem to have a much lower risk tolerance. The baby boom generation, those born from 1946 to 1964, grew up through investment doldrums in the market, but since the early 1980s, they have experienced the longest running bull market of the twentieth century. They have a relatively high tolerance for risk. Until recently those born after that time have never experienced anything but a bull market, and some of their friends have even become millionaires through high-tech start-ups, stock options, or their company's 401(k)s.

Regardless of the generation a donor is from, whatever his inclination for conservative or aggressive investments, he has the same concern: My dollars need to be at the community foundation to pursue my charitable interests, and I need to know that my dollars will be safe. Even the most experienced high-risk-tolerant donor will often say, "I hope you are not too conservative, but I don't expect you to invest your funds like I do." Donors seem to know inherently that we need to answer not only to them, but also to the whole community, not to mention state and federal regulatory agencies.

The second aspect of the need for security pertains to confidence in the community foundation's corporate culture and people. The story of my donor who wanted to know if we could "handle his money" did not stop there. Harry has met with our president and other key foundation personnel, and has attended our donor briefings on issues in the community. He has had me over to his home for dinner. At that dinner we watched a movie together and talked about the meaning of life over a glass of wine and a cigar. He needed to be secure not only in our trappings of professionalism but in who we are as people. Often, this need is underscored by the long-view concern:

"But Joe, these dollars will be here long after you and I are gone." Trust in the future is attained only through a clear elucidation of past performance and current demonstration of the corporate culture.

Finally, donors need to know that their charitable wishes will be followed now and in the future (within practical reason). Unfortunately, trust in the nonprofit sector and its assets has been called into question over the past few years. The scandals involving United Way of America, the fundamentalist religious groups, and the Foundation for New Era Philanthropy have sown seeds of suspicion within the potential donor community. Activities within other sectors of philanthropy have not helped. Private foundations, for example, have gained notoriety recently for their U-turns in grantmaking policies and priorities despite the clear intentions of their founders. A high-profile case in Los Angeles concerned a private foundation changing from the original donors' priorities of supporting modern art to their children's priorities of supporting American Indian issues. Friends and advisors to the original donors could only watch with regret.

Donors who previously trusted the sector do not always base their judgment on the assumption that good words and intentions indicate reliable management and positive outcomes. Each year, more and more community foundations are asked, "How do I know you are who you say you are?" Foundation executives must know that this due diligence is not a bothersome process but one step in establishing a relationship with the donor that rebuilds the trust in the nonprofit sector as a whole.

Leadership Challenge 3: How Does Our Openness Ensure Security and Trust?

The work of community foundations is a case in which familiarity does not breed contempt. With community foundations, familiarity breeds confidence.

A community foundation will ensure institutional security by living in a glass house. The donor, the nonprofit community, and the public in general must have freedom to evaluate information about the way community foundations operate, manage funds, assist donors, make grants, and set priorities. Lack of active forthright knowledge breeds insecurity.

The community foundation must be a leader in the spirit of full disclosure about financial information to the community. The California Community Foundation was one of the first foundations of any kind to post its full annual report, audited financial statements, and IRS 990 tax returns online. The use of the Internet is ideal not only for such disclosure, but also to share grantmaking guidelines and processes to the community.

An even greater commitment to institutional openness needs to occur as community foundations become larger. I've noticed that as they grow, many institutions—whether nonprofit, for-profit, or governmental—tend to become more withdrawn and distrustful. It is precisely at this time of great growth and increasing influence that transparency and openness are needed by community foundations as an example of durable commitment to the community.

Leadership Challenge 4: Does Standard, Conservative, Balanced Investment of Our Funds Constitute the Only Way to Fulfill Our Mission and Provide Value to the Community?

In this challenge, the community foundation is invited look at all the different investment vehicles used to leverage permanent assets to achieve its mission and benefit the community. Though security is the theme of this section, it would be imprudent not to examine all the ways that the community foundation could fulfill its mission in a responsible yet innovative manner.

Several private foundations have pioneered an alternative view of investing, and it is time that community foundations look at the opportunities. This type of investment can take various forms:

- *Program-related investments.* Pioneered by the Ford Foundation in the 1970s, this strategy allows foundations to support organizations through highly valued at- or below- market-rate loans.

- *Socially responsible investing (SRI).* This mode of investment became popular when many foundations and investment funds boycotted companies with enterprises in South Africa during apartheid. This was the first example of a social screen that is now employed by many foundations as a representation of its mission (no tobacco stocks, no defense-related stocks, etc.). SRI can also employ an active voting strategy to facilitate change in companies with social issues before its shareholders.

- *Local community redevelopment and investment.* Funds are beginning to emerge that invest in federally defined urban empowerment zones or other redeveloping areas. These regions overlie the catchment areas of grantee organizations of the foundation (areas of need). This is a complementary way that a foundation may support a blighted geographic area with both social service grants and prudent investment into local enterprises.

SOCIAL/BELONGING TO A COMMUNITY OF DONORS

Maslow begins the progression through the higher needs with the social or belonging aspect. He describes this need as filling a natural void, 'Now the person will feel as keenly, as never before, the absence of friends, or a sweetheart, or a wife. Or children. He will hunger for affectionate relations with people in general, namely, for a place in his group, and he will strive with great intensity to achieve this goal."

The community foundation by definition is a natural community of donors, living and dead alike. There is no other institution in the world that can state the claim of partnerships with thousands of donors, each with a personalized philanthropic mission, and served with greater efficiency through the resultant economies of scale. But this still sounds transactional in nature.

In the past, a donor to the community foundation was part of the hundreds of other donor advisors or future testamentary donors at a community foundation, but would never know his institutional neighbor funds (donor advised funds in particular). Each fund had acted very much like an island unto itself. This is changing.

It's changing because I believe Groucho Marx was wrong when he said, "I'd never belong to a club that would have me as a member." People wish to belong to something familiar that still allows them independence. This is proven each time I show a potential donor the community foundation's annual report. Their eyes make four noticeable actions. First, they look for someone they know. They are searching for familiarity, someone to call to ask how this philanthropic arrangement goes, to bolster their comfort level. Second, they look at the leadership, the board of directors. Is there anyone here that I know, that I can call, or that I recognize? This roster is a primary indicator of organizational personality, and they want to know if they could get along with these people. Third, they look at the number of donors to the community foundation. Is this popular or elitist? Am I the first one in line to this organization? How many other people have come before me and are still here? And, finally, where does the foundation make its grants? Do I feel comfortable with the priorities and values of the organization? This is another institutional personality indicator.

Borrowing from other traditional nonprofit organizations, and also meeting this social need, community foundations are increasingly bringing donors together for a variety of reasons. At my community foundation, we invite donors to regularly scheduled luncheons with prominent speakers on a timely global, national, or local community issue. The purpose of these meetings is for donors to become acquainted with one another, to share their charitable interests, and possibly to forge a philanthropic partnership that initiates collaborative or enhanced grantmaking.

Other community foundations are searching for ways to meet this growing social need. The SV2 program started by Community Foundation Silicon Valley is a specialized donor collective. Donors, most of whom are Silicon Valley high-tech executives or engineers, contribute to a fund and participate in a communal grantmaking process. Many community foundations hold an annual meeting for the entire community, where donors, grantees, and community leaders can gather to receive a state of the foundation report and network.

Many times, donors enjoy the community foundation atmosphere of independence with the option of socializing or collaborating. Any person who has been part of an alumni association, church bazaar, community organization fund raiser, or a family gathering, for that matter, knows that sentiments and pocketbooks are leveraged with subtle (or not so subtle) undertones of guilt. The constant bombardment of messages about the needs of the group and the donor's responsibility for subsequent support can numb a donor into inaction or, worse, cynical distrust.

In the midst of such pressures, the community foundation can become a philanthropic oasis, allowing donors to drink together from the well of knowledge as well as autonomy. This pressure-free atmosphere allows donors to become acquainted with other donors of like mind and interest for potentially synergistic results.

Leadership Challenge 5: How Can Technology Be Used to Create a Better Community of Donors and Foundations?

The term *community* has been appropriated by the Internet industry. Internet writer and philosopher Howard Rheingold describes it in these terms:

> People in virtual communities use words on screens to exchange pleasantries and argue, engage in intellectual discourse, conduct commerce, exchange knowledge, share emotional support, make plans, brainstorm, gossip, feud, fall in love, find friends and lose them, play games, flirt, create a little high art and a lot of idle talk. People in virtual communities do just about everything people do in real life, but we leave our bodies behind.[10]

There is potential for a powerful virtual community for our foundations.

I have heard some people call it our "magic" or our "power," but community foundations, collectively, have access to more information on local nonprofit organizations and their efficacy than any other collection of like institutions nationwide. Currently, the sharing of this information is executed by phone, fax, and e-mail; newsletters; and annual reports. The potential of collecting and sharing this vast and valuable programmatic information via a common network is huge. Donors in Los Angeles could find the best-managed and most affordable child care center in their hometown in the Midwest or in any other town or city for that matter. Community foundations conducting studies on school reform could log onto the collective white papers covering this issue from San Francisco to Chicago to New York. Private foundations could access the opinions of local community foundation program experts on such specialized issues such as the environment, the arts, or animal welfare.

This adds new meaning to the term *community of donors*. With the use of technology, the community of community foundations could be both a repository for a vast wealth of local knowledge and a place to interact with like-minded supporters or learners.

Leadership Challenge 6: Strategic Partnerships

The community foundation is positioned to build community, not only with its donors, but also with disparate groups that deal with philanthropy. Philanthropy can run the gamut from organizations that are at the heart of charitable giving (of financial resources or services) to those who serve it as vendors, to those who participate at its fringe. Community foundations can serve as potential partners to a number of organizations, including the following:

- *Private foundations.* As an extra set of eyes and ears in grassroots nonprofit communities
- *Financial institutions.* As an extra arrow in their quiver of service to their clients with charitable interests

- *Nonprofits.* As a funding source, knowledge provider, and philanthropic sounding board
- *Emerging "transfer of wealth" economy.* As a balance between an innovator and experimenter with charitable giving methods
- *Nonprofit incubators* (tides, community partners, etc.). As a referral source of those who want to do as opposed to those who want to fund

The community foundation is at the hub of nonprofit and philanthropic activity. This central position allows it to act as a broker of resources or excess capacity to community needs. This convening role is a way to bring more to the community table than mere grants.

ESTEEM TO MEANING

Maslow contends that the need for self-esteem is "based on the real capacity, achievement, and respect from others."[11] He asserts that one must first have esteem for oneself, and then desire the esteem of others. What community foundations often experience is somewhat different.

Donors come from a position of abundance. In our society, such abundance attracts the esteem of others in the form of admiration for the effort or ingenuity of attaining the wealth, or a desire for sharing in that wealth. In the nonprofit world, this esteem is most readily apparent by the way we recognize donors—with names on buildings, award events, and the like. These are time-honored methods that have produced much good in this country. But for many, such recognition is seen as lavish or as an exchange for glory.

The esteem of others may come from position, money, and power, but it is the inner search for meaning and purpose that provides a sense of inner security, contentment, and true self-esteem. Philosopher and business consultant Peter Koestenbaum was profiled in a recent issue of *Fast Company*. In the article "Do You Have the Will to Lead," he states, "Unless the distant goals of meaning, greatness, and destiny are addressed, we can't make an intelligent decision about what to do tomorrow morning—much less set a strategy for a company or for human life. Nothing is more practical than for people to deepen themselves. The more you understand the human condition, the more effective you are as a business person."[12]

Now what does all this talk about meaning mean for donors and the community foundation? It is generally recognized that our type of foundation is not accustomed to giving the type of recognition that many major donors traditionally receive. We do not build buildings for naming or give big awards dinners. Community foundations can facilitate grants that support such activities, but it is not the way we operate our business or acknowledge our donors.

Community foundations are in the exclusive position of being a public charity that can, to use Koestenbaum's phrase, assist a donor in examining the "distant goals of meaning, greatness, and destiny." Community foundations do this best by matching the needs of the donor to the needs of the community.

Many donors who come to community foundations are what may be called "accidental philanthropists." Ask them how they made their money and they'll simply say hard work and being at the right place at the right time. (They wink and say they were lucky.) Ask some donors why they give, and they will say half-jokingly that their accountant stressed the need for a deduction—and of course they wish to give back to the community. Ask them what they want to support; they will say their alma mater, children's school, church or temple, some causes that their friends support (the social need), and some things that they got in the mail (some wrinkled direct-mail pieces are pulled from their pocket).

Then we ask our questions. But what do *you* wish to give to? What do *you* feel passionate about? What do *you* love about your community? These questions are met with a moment of blank stares, a glance at the brochures, and then a moment of unaccustomed introspection in relation to the community. What follows later is often a steady stream (that may turn into a flood) of feelings, experiences, opinions, and passion—children's health, education, pets, domestic violence, and the like. This sets the framework for our relationship: Go here, don't go there; go slow on this, I want this tomorrow; let me know what you find, I want to see for myself. This is the very first step of defining philanthropic meaning, which in many ways affects and forms personal meaning and self-recognition.

Gratitude and self-recognition has become big business in the nonprofit world. Organizations need gratitude events to raise precious general operating dollars and recognize significant donors. But again, that is not the community foundation's role. Community foundations give donors the capacity to learn more about what they are passionate about. Community foundations give donors a customized course to pursue their charitable dreams, whether actively or passively. Community foundations provide donors all the avenues to seek external gratitude while at the same time allowing the donors to quietly thank themselves.

Leadership Challenge 7: How Do Community Foundations Act and Manage Like One Foundation When We Look Like Many?

In order to help the donor discover meaning—that is, discover the wants and desires behind their habits of the heart—all the various departments of the community foundation must work closely together.

Each week, the president and vice presidents of my community foundation come together for a management team meeting. In those sessions, it becomes clear that we are an organization that, if not schizophrenic, at least has the potential for multiple personality disorder. The Program Department oversees our discretionary grant-making program. At times, this department acts more like a private foundation. The Development and Donor Service Department handles potential donors and current donor-advised fund relationships. Occasionally, this department can act like a traditional planned giving or major gifts department. The Finance Department administers the funds under management and the accounting, cash flow, and budget of our operations, sometimes seeming like a bank trust department. The Communication Department produces our publications and Web site and conducts media relations, like a traditional public relations firm. Overlay on this the hundreds of funds and trusts with various charitable beneficiaries and intentions. As our chief financial officer likes to ask, "Are we one foundation or are we many?" The reality and dynamics are complex but the goal of "one" is clear.

Attaining unity in management tough. The following are some questions that have assisted many community foundations in the process of strengthening the ability of their diverse arms and legs to function as a strong single body:

- *Is there one individual whose primary responsibility it is to make sure all the departments are working together?* This may not be the president, depending on the size of the organization or the president's community leadership demands. If this person also leads a particular department, he will need to put the needs of the organization above his own departmental priorities.
- *Does planning for the organization happen only within departments or across functions?* Cross-functional participation should happen in as many venues as possible, from staff event training preparation and department goal setting to the annual work plan and long-range planning.
- *Is ongoing interdepartmental communication forged into the very structure and spirit of the organization?* At the California Community Foundation, most all departmental meetings have regular seats saved for representatives from other departments. At the monthly all-staff meeting, presentations spring from all departments regarding organizational processes, myths, or mysteries ("I never knew how that got done").
- Recalling to Leadership Challenge 1, *How does our process for hiring incorporate interdepartmental participation and exchange?* Often, when we hire an individual to fill a new position, representatives from other departments are asked to participate in the interview process. This not only allows for cross-functional input, but it demonstrates to the potential new hire the manner in which the foundation operates.

Leadership Challenge 8: How Will the Community Foundation Serve the "New New" Donor?

This topic is explored further in the third chapter of this book. Still, I would like to share an observation. In recent issue of *Fast Company*, leaders from fast-growing companies ("Fast Pack 2000"), business thinkers, and educators gathered to discuss a wide range of topics, which included "Can Hope Scale Up?" A friend to the community foundation world, Bill Strickland, was one of the first speakers. He told the story of his enormously successful Manchester Craftsman Guild and Bidwell Training Center in Pittsburgh. The first response in the roundtable came from Gil Bashe, CEO of HealthQuest, a health care and marketing services start-up:

> My reaction to everything that you have told us is that everything that you are doing is spectacular—but it isn't good enough. Here's what I mean. You can go from city to city in the United States and find people who are creating powerful institutions that deal with kids and poverty. St. Louis, Seattle, Boston, San Francisco and other cities across the country have these programs. But that's not enough. You tell us that it could take 30 years or more to return hope to our inner cities. But we don't have 30 years. It's got to happen in 5 years. So the question is, "How do we get programs like yours into 100 cities within 5 years?" We need to figure out how to get that done, because the problem is growing faster than the solution.[13]

As Mr. Bashe applauded Bill Strickland, I applaud his sense of urgency. But it is in this example and my experience that these are the identifiable tendencies of the new (which often means high-tech) donor:

- *Do It Themselves.* Often, their answers lie in a new organization instead of supporting the tried and true. This entrepreneurship could be very good for the nonprofit sector.

- *Do It Fast.* From 30 years timeframe to 5—this is an admirable goal.
- *If It Is Not Done, Then What.* That is the main concern for many nonprofits. Beyond the aggressive goal and initial pledge, what other commitment is there? And if this is not met (in five years) then what?

Community Foundations can lend an active and long-term perspective to many of these new donors.

These entrepreneurial donors have derived meaning from the creation of something new, most often through a technology company. Once they have become financially secure, they will again look to create something new in the world of business *and/or* philanthropy. Community foundations need to think strategically about how to serve these restless donors and doers. We are familiar with those who want to fund an organization. How can we help facilitate a person's need to look at philanthropy in a new or different way? What if they wish to establish a whole new organization?

Community foundations hold a vast wealth of knowledge and experience that would be very useful to these venture philanthropists. The challenge is twofold: (1) how to get out of our mindset of only serving those donors that fit within our 85-year-old paradigm and (2) how to provide information or consultation that can aid the social entrepreneur without getting in his or her way.

SELF ACTUALIZATION TO IDENTIFICATION

Maslow defines self-actualization in the following way:

> Even if all these needs are satisfied, we may still often (if not always) expect that a new discontent and restlessness will soon develop, unless the individual is doing what he is fitted for. A musician must make music, an artist must paint, a poet must write, if he is to be ultimately happy. What a man *can* be, he *must* be. This need we may call self-actualization.[14]

This theory manifests itself in the world of community foundations in three ways. First, it reveals itself in the way that the avocation for philanthropy becomes a primary way toward fulfillment; identity; and, potentially, self-actualization. Second, the decision to choose philanthropy is rooted in the philosophical concept of identification. Finally, the mode or vehicle of philanthropic self-actualization is as important as, if not more important than, the eventual beneficiary issues, causes, or organizations.

Maslow uses the examples of a musician, artist, and poet in his definition. It can be assumed that any vocation, if it satisfies and completes the individual, may lead to self-actualization. But my experience offers an alternative path to this higher state.

Time and time again, donors tell me that if there is one thing that wealth gives them, it is freedom. Wealth allows the freedom to choose a new avocation separate from their wealth-building vocation. Boston University researcher and sociologist Paul Schervish, an expert on the subject of wealth and philanthropy, has similar findings:

> In the material realm, such freedom is the ability to experience almost every situation from housing and vacations to education and work, as opportunities for choice rather than conditions for compromise and deprivation. For instance the fact that the wealthy do not have to work ironically results often enough in their wanting to work, they are free to select and shape their work so that it becomes a source of satisfaction, self-actualization, and effective accomplishment.[15]

Self-actualization is a recognized possibility within the world of wealth and activity.

For some, it allows the start of a new business; for others, it means more time with the family; for many, it signifies an opportunity for volunteerism and philanthropy. I find this continually with donors: "Financial security is here, now I get to do something worthwhile with my spare time and money." The very language of the donor is consistent with phrases such as "Now I get to do something good," or "Now I get to have some fun," or "This is like a second career," or the existentially transformational language of "I'm a different person" or "It's like being born again" (without the Evangelical context).

But why do these individuals even come to the door of philanthropy when all other needs are satisfied? Schervish addresses this issue with his concept of identification. He notes that people give to those causes that they most connect with. He explains:

> It is for this reason that I have found that donors contribute a bulk of their charitable dollars to causes from whose services the donor directly benefits. It is not by coincidence that schools, health and arts organizations, and (especially) churches attract so much giving. For it is here that donors, because they are also recipients, most identify with the individuals—namely themselves, their families, and people much like them—whose needs are met by the contribution.[16]

Schervish calls this familiar and traditional mode *consumptive philanthropy*. The other type is *adoptive philanthropy*: "Where donors support individuals on the basis of a feeling of surrogate kinship."[17] *Kinship* is an interesting choice of terms. It connotes a familial relationship, but, unlike consumptive philanthropy, giving does not descend from an ivory tower. Adoptive philanthropy allows a donor to share the experience and vulnerability of the recipient. From that empathy comes the natural instinct to assist the woundedness you see that you feel within yourself. Adoptive philanthropy understands that "there but by the grace of God go I."

This impulse is understandable for organizations such as the Salvation Army or the family-counseling agency, but how do donors achieve identification with a community foundation? I bring us back to the story of Barney at the very beginning of this chapter: "I guess you'll be me. . . ." The community foundation is asked to be Barney—in all his wisdom, inventiveness, entrepreneurship, risk taking, stubbornness, curiosity, and humor. This resolution of trust is awe inspiring. It reminds me of the scene in Brönte's *Wuthering Heights,* when Cathy exclaims, "I'm Heathcliff!" at the realization that the trust and love between the two had actually made them one. Similarly, Peter Drucker, in the long-range planning session he held with my community foundation's board of governors, quipped, "One of the main reasons you exist is so that donors don't look stupid many years later." The board enjoyed a good laugh at that remark, but Drucker remained dead serious. He then went on to say that this type of confidence is not to be taken lightly. Giving over one's judgment and reputation is a special and serious business.

Therefore, it was not the cause Barney mainly identified with; it was the vehicle to attain the cause. His identification was not with the client or vocational scholarship recipient; it was with the entity that would be his eyes, ears, and spirit. Over my five-year relationship with Barney, we worked through all the needs, from basic to higher, from transactional to transformational. The flexibility, permanence, and indeed soul of the community foundation allowed him to view philanthropy as his final and best calling, and maybe the means to self-actualization.

Leadership Challenge 9: How Do Community Foundations Need to Work in Order to Meet the Highest Needs of the Donor and the Community?

This final management challenge is the great debate of community foundations nationwide. It is related to Leadership Challenge 7, which addresses the issue of one foundation or many. It works much like the children's game "Crack the Whip": We work and play together, beginning the game with our hands together. Our intention is to stay together, but as we get wrapped up in our work, operational concerns and the needs of our constituencies act as centrifugal forces that cause institutional breakup—a couple of kids crying on either end of the field.

Community foundations must, like a participant in any good personal relationship, work hard at it every day. The following temptations always seem to rear their ugly heads:

- *Temptation 1: Define the foundation by one constituency.* Community foundations are beholden to their organizational history and development. Some community foundations have almost all donor-advised funds; others have significant discretionary dollars. No matter what the proportion, defining the foundation as only one type of organization eliminates the potential for balance.
- *Temptation 2: Foster competitiveness within the foundation.* This is also addressed in Leadership Challenge 7. I have witnessed the destructive effects of internal competition. This phenomenon is not so affectionately called the "silo" effect within the community foundation world, in the sense that all stay in their own little tower and occasionally tosses a missile at everyone else—each department fighting for position or prominence in the eyes of the chief executive board, or community. Unfortunately, I have seen managers that feel that such competition brings out the best performance in everyone—but this allows for only one winner and many grumbling and potentially vengeful losers.
- *Temptation 3: Hypocritical management or not walking the walk.* It is in vogue to talk about organizational balance. It is another matter entirely to execute it. Unfortunately, leaders need to follow what is said with the everyday implementation of organizational interdependence. Management hypocrisy is like throwing gasoline on the fire of internal discord. This hypocrisy manifests itself most often in the budget, planning, and personnel administration of foundations (resources not following intentions).
- *Temptation #4: Leveraging the needs of one constituency against the needs of the other.* This happens most often when one side of the organizational equation is seen as the potential devotee of the other. This potentially leads to a feeling of exploitation. For

example, if donor advisors are constantly solicited for donations to the grantmaking priorities of the foundation, the donors may ask, "Whose needs are you serving now?" On the other hand, if donors are never given the wisdom and insight of the program department, this section of the foundation may feel underutilized or overlooked.

THE KEY TO THE FUTURE

Barney, the donor mentioned at the outset of this chapter, built his life through creativity, risk, entrepreneurship and a common-sense business style. Yet inside his almost industrial exterior, beat a very caring heart. Through the many conversations with him, he tinkered with his estate and philanthropic plan. It became obvious that he was shaping identity through the ages through our institution. And he needed to identify as closely as possible with the foundation and me in order to leave this world secure in his deliberations, choices and perpetual persona.

This is the key for community foundations: to keep foremost and active the original aims of each Barney who entrusts their funds and vision; to ensure they perform as efficiently as possible without being hidden by bureaucracy, guidelines, forms and processes; and to know the weight of their work—to become the donors we serve. The community foundation, once described by a good friend as "an organization with a corporate head and a community heart," is well positioned to carry this torch.

Our wonderful challenge is to serve Barney through both sound management and a keen awareness of the community's needs, and to do so in ways that match his professionalism, personality and dreams.

A PHILANTHROPIC LINE IN THE SAND: WHO CAN SERVE THE HIGHER NEEDS OF DONORS?

The most controversial issue to arise from the community foundation world is the emergence of commercially sponsored gift funds. These operate as depositories for donor-advised funds—basically, a charitable check-writing service. The for-profit corporate entity creates a nonprofit depository that invests all its money at the originating entity. The largest of these is Fidelity's Charitable Gift Fund. Launched in 1992 and currently holds more than $5 billion in charitable assets currently. Since then, a number of commercially sponsored gift funds have been approved by the IRS as public charities. None have been as successful as Fidelity.

The most controversial aspect of this development for community foundations has been the prospect of competition with another entity with definite competitive advantages. Some have contended that because of these funds' symbiotic relationship with their parent for-profit corporation, they should not enjoy public charity status. The following is an opinion article authored by the lawyers from the Los Angeles–based firm of Rodriguez, Horii & Choi:

> Some or all of the features set forth in this prototypical fact pattern are present in the programs of such Financial Institutions.
>
> 1. The Foundation uses a trade name of the Financial Institution.
>
> 2. Representatives of the Financial Institution serve on the governing body of the Foundation. In some instances, these representatives dominate the governing body. In other instances, they constitute an influential minority of the board.
>
> 3. The donor retains the right to recommend to the Foundation's fiduciary manager (hereinafter, the "Trustee") qualified tax exempt organizations to receive distributions from the donor-advised fund from time to time. If the donor's recommendation is not accepted by the Trustee, the Trustee will make a reasonable effort to solicit the donor's recommendation for an alternate distribution.
>
> 4. The donor is sometimes a client of the Financial Institution.
>
> 5. The marketing campaign of the Foundation promotes the trade name of the Financial Institution, and the Foundation is held out to be an added service offered by the Financial Institution.
>
> 6. All of the assets contributed to the Foundation are managed by the Financial Institution, either because the Foundation has entered into a long-term contract with the Financial Institution or because there is an understanding that the Foundation will only use the services of the Financial Institution to manage the funds. Typically, money management contracts are not the subject of competitive bids, and the Foundation does not test the market

for better prices or better services than those provided by the Financial Institution.

7. The Financial Institution charges the Foundation a fee that is identical to the fee charged to the Financial Institution's other clients.

8. In most cases, the Financial Institution's sole or primary business activity is the management of other persons' money for a fee.

ISSUE

Based on the foregoing facts, the question to be resolved is: *Is the Foundation ineligible for tax exemption under Section 501(c)(3) of the Code because it is operated for a substantial nonexempt purpose?*

CONCLUSION

A Foundation organized and operated in the manner described above should not be eligible for tax exemption under Section 501(c)(3) of the Code. Despite the fact that the Foundation can be shown to be operated for charitable purposes, the Foundation's activities that further the commercial interests of the founding Financial Institution constitute a substantial nonexempt purpose that should be viewed as fatal to its tax exemption under Section 501(c)(3) of the Code.*

Many in the community foundation field have gone back and forth on the most appropriate way to address this challenge. Some feel that since there is an apparently valid challenge to their *public charity* status, we should challenge them in the regulatory and legislative world. Others wish to forgo that political battlefield and concentrate on the community foundations' core competencies of local and personal service to our donors and communities.

I do not have any more fuel for that debate, but I do wish to make a distinction based on some conclusions within this chapter. I believe the financial institution sponsored gift funds can only fulfill the base needs of the donor, Operational Effectiveness and Management Confidence, which are essentially *transactional* in nature. The three following higher needs, Community of Donors, Meaning and Identification, can only be served through a community foundation. These services are more *transformational* in nature (see Exhibit 2.3).

Philanthropy and various charitable services have recently been using the terms transactional and transformational quite liberally and without attribution. I now use these terms term in full recognition of Bernard Bass and his seminal work on transactional and transformational leadership.**

---

*Albert Rodriguez, "William Choi and Ingrid Mittermaier, The Tax Exempt Status of Commercially Sponsored Donor Advised Funds," *The Exempt Organization Tax Review*, July 1997, p. 95–96.

**Bernard Bass, *Transformational Leadership*, Mahway, NJ: Lawrence Erlbaum Associates, 1998.

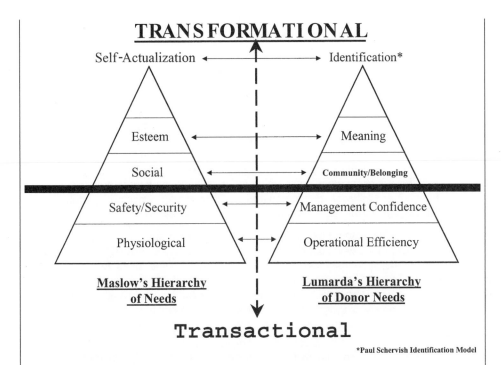

Exhibit 2.3   Transformational–transactional hierarchy.

In his book *Transformational Leadership,* Bass describes the transactional mode of operating:

> A transactional culture concentrates on explicit and implicit contractual re-
> lationships. Job assignments are in writing accompanied with statements
> about condition as of employment, rules, regulations, benefits, and disci-
> plinary codes. The stories that make the rounds repeatedly, the jargon
> used, the values emphasized, the assumptions shared and the reinforce-
> ment systems in the transactional culture usually set a price for doing any-
> thing . . . Commitments remain short term and self interests are under-
> scored.

In the transformational mode a different spirit exists:

> In the organizational transformational culture, there is a sense of purpose
> and a feeling of family. Commitments are long-term. Mutual interests are
> shared along with a sense of shared fates and interdependence of lead-
> ers and followers.
>
>   Leaders serve as role models, mentors, and coaches. They work to
> socialize new members into the epitome of a transformational organiza-

tion culture. Shared norms cover a wide range of behaviors. The norms are adaptive and change with changes in the organizations environment. Emphasized are organizational purpose, vision, and missions.

The transformational mode of operating does not disqualify the discipline of the transactional mode, but rather, complements it.

As with leadership, transformational culture can build upon the transactional culture of an organization. The inclusion of assumptions, norms, and values that are transformationally based does not preclude individuals pursuing their own goals and rewards. This can occur at the same time if there is an alignment of individual self-interests with a central purpose, and there is accompanying coordination to achieve the integrated goals. Leaders and followers go beyond their self-interests or expected rewards for the good of the team and the good of the organization.

Commercially sponsored gift funds can match and even possibly surpass community foundations in the world of transactional efficiency. They should. They share back offices and marketing departments with multi-billion dollar mutual funds. But many dealing within the financial institution and mutual fund industry, the primary goal of all of their enterprises—whether for profit or nonprofit—is simple and focused: to attain and retain assets. This is a very different vision than the one for community foundations.

Where the gift funds do not touch community foundations in terms of service and performance is in the higher needs, which are *transformational* in nature (see Exhibit 2.3). That is, donors to community foundations have the opportunity to learn and share more about their local community and the nonprofit community as a whole than they could with any commercially sponsored gift fund. And through the growing network of community foundations nationwide and around the world, donors to community foundations may learn about and make grants to the best children's programs in their backyard, in Peoria, Illinois or Warsaw, Poland. They may also join with other donors to learn about and collectively grant to the issues or causes they care about. Even the commercially sponsored gift funds concede this point. As then-president of Fidelity's Charitable Gift Fund, Jamie Jaffee, stated in the *Chronicle of Philanthropy* (November 28, 1996), "We have not built a big program staff and we have not done a lot of donor education because we don't want to duplicate what community foundations do. They can do a far better job."

Additionally, other than many financial institution cultures, community foundations have the long-term needs of both the donor and the community-in mind. They realize many relationships take time and patience for mutual knowledge and understanding to grow and develop. Short-term goals should not influence the manner in which a foundation approaches the needs of their donor partners. Trust is best built without the pressure of an impending or immediate fiscal bottom-line.

Community foundations, along with local management and transactional efficiency, offer experience, personal relationships and prudent judgment. For the donor who wants nothing more than transactional service, commercial gift funds may be the way. For those who desire wisdom, attentiveness and a local relationship, community foundations are the sensible choice.

NOTES

1. Abraham Maslow, *The Maslow Business Reader*. New York: John Wiley & Sons, 2000, p. 2.
2. *Id.*, p. 1.
3. Debra Blum, Marina Dundjerski, and Domenica Marchetti, "Gifts Up 5% at Top U.S. Charities," *Chronicle of Philanthropy*, October 31, 1996, p. 1.
4. Harvey Lippman, "Faltering Economy Slows Asset Growth at Community Foundations," *Chronicle of Philanthropy*, October 18, 2001.
5. Maslow, *The Maslow Business Reader*, p. 254.
6. *Webster's New World Dictionary*, Third College Edition. New York: Webster's New World, 1988, p. 569.
7. Treas. Reg §1.170A-1(b).
8. Peter Drucker, *Managing in a Time of Great Change*. New York: Truman Talley/Dutton, 1995, p. 239.
9. Robert Lenzer and Ashlea Ebeling, "Peter Drucker's Picks," *Forbes*, August 11, 1997, p. 99.
10. Harvey Rheingold, *The Virtual Community: Homesteading on the Electronic Frontier*, New York: Harper Collins, 1993, *www.well.com/user/hlr/vcbook/vcbookintro.html*.
11. Maslow, *The Maslow Business Reader*, p. 261.
12. Polly Labarre, "Do You Have the Will to Lead," *Fast Company*, March 2000, p. 224.
13. Adrienne Tomine, "Fast Pack 2000," *Fast Company*, March 2000, p. 236.
14. Maslow, *The Maslow Business Reader*, p. 261.
15. Paul Schervish, "Developing Major Gifts," *New Directions for Philanthropic Fund Raising*, Summer 1997, p. 89.
16. *Id.*, p. 99.
17. *Id.*

CHAPTER 3

Impact of the New Economy on Foundations

by Bill Dietel, Tory Dietel Hopps, and Jonathan Hopps

PERSPECTIVES

Has the "New New" Thing* spawned a "New New" Philanthropy? The innovators and business moguls who have built the Information Age have taken on philanthropy in much the same way. As one associate once mentioned, "This group does not look to fill the barn, paint the barn, or even name the barn. They want to burn the barn down and build a new one in the same way they built their company." This not only means the exploration of new business models, but exploration *in a hurry*.

Is the approach of these entrepreneurs-turned-philanthropists any different from Andrew Carnegie's, who left the architectural blueprint of his libraries along with his money at the turn of the century? Are we really on the edge of a fundamental change in the funding and role of foundations?

Though the stock market technology bubble has been battered, there are still plenty of companies and foundations that want to participate in a transformation (or updating) of philanthropy.

Bill Dietel, former president of the Rockefeller Brothers Foundations, is a senior statesman and highly regarded for his visionary role through his career in American foundations and philanthropy. His continued work in these areas has now taken him into global foundations and philanthropy, where his instinct for creative innovation continues. He is joined by young associates, Tory Deitel Hopps and Jonathan Hopps, who are consultants to foundations, nonprofits, and philanthropists.

*Michael Lewis, *The New New Thing*. New York: Nort & Company, 1999.

INTRODUCTION

Today, foundations—the stalwarts of philanthropy—are being challenged to meet the profound and pervasive impact of the new economy. The last decade has witnessed a period of unsurpassed technological advancements and economic growth, creating a shift in the mindset and practices of the old industrial age economy. The one undeniable by-product of this time is the mega-wealth generated by the innovators and financial participants in the creation of the new economy.

The forecast for wealth transfer is well documented.[1] The conditions are right for a tidal wave of trillions of dollars to transform the nonprofit sector. The marketplace has brought forth new interests, aptitudes, energy and intellectual capital in a stunning fashion. Many observers claim the country is at "a combustible moment"—the onset of a period of renaissance in philanthropy.

As the new millennium opens, there is a new cadre of participants in the world of philanthropy, utilizing a wide range of philanthropic vehicles of which private foundations, as we have known them, are only one arrow in the giving quiver. Some of the new wealth holders are innovating on established techniques and structures and developing new mechanisms to address the issues that arouse their philanthropic concern. The historic shape of private philanthropic organizations is being challenged.

There are many forces at work creating this new climate for philanthropy. Among them are the changing demographics of the wealth holders, the use of technology, the personal and passionate involvement of donors, the shift in the relationship between government and the for-profit and nonprofit sectors, and an increase in the media's focus on and the public's interest in philanthropic issues.

A few statistics help to explain the current optimism about the future of organized philanthropy. According to the Foundation Center, the number of foundations—private, community, corporate, and operating—now stands at an all-time high of 46,832. Fifty-two percent of all foundations have been formed since 1980 and foundation assets have grown from $8.7 billion in 1989 to $385 billion in 1998.

Introduction

Grantmaking by foundations in the United States grew by 17.2 percent in 1999, and total dollars went from $19.5 billion in 1998 to $22.8 billion in 1999.[2] While the increase in the value of foundation assets is primarily the result of the bull market, the commitment of new capital to foundations is also at an all-time peak.

This chapter seeks to provide an overview of the impact of the new economy on organized philanthropy, and, in particular what it means for private foundations. The wave of change continues to form even as this book goes to print. According to *The Economist*, "the lesson is that any analysis of the economic consequences of the current burst of innovation . . . should proceed with care."[3] Thus, we write this chapter with optimism for the future, yet recognize there are events which have already shifted the tides, such as September 11, the e-commerce meltdown, the corporate accounting scandals, and the current beat market, as well as unforeseen events on the horizon.

As students of the sector, we focused our research for this chapter on discussions with some new economy philanthropists, individuals who run their own foundations, service providers to the foundation field, and directors of traditional foundations. We sought especially to draw on their direct experiences of the last 24 months (1997 to 1999). Our objective was to look at the structures, programs, operations, and philosophies of these new participants in the world of philanthropy.

We believe that the new philanthropy is marked by a sense of excitement, tension, suspicion, and skepticism. Edward Skloot, executive director of the Surdna Foundation, notes: "Today the relationships among business, foundations, and not-for-profits are edgy and in transition." Perhaps for the first time in our history it is possible to project a future in which nonprofits may, in fact, become capable of equal participation alongside government and business in addressing society's opportunities and challenges.

The new economy quite simply favors globalization and fresh linkages between ideas, information, and human relationships. It appears the prime goal of the new economy is to undo—company by company, industry by industry—the industrial economy.[4] Will the new philanthropy wittingly or unwittingly undo traditional philanthropy? The quality of "dynamism" in the new philanthropy is one of its hallmarks.

Many have termed the new philanthropy *venture philanthropy*,[5] which implies the application of lessons learned from the marketplace experience to philanthropy. For the purpose of this chapter, we will use the *new philanthropy*, which we define as the philanthropic endeavors of the newly wealthy, specifically when they take the form of foundation-like structures and procedures. We do so because we believe there are a host of factors impinging on philanthropy that are more than just the lessons learned from the marketplace.

While some pit the new philanthropy versus established philanthropy, we agree with Tom Reis, Program Director of Venture Philanthropy at the W.K. Kellogg Foundation, who states, "The healthy response to the new economy foundations is not an 'either/or' response. It is an 'and/both' response. Any organization that has been established for a while tends to atrophy. We need freshness, innovation, new ideas, and tools emerging from philanthropists, along with the wisdom and experience of established philanthropies, which can provide added value to organized philanthropy." Before we can fully understand the changes being wrought in the foundation field as a result of the activities of some of the new wealth holders, it is helpful first to consider some of the major characteristics that delineate these recent entrants to philanthropy.

SO WHAT'S NEW AND DIFFERENT ABOUT THIS NEW BREED OF PHILANTHROPISTS?

Historically, the major philanthropists of the first approximately 80 years of the twentieth century expressed their most effective philanthropic activities through the device of the private foundation. It is important to note that these men and women of great wealth also tried to achieve their philanthropic goals through a variety of other means as well, but they left their most distinctive mark on American culture and society primarily as a result of their perfection of the private foundation. Their attempts to carry over the lessons they had learned from their own commercial, financial, and industrial experiences to both the private foundation and the nonprofit organization presaged in many respects the experiences of the current generation of entrepreneurs and venture capitalists about whom we read in the media today.

Generalizations about any social phenomenon as complex as American philanthropy of the twentieth century is fraught, but it helps to sharpen the apparent differences between the old and the new breed of philanthropists and foundation creators and leaders if we particularly note the former's belief that through research and analysis, it was possible to focus foundation giving on critical issues of the times and to do so most effectively by creating strongly led and well-managed nonprofit organizations to address these issues (e.g., the General Education Board; the Brookings Institution; and, on the international front, the Consultative Group of International Agricultural Research Centers). Of course, these philanthropists also supported organizations already in existence, which they believed performed important services to the community. The vast majority of foundations with notable exceptions created before 1990 or thereabout helped projects and programs and institutions in their immediate backyards and did not conceive of themselves as the generators of new intellectual capital for the nonprofit sector nor as innovators in institution building for the nonprofit sector, and assuredly they did not think of themselves either as mentors to or investors in the nonprofit sector.

With the caveat that all efforts at describing a diverse group of individuals run the risk of distortion and exaggeration, the following descriptions are generic characteristics of the new economy wealth holders. We suggest this description to help us explore the significance of the contribution of this new breed of philanthropists.

Not surprisingly, the new economy wealthy have an expertise in business creation and development and in finance and management. They live in business environments where technology and the speed of "real time" play important roles in their vocational success. They are quick learners, share information readily and continually, and have a "can do" response to difficulties and opportunities. They are often big risk takers, are comfortable working in partnership with others, and have learned, often painfully, how to garner significant capital to support their ideas and dreams. As a group, they move toward new opportunities as opposed to coming up with solutions to problems and, when necessary, have created markets where none existed before. In addition, in many instances their experiences have given them an appreciation for the importance of a strong infrastructure to the success of any venture.

It is also worth noting that participants, other than the traditional white male, are stepping onto the playing field of philanthropy. Today's players come from diverse socioeconomic backgrounds; their educational backgrounds are more varied; and a host of ethnic groups, women, and an emerging and public group of gay and lesbian philanthropists are prominent participants. Not only are new entrants more diverse in their backgrounds, but also many are entering the field at a significantly younger age. Tom Reis is on target when he notes that today's new and younger philanthropists "have a longer period of time for their philanthropy to develop. . . . [It] is going to evolve dramatically because they are going to be in to it (far longer)."

Certainly, the language used in business and investment is becoming the *lingua franca* of twenty-first-century philanthropy. All about us we are urged to heed the importance of measurement and evaluation, going to scale and market focus. The perception is that the nonprofit that cannot speak convincingly of its ability to deliver a significant return on investment is in danger of rejection.

As Vanessa Kirsch, founder and president of New Profit, Inc., a venture fund to provide mezzanine funding for social entrepreneurs, reminds us, "There is a growing philanthropy that is about investment." While the qualities of some of the new philanthropists bring to bear on the field of philanthropy are energizing, we believe we must take heed, for as Jed Emerson, president of the Roberts Enterprise Development Fund and Bloomberg Senior Research Fellow in Philanthropy at the Harvard Business School warns,

"There is a population that think 'All the [not-for-profit] sector needs is a little business savvy'—if it were that easy, it would have happened a long time ago." Emmett Carson, CEO of the Minnesota Foundation, reminds us that it may be far easier to apply principles of venture capital investing to the program-related investments of foundations than to their grant making activities.[6] With an overwhelming drive for the "new new" to present itself in everything connected with the high speed, high energy and high finance of today's economy, the push into the world of philanthropy and foundation operations is not all a bad thing. There is and will be an awkward period in which there will be a shakedown where the old foundations will adapt and adopt some new ways of doing things and the new will begin to understand the complexity and messiness of addressing some of our most pressing social problems through grantmaking. The proof will be in the pudding, and the pudding is still congealing, and quite possibly we might come to learn that the best state for the pudding is one of fluidity.

How Do the Newly Wealthy Enter into Philanthropy and What Exactly Are They Trying to Accomplish?

While some new philanthropists are entering into the field with little experience, others are sophisticated in their thinking and approach. The range of donor experience and education is as wide as the number of new wealthy.

Shannon St. John, executive director of the Triangle Community Foundation, who is an innovator in her region of North Carolina, claims, "Entrepreneurs are a fiercely independent breed." She describes the typical entrepreneurial characteristics as "wanting leverage, wanting to see measurable impact and wanting to be creative." And Paul Brainerd's observations are noteworthy: "There is something different about this new brand of philanthropy. It's more hands on; it expects results, it's optimistic, and it's very spirited in its approach, and these differences are generational and professional."

According to Jed Emerson, when George Roberts created the Roberts Enterprise Development Fund, he thought: "If I can create great economic value with this model, then why wouldn't some of those same principles be at play in this other space where you're trying to create social value?" George wanted to "pursue more of a free enterprise, a free market approach to our philanthropy, and the challenge then became . . . how do you best do that?"

Christine Letts, Associate Director of the Hauser Center for Nonprofit Organizations at Harvard University, says that when she counsels people on philanthropy, she tries to "help them to understand all the implications and choices they have, and to understand the notion of fit. . . . If they're going to talk about making a big social change, then they probably ought to do something different than give out one hundred $10,000 grants." Virginia Esposito, president of the National Center for Family Foundations, notes that when talking with new economy philanthropists, "Giving frequently starts with what has been important to them in their own development. This is why you see a lot of new wealth folks making gifts to their colleges and universities. There is this wonderful fundamental need to connect what is changing in your life with what has been important in your life . . ."

Bill and Melinda Gates used their business acumen when designing their foundation. Patty Stonesifer, executive director of the Gates Foundation, says, "Bill and Melinda really believe that the twenty-first century has some unusual and exciting changes for the world. They realize that given a time of such rapid and exciting change, philanthropy could perhaps address needs that have been impossible to address and do it in new ways." Susan Packard Orr, chair of the David and Lucile Packard Foundation, puts it this way when she speaks with the newer philanthropist(s): "Some of us have been at this for a while. We probably have a few things that you might be able to learn from, so come look at us, but don't take this to mean we have all the answers and we know how to do it necessarily. Everybody has to do it their own way."

We observe a spectrum of understanding among the new philanthropists and a wide range of expectations. There is also a high demand for philanthropic information and education and a sense of urgency consistent with their for-profit experience. We believe that it is critical for individuals to discover and articulate their passion, style, and the impact they hope to have before embarking on their philanthropic quest.

What Are some of the Challenges That Face These New Philanthropists?

We agree with many of the most astute observers of the contemporary scene that we are in the middle of major-sector boundary shifts. Private entrepreneurs are eagerly invading the domains of government and nonprofits in their enthusiastic pursuit of change in the faltering delivery of services to people.[7] Many of the people we interviewed about the impact of the new philanthropists, however, questioned their ability to stay the course and go the long distance often required to bring about social change.

Many of the new philanthropists find that results do not happen in the short term and a lot of their business success has come from their ability to make things happen very quickly. Unfortunately, much of the work in philanthropy cannot be done quickly. "It is too early to tell how well these people will be able to adapt to a longer timetable," says Meriwether Jones of the Aspen Institute and director of the Community Strategies Group.

Christine Letts also questions the tenacity of some of the new philanthropists . . . "because they're used to getting in and out . . . being comfortable with change is a double edged sword . . . they may not seem to be able to stick with it long enough, year after year." The "flipping" idea that characterizes much of the e-com world, at least at first glance, does not seem to fit the nonprofit world. Understandably, new philanthropists are success oriented and want results from their giving that can be measured tomorrow in quantitative terms. There is often an unwritten assumption that if something cannot be measured quantitatively, it is suspect. The jury is still out on whether these donors can distinguish between and among short- and long-term and qualitative and quantitative results. Meriwether Jones says it is "unclear whether they have the staying power once they realize how frustrating grantmaking can be relative to the immediate gratification they are accustomed to . . ."

The new philanthropy is a mixture of objectives, styles, and institutions. The Gates Foundation is part of this spectrum of new giving and so are the thousands of new, small, often family-oriented foundations with assets of under $100 million. The myriad of donor-directed funds whose power to affect change is still being tested, and the admittedly exciting and challenging new partnerships and concepts imported from the business world, have not yet been fully evaluated.

What's Being Challenged and Why?

If we are indeed at a combustible moment in philanthropy, there is a multiplicity of reasons for this condition. Result-oriented new philanthropists are raising questions about process, about relationships, and about outcomes. They want results and are eager to apply the techniques that are hallmarks of their for-profit success to the foundation side.

Frustration with Nonprofit Operations

The transition from the business world to the nonprofit sector can be frustrating for this new brand of philanthropist. Eager to make a difference and eager for results, the new philanthropist expects to adapt best practices from the business sector to the nonprofit sector, and that can be an exasperating experience. This frustration creates tension, but tension creates innovation.

The foundation program officer makes a grant recommendation and then awaits results that he or she hopes can be measured. The investor in a new and high-risk business brings a different mindset to his involvement. He insists on a board seat and expects to play a vital role in building the company. This is contrary to historical foundation practices.

As Vanessa Kirsch discovered, "The funders who are investing in our fund are people who articulate the frustrations of philanthropy within the first five minutes of talking with me." New economy philanthropists exhibit less tolerance for unbusinesslike procedures and thinking. This attitude pervades their reaction to governance, fund raising, and especially management.

It has long been the case that there is a wide gap in the management training and experience between the men and women who operate businesses and those who lead many, if not most, of our nonprofits. "Almost no one has chosen to work in philanthropy because they understand organizational development or management," Edward Skloot points out. "As a result, most foundations cannot diagnose, let alone treat, bad management on the part of their grantees." This is partly due to the fact that professionals who are experts in areas of program interest dominate foundation staffs.

Cora Mirikitani, director of the new Innovation Fund at the Irvine Foundation, summarizes it this way: "I think the idea of venture philanthropy implies that you're going to get more involved in the business. I don't know if that is a good or bad thing. . . . We're breaking new ground here."

Much of the power the new economy types bring to the nonprofit sector stems from their networks and their ability and willingness to forge strategic partnerships to deliver talent or resources necessary for success. Applying these proven techniques to the nonprofit sector requires a fine balance between speed and sensitivity for the current nonprofit model.

Honest Communications

The traditional grant giving and reporting structures used by many of our country's foundations are now being called into question.

Grantors have not been effective in persuading grantees to communicate the major stumbling blocks to their success honestly and regularly. The desire to be seen as successful in the eyes of a funder is often enough of an incentive for nonprofits not to enter into full disclosure.

Both the traditional and new philanthropists, then, face the challenge of how to develop more honest relationships between funders and their funding recipients. Rachel Bellows of divine interVentures puts it this way: "During the time I was involved with conventional philanthropy, I found the single greatest obstacle to smart program development and effective measurement of impact is that we had no capacity to have honest conversations with our constituents; there is no transparency."

Lack of Market Forces

Many of the new philanthropists we talked to were vocal about the lack of "market forces" at work in the field of philanthropy. For many, if there is no market at work, it is nearly impossible, almost by definition, to know whether or not you have invested wisely and whether your strategies are in fact successful.

"It is not like other marketplaces . . ." adds Bellows, "where if you miss with your target market, you know, because they are no longer purchasing your product. . . . Since there is no market in any real sense of the word, you try to make it a partnership, but it is not a partnership because we (foundations) . . . have the power—we have the capital. We need to be able to enter into a fundamentally different relationship with not-for-profit organizations."

Put in more dramatic language, Bellows insists: "What you have in the not-for-profit sector is a hermetically sealed condition, ecology, where they are in a death dance with philanthropy. You have this enormous lag time between the failure of your delivery on your objectives and the moment when your constituency, your market, wakes up and says, 'Hey look what you've done' . . . (or not done)."

Speed and Efficiency

The nature of the new economy experience in operating in real time has brought the need for speed and efficiency over to a sector that has traditionally been operating at a much slower pace. In the business and commercial worlds there is an inexorable pressure to find new and more efficient ways of doing things, to embrace doing things differently. In order to be more efficient, the sector must build internal capacity, including technology, appropriate application of technology, and staff training in utilization of those systems. This is an area in which the nonprofit sector is underresourced.

Level of Engagement

Another issue, which is hotly debated, is the question of how close funders should get to the board leadership of the organizations they fund. Some, like New Profit, Inc., believe it is imperative to hold seats on the boards of nonprofits in which they invest. As Vanessa Kirsch explains, "We really do our homework . . . we work hard at setting the standard with organizations and then there is alignment around commonly held performance standards which is important." This approach appeals to some, but by no means all of the new venture philanthropists. Regardless of whether funders serve on boards or not, the models being used by many new philanthropists provide more interaction with boards than typical funding relationships of the past. Jed Emerson believes many of the new models "allow the board of a not-for-profit to develop a different type of relationship with the funders, when, historically, there really has been no meaningful relationship."

Whether these philanthropists serve on boards or not, the bottom line is that their commitment in one way or another to improving the governance and management of the nonprofit sector is real and potentially very powerful. Edward Skloot observes, "More remarkable still is the fact that people who have succeeded (in the new economy) are now viewed as possible partners, even mentors, to the not-for-profit leaders, whose entire training has been a struggle to conserve funds."

NEW MECHANISMS AND DEVICES FOR FOUNDATIONS

While conducting our interviews, we were especially interested in learning about new mechanisms and devices being used to effect change by the newest participants in American philanthropy.

Technology

The role of technology is at the top of the list of new devices and mechanisms being utilized by the new economy philanthropists and at a rate and in ways that are significantly different from the practices of most established foundations. The new philanthropy is using technology to address and to facilitate the need to be more rigorous with communication, continual monitoring, facilitation of grant-making, and sharing of information. The chasm between the for-profit sector's use of technology and access to the most sophisticated systems and the nonprofit sector's use of technology is enormous. The increased use of technology by new philanthropists has been heralded as having the potential for incredibly positive impact. Technology "has the potential of making things more transparent. It has the ability to save a lot of cost and facilitate communication, which are needed in terms of relationships between communities and foundations," says Christine Letts.

When talking about the new philanthropists she has worked with, Shannon St. John points out, "Everything is by computer, so we have to be able to gear up to meet their technological expectations and their time expectations." Vanessa Kirsch drives the point home when she says, "Technology is integral to everything we do . . . starting with the fact that we only communicate with our investors with e-mail. All our portfolio organizations have pretty strong Web strategies and are using it for communications: one to lower cost and, two, to build knowledge."

It is important to note, however, that many of technology's most ardent advocates recognize that there are limits to what it can and cannot do. As Carol Welsh Gray, director of the Center for Venture Philanthropy at the Peninsula Community Foundation, says, "Face-to-face is still very valuable, especially when you're having difficult conversations." There will always be a need for high touch interaction in the field, and technology cannot replace the very critical human element of philanthropy.

Lean Operations

New economy donors exhibit some anxiety about the creation of big bureaucratic foundations. Many people spoke to us about the reluctance of new economy philanthropists to employ large staffs or even modest-sized staffs. Several different motivations seem to be at work here—the fear of bureaucracy, the desire to be facile, or the need to be personally engaged.

Emerson said, "We operate from a philosophy that we don't really want to increase our own staffing as much as build the capacity of other organizations to execute their strategies more effectively." What does smaller staffing mean for the new foundations? According to Christine Letts, "If they don't have a lot of staff, they are either going to give out huge grants or they are going to be using a lot of consultants."

In addition to using consultants, there is a model of using intermediaries, and the Gates Foundation is a good example of that approach. "We are purposely keeping our staff very small and relying on external advisors and expert organizations to advise us," says Patty Stonesifer.

There are, of course, some problems with these models. First, there is the anomaly of an organization managing a large endowment whose own organization is undercapitalized in terms of human resources. It is difficult to undertake some kinds of grantmaking without some in-house expertise. As Chris Letts warns, "Using a lot of consultants can be quite problematic. You end up with a lot of knowledge and experience that resides in people outside the foundation."

In addition to smaller staffs, there is some indication that a higher percentage of new foundations are structuring themselves to terminate and not last in perpetuity, while statistics are not yet available to reflect the scope of this trend. This phenomenon further decreases the likelihood of bureaucratic structures.

Continual Due Diligence

Another area of change in some new economy foundations is the attitude toward due diligence. Historically, foundations have done their due diligence before the grant decision was made; now there is a growing emphasis on a continuous kind of due diligence. In the traditional model, due diligence all happens ahead of time. It involves a major change to move your capacity from before the grant to after the grant. Christine Letts thinks this is "a great culture shift. It's a capacity shift."

Jed Emerson says, "We're involved in continual due diligence." This type of due diligence tries to address the concern about transparency. Many new funders believe it also improves the chance of a higher return on investment and ultimately success. Carol Welsh Gray believes she is not taking riskier investments in nonprofits: "I simply think that I am managing the risk along the way, which increases the chances of success."

Performance Measurement and Evaluation

Performance measurement is an area of heated discussion in the field of philanthropy. Reactions to this issue run the gamut. Some feel adamantly about it, and some institutions have decided to invest increasingly in research on the subject. Others remain skeptical, arguing that American philanthropy seems to go through cycles of interest and confidence in measuring success.

"When you have people who are driven primarily by marketplace experiences, they do expect measurements. I miss the obvious measurements of success or failure that you do get from the markets but you don't necessarily get from philanthropy," confesses Patty Stonesifer. "If you invest in the marketplace, you get very immediate indicators that you were unwise, but in philanthropy you get 'thank you very much, that was wonderful.'"

Michael Bailin, president of the Edna McConnell Clark Foundation, believes "if you're really concerned about impact and measuring the social yield of your investments, you've got to invest like an investor, invest in something that has a good chance of working. There needs to be a way of tracking things as you proceed so that you know what is happening, or if things aren't happening, you can take corrective action."

Some new philanthropists eschew the very word *evaluation* because they find it misleading. "We're not going to use that word," says Jed Emerson. "Oftentimes mainstream 'evaluation' is retrospective; it's punitive, and it doesn't inform practice . . . I think if all foundations said 'for every fifty thousand dollars grant money we put out, we're going to put out twenty thousand in building information management capacity,' . . . over a five- or ten-year period you would in fact have a very sophisticated network of performance and reporting systems."

One of the most experienced students of the nonprofit sector, Elizabeth Boris of the Urban Institute, comments, "The social side of our economy is very difficult to capture in a bottom line and the desire to have nonprofits adhere to a bottom line and talk in those terms goes back more than a decade. It is not the invention of new philanthropy."

At first glance, performance measurement and evaluation practices are not easily transferable to the nonprofit world. As foundations embrace and invest in technology, said practices might become more practical.

Partnerships

Another mechanism that appears to be growing in importance and popularity is that of strategic partnerships and collaborations. New economy philanthropists bring their comfort level with partnerships to the table in their funding. As a result, some believe the chances for successfully addressing really big social problems is greater. Patty Stonesifer describes, "The most defining part of our philanthropy thus far is that it has been very collaborative. Bill Gates is the first one to say that most very large societal problems require both governments and marketplaces to address them because of their size. . . . (It's a three-legged stool) and one leg is a lot smaller than the others—the not-for-profit leg." As we see it, it lacks the financial and political heft of the other two legs. Without radical changes, it is unlikely to be coequal with government and the for-profit world in the future.

Some hope that this new interest in partnerships will help to bring the foundation field out of its "insulation" and enable both funders and nonprofits to have a louder voice and stronger impact. Says Cora Mirikitani, "We really are anticipating we will have to learn something new and that's different. . . . It requires we give up some power, in a sense, that we expose ourselves to some risk in a way that is quite unusual for us."

Partnerships and collaborations are seen in the growth of giving circles, gatherings of niche funders, and creation of entrepreneur funds. Each of these raise the level of dialogue about philanthropy, provide access to a variety of philanthropic devices to a wider audience, and involve new groups of people in philanthropy at earlier ages and stages in their success, all of which is good for the field and the nonprofit sector.

Long-Term Funding and Larger Grants

We are also seeing innovations in funding patterns and policies that offer hope that some of the nonprofit sector's concerns will finally be addressed on a multiyear basis by the funding world. The vogue in foundations the past 20 years has been program funding and one-year funding. The new economy philanthropists appear to be bucking this trend or, at the very least, are talking in terms of "longer-term" funding. Some are making a conscious effort to build institutional capacity rather than focusing their funding on programs and projects. This approach is both old and new. It differs from the patterns of foundation funding in recent decades but also harkens back to the early focus of the Rockefeller Foundation, Carnegie Corporation, and the Ford Foundation. Tied to the rising interest in long-term funding is the slow increase in the size of grants. As funders increase their amounts and commit to supporting organizations over longer periods of time, there is a higher potential for the relationships between funders and grantees to become more dynamic and thus more helpful.

NEW ECONOMY MODELS AND THEIR IMPACT ON PHILANTHROPY

Are some of the new economy foundations really shaking things up, or is it the old wrapped in a provocative new package, or, perhaps, mostly hype? Let us start by describing some examples of this new philanthropy.

Paul Brainerd founded Social Venture Partners (SVP) (which operates outside the purview of the Brainerd Foundation). "SVP employs mechanisms used in the private sector to fund young, innovative ideas and to nurture them." This organization is more like a giving circle in which each partner contributes or invests a minimum of $5,000 a year; some give more, and they make a commitment of two to three years at a minimum. The funds are spent out each year, so it is a recycling fund. The Seattle Foundation handles the back-office services. Brainerd says, "In one respect we're a training ground for individuals to get experience in philanthropy . . . we've spawned off two or three family foundations."

The Gates Foundation has developed a three-part strategy for its philanthropy. As described by Patty Stonesifer, "Our strategy is to rely on the experts, the people doing the innovative work in public health, education, and libraries around the world. In partnering with outside organizations we try to act as a convener and a catalyst for

99

change. Business, governments, NGOs (nongovernmental organizations), UN agencies, and philanthropists all have a role to play, and if we are able to help bring them together to address a common goal then we can make important progress."

Carol Welsh Gray explains the work of the Center for Venture Philanthropy this way; "Our model combines understanding of the nonprofit world and lessons in philanthropy with an adaptation of five key elements of modern venture capital practices. We invest for the long haul in three- to six-year business plans, have a managing partner relationship, provide cash, as well as expertise, emphasize accountability-for-results and quarterly benchmarks, and think about the exit strategies."

In Silicon Valley, the Entrepreneurs Foundation, a two-year-old philanthropy, is aggregating money and personal commitment. It receives shares of start-up companies from their owners. When the shares go public, the Foundation sells them and invests the proceeds in entrepreneurial nonprofits. To date, 63 companies have joined the foundation.

Another model is the Entrepreneur Philanthropic Venture Fund of the Triangle Community Foundation. Shannon St. John explains: "The Entrepreneur Philanthropic Venture Fund is for entrepreneurs who make a donation of $50,000 to create a pool of $500,000 to be a resource for early stage entrepreneurs who become philanthropists but don't have cash. They can draw down from that pool explicitly for the purpose of making charitable grants. And in return, they put up shares of their company as collateral." Each of the aforementioned examples is long term, ranging from 3 to 20 years of investment.

New or not, these approaches are capturing the attention of the foundation world. Emerson believes, "Now the mainstream has to take us seriously as opposed to just tolerating innovation. We have increasing capital under our belts, an emerging track record our ideas are resonating at a deeper level. Even though there are probably no more than 10 foundations that are really doing things fundamentally differently, under the Venture Philanthropy, based on the response we sometimes get, you'd think we are the Huns coming over the wall—which leads me to believe we must be doing something right!"

Jonathan Fanton, president of the MacArthur Foundation, speaking on behalf of many of his colleagues, cautions that newness can often be more a matter of language than reality. "Newly founded foundations use the term 'investment' to describe what some older foundations like MacArthur have tried to do for a long time. But it is helpful to be reminded that setting clear goals and measurable outcomes for program areas is a healthy process." The distinction between an investment and a grant is not always clear either to the public or to the recipient nonprofit.

More than one observer welcomed the blooming of the many new approaches to philanthropy. It is too early to tell whether these new models and devices will become trends and fundamentally alter the nonprofit sector. But in our opinion, Edward Skloot has put his finger on what needs to be emphasized: "The three things the not-for-profit sector needs most are capital, technology, and a culture of sharing knowledge. Now, the mega-wealthy can provide the money and the technological capability to help answer some of our most pressing social questions—and nudge older philanthropy too. What Gates, Brainerd, and others are doing could well serve as a model for the thousands of dot.com millionaires. First, they are building on their strengths in technology and information systems. Second, they act with strategic focus . . . Third they take a long view . . . Taken all together this is the outline of a new, high-engagement enterprise."

HAVE ESTABLISHED FOUNDATIONS RESPONDED TO THE NEW APPROACHES AND CHALLENGES?

Some of the established foundations have begun making changes—some small, others more significant.

Perhaps the most dramatic and influential changes in grant-making by major established foundations have occurred in the Edna McConnell Clark Foundation of New York and the Irvine Foundation in California. They are in the process of effecting major restructuring of their organizations as well as their grantmaking.

In New York City, the Edna McConnell Clark Foundation is actively retooling the entire foundation to become a long-term institution builder. Michael Bailin, president of the Foundation, and his board are now in the early stages of changing an old-line foundation to embrace elements of the new philanthropy by clarifying their focus and developing partnerships with organizations that are prepared to create and implement a strategic "growth plan."

Bailin notes that the genesis of the change at Clark stems more from his years at Public/Private Ventures on the other side of the grantmaking table as opposed to seeking to implement what is labeled as *new philanthropy*. Still in the early stages of this pilot program, they have begun to alter drastically how they identify and evaluate organizations that they partner with. They are focusing on more evolved organizations and or those who have proven success or are ripe with potential. The partnership combines technical expertise, bringing other funders to the table, being more engaged in improving organizational performance, and making up to a five-year commitment with several millions of dollars in grant money. Both the style of the foundation's choice of partners and the magnitude of their financial support suggest that Clark is engaged in a pioneering effort.

The Irvine Foundation, under Dennis Collins's leadership, has established within itself the Innovation Fund. According to Cora Mirikitani, director of the Innovation Fund, which appears to be a research and development department of the Foundation, it is getting launched with $6 million in funding. In effect it will act as a venture investment fund that will be seeking a variety of ideas and products and services coming from both the commercial sector and the nonprofit sector, involving elements of the new technology.

Mirikitani says, "Hopefully the fund will be more flexible and develop more creative solutions and new partnerships to solve problems." In addition, the Innovation Fund is going to be launched strictly online. It is positioned to have guideposts, but not rules; therefore, the amount invested as grants will be determined based on need and not on the basis of predetermined program categories.

"I think our intention in making this fund a little bit more agile, a little bit more responsive, a little bit more opportunistic has really caused us to examine the way that we operate normally as a mature philanthropy. We have a lot to learn. It is more than a difference in styles," says Mirikitani.

The effort to adapt to changed conditions and opportunities is not confined to the larger foundations. For instance, the Maine Community Foundation has created a new subsidiary called Common Good. Common Good will help nonprofits become more efficient and cost effective in their social-purpose enterprises by providing significant technical assistance as well as funding. Common Good is actively recruiting a new set of philanthropists in the state.

Undergirding all such efforts is the recognition that society needs to find more effective ways and means of incubating and supporting social entrepreneurships. There is now a keen interest and growing commitment on the part of established foundations like the Ford Foundation, the Rockefeller Brothers Fund, and the Kaufman Foundation to create curriculum and educational opportunities for would-be social ventures. The foundation world is recognizing the need to train a cadre of nonprofit leaders for tomorrow in a nontraditional fashion. This is also happening on the other side of the Atlantic with the work of Sir Michael Young and James Cornford at the School for Social Entrepreneurs in London.

WHAT ARE THE POSSIBLE IMPLICATIONS AND WHAT ARE THE CHALLENGES POSED BY THE NEW PHILANTHROPY?

The new innovations in philanthropy have implications for the future as well as challenges.

We see that old boundaries are being tested and lines that used to demarcate the worlds of the profit and nonprofit sectors are being blurred. Gene Steuerle of the Urban Institute warns, "There is a lot more tension coming about because of the mix of not-for-profits and business." As a result, the new philanthropy and more highly engaged forms of "investment" in the nonprofit sector "may very well become a matter of interest to both legislators and regulators." Cora Mirikitani describes the new philanthropy as "the brave new world."

New partnerships and investment strategies may call for more new philanthropic vehicles. "I think they (new economy types) are going to create new structures. They are pushing in that direction already. They are trying to talk to the Treasury to set up 'our kinds of institutions' . . . these institutions are not quite business and they are not quite philanthropies. Neither set of rules fits them," says Elizabeth Boris. The new philanthropy at its most promising brings new human resources and fresh intellectual capital as well as massive infusions of financial capital to the nonprofit sector.

Nearly everyone we interviewed for this chapter believes the issue of the speed of change alone will have implications for the future of philanthropy. Perhaps the most positive view of the implications of change comes from Cora Mirikitani: "The rate of adaptation is much faster . . . I think that if we can keep up and don't get discouraged and don't get scared away, we'll get smarter a whole lot faster."

Another result of the growth in sheer numbers of new foundations is the growth of new services and supporting organizations being developed. Information and support materials are being produced to teach new philanthropists how to create, govern, manage, and evaluate the various opportunities for doing philanthropy. As the number of alternative ways of spreading charitable largesse expand, it is more than probable that the role of the foundation will also change. It is too early, however, to predict with any accuracy what forms foundations will take in the future. This much is certain: The definition of a foundation is changing before our eyes. Since the new economy and the resulting new philanthropy are so new, society at large will want to track their maturation, examine their impact, and explore their interaction with both government and the for-profit sector.

From today's perspective, it is difficult to imagine a time in the foreseeable future when total government funding could be replaced by private philanthropy dollars. However, we can visualize a time when the balance between government and the private sector will shift significantly. New ideas, institutions, and leaders will be needed to help society adjust to the changing circumstances. As a number of our interviewees pointed out, the private sector and private money have great potential for leadership and leverage.

In addition to the big foundations (those with assets in excess of $500 million), small foundations in the future will also make a significant impact if they choose to exploit some of their hidden power in an imaginative way. Joe Pierpont, co-executive director of the Association of Small Foundations (ASF), believes, "Small foundations represent the most powerful, but neglected, legislative force for changing public policy in the country." On average, Pierpont sites 50 percent of the members of ASF personally know their congressperson, senator, and state legislator. It would not be surprising that in years ahead, like in the past, periodic challenges to foundations would take place, in which national and state legislators who were unsympathetic to them would look to place restrictions on them. Therefore, this growing number of small foundations and their donors could have tremendous opportunity to uphold the institution and protect as well as guide it. Unfortunately, history does not encourage us to believe that private philanthropy will regulate itself.

Elements of the new philanthropy call the historic relationships in the nonprofit sector into question. How organizations and funders work together in some of the new philanthropy models will be very different.

If the new philanthropists find the time to become highly engaged, will they find the nonprofit partners willing to engage with them? "I think where venture philanthropy is value added is when there are very complex initiatives that will need and really benefit from problem solving along the way," Carol Welsh Gray points out. ". . . It is very labor intensive work . . . and it requires strong leadership." From the perspective of the nonprofit, "You have to feel pretty good about yourself as a not-for-profit leader in order to open up yourself and your organization for problem solving with investors. A strong sense of trust must be in place with roles, boundaries, and expectations clearly defined and honored by both sides." In describing the organizations that exited the Roberts Enterprise Develop-

ment Funds program, Emerson warned: "The cultures of these organizations were so embedded in traditional nonprofit ideology that at
the end of the day, they didn't have what it takes to run their businesses in a disciplined way."

Vanessa Kirsch, one of the most optimistic of social entrepreneurs, loses sleep wondering "whether there might not be
enough pipeline organizations (not-for-profit) for the new economy
wealth. . . . I don't know how many such organizations exist today,
but I'm convinced that it is not a big number. I hope very much that
other organizations like mine will be started so we can make major
additions to the pipeline."

Although most people working in the nonprofit sector might
have difficulty in recognizing the problem as Kirsch presents it, we
believe she is correct in thinking,". . . There's going to be so much
money coming down the pike that a lot of not-for-profit organizations are going to be passed over because they will not have the capacity to take the new philanthropic money available. They don't really have the needed leadership, knowledge, and human resources
required and, most regrettably, they are unable to think and act
strategically."

We need to be reassured that along with the new economy's
love of speed, there will not come an intolerant attitude toward the
length of time it often takes to address society's most complex social
issues. We crave evidence that the new philanthropy will address
some of the most intransigent systemic issues. The labors in the past
of the large foundations on race relations, civil rights, and public education are a constant reminder of how important research, analysis,
communication, and public policy advocacy are to change. Our national experience is that leadership and patience are absolute requi-
sites for profound change.

CONCLUSION

All facets of twenty-first-century life, including philanthropy, will be
avidly analyzed and studied in the decade ahead. Thoughtful people

will watch to see what the contribution of the new philanthropy in fact will be to society. Looking ahead, here are some of the questions that we intend to pursue:

- Will the new philanthropy continue to have appeal for both new and established philanthropists and, if so, to what degree?
- How will these initial innovations morph over time within the institutions that currently embrace them?
- Will innovations described here and others begin to be adapted or adopted by more established foundations, and, if so, what will the impact be on the sector as a whole?
- Will a "capital market" for nonprofits be the result of this new wealth, and, if so, will it cause the kind of competition and survival of the fittest that has been a part of the for-profit sector and thus begin a period of shakeout in the nonprofit sector?
- What will the future leaders of the nonprofit sector look like, and what will be the requisite skills and experiences?

We believe the answers to these questions will come from a new kind of high-performance philanthropy that will blend the strengths of the traditional and the new philanthropies.[8] It would be a grievous error to set up a false competition between the two. Clearly, foundations will have to walk the path that Paul Brainerd so aptly describes as "walking a tightrope between focus and openness to new approaches and new ideas."

Rachel Bellows, the iconoclastic critic of philanthropy, raises profoundly disturbing questions for everyone interested in and dedicated to organized philanthropy when she insists on the fundamental dichotomy of twentieth-century philanthropy. She rightly states that as long as power—and financial capital is undeniably power—remains in the hands of the donor, there can be no transparency in the donor–donee relationship. If there is no market, then demanding accountability and insisting on measurement of performance are really a mug's game, no matter how much intellectual capital, human resources, and money are expended on them.

Much is expected of the new philanthropy. The new economy philanthropists and the media both have contributed mightily to these heightened expectations. Their direct and indirect comparisons of themselves and their new style of giving with their predecessors has both annoyed and intrigued "the traditional foundations." On the one hand, their entry on the philanthropic stage has been applauded by the donee audience, which has been pleading for decades for not only more capital but also for a fresh understanding of their need for more timely and longer grants and more imaginative relationships with the donor actors. On the other hand, the initial, sometimes fierce, rhetoric about pro-action has struck a note of apprehension in the donee audience.

Some of the new economy philanthropists—perhaps Bill Gates is the most visible and promising example—are making a serious effort both to address the causes of some of the world's most destructive problems and to act through existing nonprofits in partnerships and to bring these institutions and coalitions rapidly to scale. The Gates model is having an impact on the established foundations, but it is slow going to change the procedures and practices that all too often have been concerned primarily with low risk and security in grantmaking.

In the early 1980s, Edward Skloot went looking for entrepreneurs and people possessed of the venture capital spirit in the nonprofit sector, he came away with few examples for emulation. If he repeated his study today, we believe he would be heartened by the results.[9]

We believe the new entrants in the field of philanthropy will have systemic impact over time. We hope the combination of fresh ideas, significant capital, new forms of partnerships, and an openness to innovation and risk taking will result in something more than change at the edges of the philanthropic field. Then and only then may we be on the verge of something truly worthy of the term *renaissance* to describe the dynamics that this chapter attempts to explore.

NOTES

1. Paul G. Schervish and John J. Haven, *Millionaires and the Millennium: New Estimates of the Forthcoming Wealth Transfer and the Prospects for a Golden Age of Philanthropy*. Boston: Boston College, October 1999.
2. Foundation Center, *Foundation Yearbook 2000, http://fdncenter.org*, FC Stats, Foundation Growth Trends.
3. Pam Woodall, "Untangling e-conomics," *The Economist*, September 23, 2000, p. 5.
4. Kevin Kelly, *New Rules for the New Economy: 10 Radical Strategies for a Connected World*. New York: NY, Penguin Books, 1998, p. 112.
5. Christine W. Letts and William P. Ryan with Allen Grossman, "Virtuous Capital: What Foundations Can Learn from Venture Capitalists," *Harvard Business Review*, March–April 1997.
6. Emmett Carson, "Grant Makers in Search of a Holy Grail," *Foundations New and Commentary 41*(1) (Jan./Feb. 2000), adapted from a presentation at the Fifth Distinguished Lecture Center for the Study of Voluntary Organizations and Service at Georgetown University, October 1999.
7. Edward Skloot, "Evolution or Extinction: A Strategy for Nonprofits in the Marketplace," *Nonprofit and Voluntary Sector Quarterly 29* (2) (June 2000) pp. 315–324.
8. Edward Skloot, "The Promise of Venture Philanthropy." Keynote address at the Sixth Annual Nonprofit Executive Series: Building the Entrepreneurial Nonprofit, Town Hall, Seattle, WA, April 10, 2000.
9. Skloot, "Evolution or Extinction: A Strategy for Nonprofits in the Marketplace."

CONTRIBUTORS

The John D. and Catherine T. MacArthur Foundation
Jonathan Fanton, President
140 S. Dearborn Street
Chicago, IL 60603
(312) 726-8000
http://www.macfdn.org/index.htm

Bill & Melinda Gates Foundation
Patty Stonesifer, President
P.O. Box 23350
Seattle, WA 98102
(206) 709-3100
www.gatesfoundations.org

Aspen Institute
Meriwether Jones, Director
Community Strategies Group
One Dupont Circle, NW, Suite 700
Washington, DC 20036
(202) 293-0525 CSG fax
www.aspeninstitute.org/csg

The Hauser Center for Nonprofit Organizations
Christine W. Letts, Associate Director, Lecturer in Public Policy
Harvard University
9 John F. Kennedy Street
Cambridge, MA 02138
(617) 496-5675
www.ksghauser.harvard.edu

Urban Institute
Center on Nonprofits and Philanthropy
Elizabeth T. Boris, Center Director
C. Eugene Steuerle, Senior Fellow
2100 M Street NW
Washington, DC 20037
(202) 833-7200
http://www.urban.org

Robin Hood Foundation
David Saltzman, Executive Director
111 Broadway, 19th Floor
New York, NY 10006
(212) 227-6601
www.robinhood.org

Triangle Community Foundation
Shannon St. John, Executive Director
P.O. Box 12834
Research Triangle Park, NC 27709
(919) 549-9840
http://www.trianglecf.org/

Brainerd Foundation
Paul Brainerd, President/Founder
1601 Second Avenue, Suite 610
Seattle, WA 98101
(206) 448-0676
http://www.brainerd.org

Contributors

The Roberts Enterprise Development Fund
Jed Emerson, President REDF/Bloomberg Sr. Research Fellow in
    Philanthropy, Harvard Business School
Presidio Building 1009, First Floor
P.O. Box 29266
San Francisco, CA 94129-0266
(415) 561-6677
www.live4punk@redf.org

Libra Foundation
Owen Wells, President
P.O. Box 17516-DTS
Portland, ME 04112
(207) 879-6280

Common Good
Kristin Majeska
17 Glen Avenue
Waterville, ME 04901
k_majeska@yahoo.com

James Irvine Foundation
Cora Mirikitani, Senior Program Director
Innovation Fund
One Market, Steuart Tower, Suite 2500
San Francisco, CA 94105
(415) 777-2244
www.innovationfund.org

Rachel Bellows
divine interVentures
588 Broadway, Suite 910
New York, NY 10012
(212) 334-6029

The Center for Effective Philanthropy
Mark Kramer, Founder/Senior Advisor
101 Federal Street, Suite 1900
Boston, MA 02110
(617) 204-5772
http://www.effectivephilanthropy.com

Merck Family Fund
Jenny Russell, Executive Director
303 Adams Street
Milton, MA 02186
(617) 696-3580
www.merckff.org

Peninsula Community Foundation
Carol Welsh Gray, Director
Center for Venture Philanthropy
2744 Sand Hill Road
Menlo Park, CA 94025
(650) 854-5566
Contact: *Margot Mailliard Rawlins www.pcf.org*

Surdna Foundation
Edward Skloot, Executive Director
Vincent Stehle, Program Officer for Nonprofit Sector Initiative
330 Madison Avenue
New York, NY 10017-5001
(212) 557-0010
www.surdna.org

Association of Small Foundations
Joe Pierpont, Co-Executive Director
4905 Del Ray Avenue, Suite 308
Bethesda, MD 20814
(301) 907-3337
www.smallfoundations.org/links.htm

Edna McConnell Clark Foundation
Michael Bailin, President
250 Park Avenue
New York, NY 10177-0026
(212) 551-9100
http://fdncenter.org/grantmaker/emclark/

The Philanthropic Initiative, Inc.
H. Peter Karoff, Founder/President
77 Franklin Street
Boston, MA 02110
http://www.tpi.org

National Center for Family Philanthropy
Virginia Esposito, President
1220 Nineteenth Street NW, Suite 804
Washington, DC 20036
(202) 293-3424
www.ncfp.org

Council on Foundations
Albert Ruesga, Director
New Ventures in Philanthropy
1828 L Street NW
Washington, DC 20036
(202) 466-6512
www.cof.org

W. K. Kellogg Foundation
Tom Reis, Director
Venture Philanthropy Center
One Michigan Avenue
Battle Creek, MI 49017-4058
(616) 969-1611
www.wkkf.org

The David and Lucile Packard Foundation
Susan Packard Orr, Chairman
300 Second Street, Suite 200
Los Altos, California 94022
www.packfound.org

New Profit Inc.
Vanessa Kirsch, President and Founder
2 Canal Park
Cambridge, MA 02141
(617) 252-3220
www.newprofit.com

Community Foundation Silicon Valley
Peter Hero, President
60 South Market Street, Suite 1000
San Jose, CA 95113-2336
(408) 278-2200
www.siliconvalleygives.org

RESOURCES

Association of Small Foundations Membership Survey Results 1999. Association of Small Foundations. Charles Scott and Joe Pierpont Co-Directors. 4905 Del Ray Avenue, Suite 308, Bethesda, MD 20814. Inquiries: Contact Charles Scott at *clscott2nd@earthlink.net.*

Association of Small Foundations: Winter 1999–2000, Vol. 3, No. 4. Web site: *www.smallfoundations.org*

Bernholtz, Lucy Ph.D. "Foundations for the Future: Emerging Trends in Foundation Philanthropy." University of Southern California, Nonprofit Studies Center Forum on Philanthropy, Public Policy and the New Economy, December 1999.

The Challenge of Change: Implementation of a Venture Philanthropy Strategy. The Roberts Enterprise Development Fund and BTW Consultants— Informing Change, Eds. Authors contributing to this report may be reached through the REDF Web Site at *www.redf.org.*

Emerson, Jed. *The Nature of Returns: A Social Capital Markets Inquiry into Elements of Investment and the Blended Value Proposition.* Boston, MA: Harvard Business School. Working paper copyright 2000 Jed Emerson.

The Foundation Center. Foundation Today Series 2000 edition. Foundation Growth and Giving Estimates, 1999 Preview. *http://www.fdncenter.org.*

Kirsner, Scott. "Nonprofit Motive," *Wired,* September 1999, p. 110.

Letts, Christine W., and William P. Ryan with Allen Grossman. "Virtuous Capital: What Foundations Can Learn from Venture Capitalists." *Harvard Business Review.* March–April 1997.

"New Philanthropists Eager to Make an Impact," *Philanthropy News Digest 6(27),* June 2000.

Odendahl, Teresa (ed.). *America's Wealthy and the Future of Foundations.* The Council on Foundations and the Yale University Program on Non-Profit Organizations.

Reis, Thomas K., and Stephanie J. Clohesy. "Unleashing New Resources and Entrepreneurship for the Common Good." A Scan, Synthesis, and Scenario for Action. January 1999. W. K. Kellogg Foundation, One Michigan Avenue East, Battle Creek, MI 49017-4058. Web site: *www.wkkf.org.*

Saxenian, Annalee. *Regional Advantage: Culture and Competition in Silicon Valley and Route 128.* Harvard University Press, 1996.

Sievers, Bruce, and Kirke Wilson. "Our Half Century." *Foundation News and Commentary* (March/April 1999): 32.

Edward Skloot. "Evolution or Extinction: A Strategy for Nonprofits in the Marketplace." *Nonprofit and Voluntary Sector Quarterly* 29, No. 2 (June 2000): 315–324.

Skloot, Edward. *The Promise of Venture Philanthropy.* Surdna Foundation, Inc., New York. Keynote address at the Sixth Annual Nonprofit Executive Series: Building the Entrepreneurial Nonprofit, Town Hall, Seattle, WA, April 2000.

Suhrke, Henry C. "Private Foundations: The Problem with 'Going All the Way.'" *Philanthropy Monthly* (July/August 1999): 27.

Suhrke, Henry C. "Private Foundations: Will Changing Leadership Mean Wiser Grantmaking?" *Philanthropy Monthly* (July/August 1999): 27.

Venture Philanthropy: Landscape and Expectations, Morino Institute Youth Social Ventures. Community Wealth Ventures, Inc., 1999.

Williams, Roger M. "Inside The Gates." *Foundation News & Commentary* (May/June 2000): 33.

Web Sites

Jewish Funders Network:	*www.jfunders.org/jewishphilanthropy.htm*
Philanthropy Journal:	*www.nonprofitnews.org*
Social Funds:	*www.socialfunds.com*
Wired:	*www.wired.com*
Philanthropy News Network:	*http://pnnonline.org/*
Philanthropy News Digest:	*http://www.fdncenter.org/pnd/current/ index.html*

Section Two

The Foundation's New Reach: The Emerging Role of Leader, Communicator, and Facilitator of Change

CHAPTER 4

The Meta-Foundation

Venture Philanthropy Starts the Next Leg of Its Journey with a Surprising New Pilot

by Jack Shakely

PERSPECTIVES

Is a foundation just the grants it makes? Are there other capacities or expertise foundations might share with the community? Can a foundation become "more than money"?

Venture philanthropy is a phrase coined by nonprofits and foundations to describe what happens when a funder does more than write the check. Different models for such expanded relationships between funders and grantees are springing up around the country, not surprisingly in places such as the Silicon Valley, Seattle, and Dallas, where entrepreneurship has found fertile ground. There is, however, a gentle tension between simply giving away money and becoming deeply involved in the leadership and management of an institution. What are some of the lessons learned?

In this chapter, Jack Shakely uses the story of a nonprofit he himself helped rescue as a test case for the potential of what he calls "the meta-foundation"—exploring the limits of what a foundation, in particular a community foundation, can contribute to the growth and infrastructural development of key organizations in its communities. Jack draws from more than 20 years of experience as president of the California Community Foundation in Los Angeles.

A CASE STUDY

Mollie Lowery sat on the sun-baked patio carved out of an old skid row warehouse and thought of llamas. Mollie had a lot of other things on her mind. As she draped her muscular six-foot frame over a lawn chair that served as her office furniture, she added and scratched off names for that day's work roster at the LAMP laundry service. The laundry was not only the single largest employer of skid row residents in Los Angeles, it was the only facility in the country whose entire work staff was made up of mentally ill substance abusers (euphemistically termed *dual diagnosed* in social work jargon). It took a lot of juggling to keep the roster filled from day to day, and Mollie knew it was touch and go to keep it open, period.

Mollie and her chairman, a generous department store executive whose own son struggled with mental illness, had created LAMP some 15 years before, and it quickly became the social service lodge pole for the entire skid row area. Originally called Los Angeles Men's Place, LAMP had long since opened its doors to women, and its acronym was now better known than the words it replaced.

The LAMP treatment philosophy had won a national reputation and much media interest. There was even talk of a television movie of the week, but the painfully shy Mollie would have none of it. She skipped an award dinner in her honor in Beverly Hills, saying the award was for her treatment philosophy, not her.

The treatment was based on an underpinning of dignity and community where each client was regarded as a "guest." There were three residential areas, LAMP Inn, for the newly arriving or recently off-the-wagon guest who needed special care, LAMP Lodge for the guest farther along in sobriety and treatment, and finally LAMP Residence, where guests had their own apartments, were free to come and go, and generally lived as residents of any other cooperative.

There was also LAMP Industries, which began with a laundry service that gave dignified, meaningful work to 20 to 30 guests daily, and provided cheap, clean towels and linens to three other skid row residential facilities, in addition to LAMP's own. LAMP Industries later branched out to include a laundromat for people on the row, a convenience store, and a crafts shop called Skid Row Access.

Finally in 1992, after more than a dozen years of days and nights on the row, Mollie retired and moved to rural Bishop, California, in the High Sierras. She opened a trail guide business, where she and her two llamas would portage city folks through the mountains, including a few of her old "guests," when she could afford to bring them up.

In less than three years, however, LAMP began to unravel. The chairman, who had functioned as unofficial development director and chief financial officer, died suddenly, and private sector support dropped 80 percent in two years. Mollie's strength in treatment—her faith in her guests—became her weakness in management. She promoted three former guests to serve as key staff, one of whom became executive director when Mollie stepped down. All three functioned well under Mollie's tutelage, but were in over their heads without her and eventually resigned, leaving the agency more than half a million dollars in debt, the laundry and convenience store shuttered, and the residences half empty.

The *Los Angeles Times* headline for April 25, 1995, summed it up: "Innovative Skid Row Program to Close Its Doors." That afternoon, Mollie Lowery got a telephone call from a foundation executive in Los Angeles. "Mollie, we've got to save LAMP," he said. "It's the only organization of its kind in the city that handles dual diagnosed patients, and now that AIDS has hit the row, it's more needed than ever. If we don't save LAMP, we'll have to recreate it at twice the cost. You can save it Mollie, and we are willing to give you the money to do it."

"I'm willing to try," Mollie said, "but I'm going to need a lot more than your money. I'm going to need things from your foundation you've never given away before, including staff, board, and expertise."

For the next three days, Mollie and the executive sat in the offices of LAMP, putting together a philanthropic partnership, a partnership that would startle, perhaps even horrify, the traditional foundation program officer. Now three years later, Mollie had just gotten word that the reopened laundry service had finally turned its first quarterly profit, and she looked up at the leaden sky and thought of llamas.

UNDERSTANDING THE "TRADITIONAL" FOUNDATION

There are few things in America more traditional than the traditional foundation, if in the sense of traditional, one means remaining true to existing values and practices. If you were a program officer of a major foundation in the mid-1950s and were suddenly abducted by aliens, you would find upon your return 50 years later that, aside from mastering the computer and fax machine, your job has remained essentially the same.

The apparent unwillingness of the philanthropic field for introspection and experimentation is curious in the face of the cobbled-together nature of foundation grantmaking, together with its almost ritualistic preference for innovation. Only a look at the history of foundation grantmaking can explain why the introduction of venture philanthropy into the mix a few years ago has stirred such a firestorm of controversy—a firestorm that threatens to obscure both the best and worst that venture philanthropy has to offer.

The program officer swept up by the UFO was very unlucky indeed, because there were very few foundation program officers, on earth or aloft, in the 1950s. There were so few *foundations,* in fact, that there was seen no need for a directory of them until 1954 (originally published by the Russell Sage Foundation in New York, the directory was taken over by the Foundation Center in the early 1960s). Foundations weren't even required to publish annual reports to the public until 1970, and there was absolutely no national recognition of foundations as a "field." Even the Council on Foundations didn't come into existence until the early 1960s, and spent most of its first two decades in New York City, acting more as a local association of foundation investment managers and attorneys than a national trade association.

Most foundations were content to fund the museums, colleges, and orphanages that had been dear to the founder, who was often deceased. Foundation staffs, what there were of them, were often trusted financial or legal advisors who monitored the family's philanthropy much as they monitored other family investment matters.

An informal study conducted for the Council on Foundations in 1970 revealed fewer than 500 foundation program officers in the entire country, with half that number employed by two foundations, Ford and Rockefeller.

A number of seemingly unrelated events changed this cozy landscape swiftly. First, the Internal Revenue Code of 1954 finally defined nonprofit organizations, giving them stature and "most favored" status in contrast to profit-making entities, to receive federal grants and contracts. Second, the "Great Society" experiment in civic improvement and social change initiated in the Johnson Administration decided to focus on these same nonprofit organizations to distribute funds to inner cities where governmental mediating structures were sparse.

Most importantly, congressional scrutiny at last got around to foundations, with the Patterson and Patman commissions of the late 1960s. Although there were very few cases of actual abuse uncovered by either commission, the notion of foundations as secretive and nonresponsive led to Draconian foundation legislation with the passage of the 1969 Tax Reform Act. (Interestingly, the Council on Foundations reports that the first use of the phrase *venture philanthropy* was by John D. Rockefeller, III, in defending foundations to Congressman Wright Patman's commission. It is clear in context, however, that Rockefeller was using the phrase to describe funding unconventional or unpopular social programs, rather than the entrepreneurial business context used today.)

The number of foundation program officers increased dramatically in the decades of the 1970s and 1980s. Foundation executives saw the huge army of nonprofit organizations in health, children's services, housing, the arts, and education and realized that it would require people in the field to select and sort out the best of these. Perhaps more importantly, the Tax Reform Act of 1969 required foundations to come out of hiding, publish annual reports, and grant a certain percentage of assets every year (originally 6 percent, now 5). Nonprofit organizations, which only a few years earlier were awash in federal grant money, were feeling the cutbacks being implemented by the Nixon Administration, and quickly embraced this "new" funding field. Foundations that had received less than 100 proposals for funding every year found themselves receiving more than that every month.

People were needed to handle the paper flow, and thousands of new program officers were brought in from three existing pools: the government, United Way, and academia. Each group brought with it a skill set that suited the old paradigm, but often was meaningless in the foundation world.

From government grant officers we inherited annual grant cycles. This was essential to government grantmakers, where the yearly dance of authorization, allocation, and obligation is well known. Foundations, however, with the single exception of some corporate foundations, are funded from a massive initial infusion of capital and can predict with some certainty how much money will be available in 1, 5, or 20 years. Even the annual payout imposed by Congress is determined over a four-year rolling average, so no adherence to annual grant cycles was ever needed by foundations.

From government program officers we also learned how to cut proposed budgets. Most government grants are as driven by political concerns as human ones, and funding a great many small programs is always preferable to funding a few large ones. Government program officers, therefore, almost always recommend more projects than available funding will tolerate, then cut budgets, giving, say, 80 percent funding to 700 organizations, rather than 100 percent funding to 500. Nonprofit organizations seeking government funding quickly learned this game, and constantly padded budgets in anticipation of the inevitable cuts.

Armed with this skill set, foundation program officers became notorious, and often gratuitous, budget cutters. It is not unusual to see a program officer spend two days cutting $1,200 out of a $35,000 request. Perhaps because program officers try to find a "value-added" aspect to their plowing through the hundreds of proposals that fall on their desks every month, the single most common fault of new program officers is in slashing budgets, thus "saving" the foundation money. These cuts invariably come from areas of administrative competence.

From the United Way, program officers brought two mindsets: Anything more than money from a foundation is intrusive and dangerous to the nonprofit recipient, and administrative overhead is bad.

Because the United Way is a collection of grantee organizations and the United Way itself is set up as a buffer between donor and recipient, the skepticism toward too much donor involvement is understandable. But what is too much?

The greatest disservice the United Way program officer brought to the foundation table was the message, which continues today, that high administrative costs equal irresponsible programming. The United Way itself, for more than 30 years, focused its advertising as much on its own low administrative costs as its service to the community, and used administrative cost ratios as one of the major criteria for member allocations. It is little wonder that decades of such nonscientific bias have poisoned so many volunteers, as well as foundation officers. Go to any Rotary Club meeting in the country, and if your table partner knows anything about nonprofit organizations at all, he is likely to believe that all nonprofits have excessive administrative costs (curiously, this is an evaluation tool never used in the for-profit sector. In fact, high start-up, marketing, and capacity-building expenses are often viewed very favorably in entrepreneurial circles, where terms like *burn rate* are buckled in swash).

The last to the program officer roundtable was the academician. Certainly, foundations could never be faulted for wishing to possess expertise in selected fields of grantmaking. This expertise, however, was almost always subject based and constituency driven. Foundation program officers began to view their "clients" not as the applicant organizations, but the constituencies these organizations represented. The nonprofit organization began to be considered merely a conduit, a way to get to a population at risk. If one nonprofit should fail, there were plenty more that could be chosen, or created, for that matter.

Moreover, if foundations funded only the tried and true, the old-line service providers, where would be the value added by the academic program officer? The legendary businessman and philanthropist Nathan Cummins once asked a packed Council on Foundations conference audience, "What would you do if it was discovered that the single best child care agency in the country was the Salvation Army? Would you send them all your money?" The collective gasps and exhalations perked up every potted palm in the room.

This desire to add value, as in the case of budget cutting, led foundation program officers inevitably to an addiction to "innovative" grantmaking. Innovation as a criterion for funding began in earnest in the 1980s, and quickly became synonymous with "new." This slavish adherence to the new induced many foundations to limit funding of organizations to an arbitrary number of years, often three.

The skill sets brought to the traditional foundation from government, the United Way, and academia were different, but there was one skill set lacking in each: understanding of good management practices. Economics guru Peter Drucker had been gently scolding foundations for years to see nonprofit organizations as corporations, not merely service providers. Not only did Drucker draw attention to good nonprofit management through his annual compilation of the nation's best-managed nonprofit organizations, he urged foundations to help nonprofits improve their "bench strength"—his sports analogy to depth in capacity.

Others joined Drucker in criticism of foundation practices that grew increasingly sharp. McKinsey and Company, which had worked with the Red Cross and the United Way of America in changing their management practices, devoted an entire issue of its quarterly magazine to nonprofit organizations and their seeming inability to take programs to scale. The McKinsey report laid almost all the blame on foundations that "actively punish success." "When a nonprofit begins to attract additional funding," the report states, "and to generate new revenue streams, foundations often end their support, arguing that the nonprofit no longer needs it. This makes growth very difficult, if not impossible. Most foundations are eager to provide seed money for innovative new programs, but fewer are interested in helping sustain and build on successes. Nothing could be more counterproductive."

To make a bad situation worse, the McKinsey report continues, the sources of funding are themselves so numerous and fragmented that most nonprofit managers spend their time fund raising, even if the grant programs don't fit the nonprofit mission.

It is a sad fact that there are very few nonprofit management-training programs anywhere in the country. Those that call themselves such are often fund-raising and grantsmanship training programs with some program planning thrown in. Management consulting firm Bain Consulting found so much need for management assistance in the nonprofit sector that it created Bridgespan Group to deliver strategic management assistance to nonprofits serving low-income youth. Although the need for this clearly is present, it is unclear if Bridgespan Group can actually turn a profit providing this type of assistance.

Universities and think tanks began monitoring and critiquing foundation/nonprofit relationships in the 1990s. Harvard especially, through Michael Porter and the Strategic Planning for Nonprofit Management seminars at the Harvard Business School, Peter Frumkin at the Kennedy School, and Christine Letts of the Hauser Center, started probing foundation practices. The *Harvard Business Review*, which barely acknowledged nonprofit corporations heretofore, began publishing four to six articles a year on the subject.

The roof blew off the traditional foundation world with the publication in the spring 1997 *Harvard Business Review* of "Virtuous Capital: What Foundations Can Learn From Venture Capitalists" by Christine Letts, William Ryan, and Allen Grossman. A year later, the same authors expanded their article into a book.[1]

Foundation program officers, who had little management skills and had discounted their importance accordingly, were being lectured at every level that good management was *all* that mattered. "Behind every effective program, and especially every sustained effective program, is an organization that performs well," Letts wrote.

This article, and subsequent pieces from Michael Porter, Mark Kramer, and Mario Marino quickly took hold with a group of philanthropists looking for a new paradigm. It was only a matter of months until what has become known as venture philanthropy swept across the country like a prairie fire. According to the Morino Institute, 40 social venture funds came into existence since January 1, 1999.

Nothing in the history of philanthropy has ever taken hold so quickly, nor stirred more controversy.

On the West Coast, Internet and other entrepreneurs loved the language of venture philanthropy, which was as familiar to them as the language of foundation grantmaking had seemed foreign. Paul Brainerd and his Social Venture Partners in Seattle, Steve Kirsch in San Jose, and Jed Emerson in San Francisco started building the venture philanthropy model, explaining the process as they made their first grants in it ("kind of like building an airplane after it is already in the air," sniffed a foundation officer, not realizing, perhaps, that this is the very analogy an entrepreneur might use as a commendation).

Of this group, only Emerson had prior experience in the nonprofit world. He also understood the complete break his group was making from the constituent-oriented traditional foundation. He wrote that venture philanthropy is "significantly different from traditional grant making in that it seeks to profoundly improve the capacity of organizations to execute their strategies." Make the organizations as strong as you can, then hold them accountable for their actions, Emerson said.[2]

Eventually, venture philanthropy came to be defined by three general strategies:

1. Long-term investment (three to six years) with a clear exit plan
2. A managing partner relationship between the donor and the nonprofit, which can include seats on the board of the nonprofit
3. Provision of funds and expertise

The key to venture philanthropy's success is wrapped up in the last strategy, where technical assistance in management, technology, and infrastructure are deemed as important as money.

We'll never know just how well venture philanthropy might have worked if the lights hadn't gone out in the "dot.com" world. But they did, and with them went much of the funding for the ventures. Undercapitalized in the best of times, many venture philanthropy start-ups found themselves out of money. The Austin Social Venture Partnership in Texas, for example, has less than $500,000 in total assets. It would be difficult to develop a long-term funding plan out of that.

In addition, this lack of funds has led to the irony of venture philanthropies so small and poorly staffed that they don't have the capacity to provide the very management and technical assistance they established as essential. According to the Morino Institute, half the funds calling themselves venture philanthropies have two or fewer employees. In a rare display of naiveté, many of these organizations are now seeking funding from the same traditional foundations they scorned only a few years prior. What many of them are about to learn is that, while most foundation program officers can't guarantee you will get funded, most of them can guarantee you *won't.*

The limited capacity of venture philanthropy funds was recognized from the beginning, but there was always an understanding, sometimes stated, often implied, that the donor would provide the management expertise. Unfortunately, even in the best of times, many management skills are not transferable between the profit and nonprofit sectors. As Peter Drucker has demonstrated, nonprofit management is not "management lite," as some entrepreneurs assume. The failed experimentation of corporate loaned executives programs practiced by Xerox, IBM, Chrysler, and other companies in the 1970s and 1980s revealed that not only did most loaned executives have unproductive experiences; the nonprofit often had to nursemaid them through the sabbatical.

Nonprofit organizations do need better management, better technology, longer-term funding prospects and hands-on partnerships with important donors. In this, the venture philanthropy philosophy is on target. But there is much missing. What is needed is a merger of the traditional foundation's size and permanence with venture philanthropy's devotion to a combination of funding and expertise over the long haul. What is needed most of all is a delivery system.

What is needed is a meta-foundation, one that goes beyond grantmaking, to become a well-staffed and funded philanthropic services corporation—one whose assets are sufficiently large to withstand any stock market fluctuation or individual donor eccentricity, which will always be in the community and near the nonprofits with which it enters into partnerships, one that understands nonprofit asset development, law, investment, communications and organizational management.

What is needed, as it turns out, is the modern community foundation, the meta-foundation of the twenty-first century.

Most community foundations are totally unaware of either the label or their elevation in status. In fact, only 40 or 50 of the largest community foundations of the country's more than 500 fit the definition. But because of the fierce competition for asset development in the past two decades; the incredible volume of gifts, grants, and philanthropic programs; and the complexity of philanthropic services regularly supplied by the modern community foundation, it stands out as the delivery system that venture philanthropy needs.

There are seven areas of expertise that the meta foundation must have to go beyond grants into management capacity building: organizational development, asset development, communications and public relations, legal services, finance and investment services, space and facilities, and loans and alternative financing. Following is a more detailed description of each area and how community foundations, sometimes by design and sometimes by historical accident, add value to each area.

1. *Organizational development.* The needs of nonprofit organizations in this area fall into three categories: board, CEO, and staff. It is in board development that community foundations really shine. Boards of community foundations must turn over as part of their commitment to public charity status, so every community foundation is

constantly seeking community leaders. Moreover, because community foundations are not typical fund-raising organizations, such as the United Way, the types of leaders being sought by community foundations are broad, including religious, academic, community, and nonprofit leaders. Community foundations also understand who the people of wealth are, and because many of these same people have donor-advised funds in community foundations, the community foundations know which wealthy people are apt to support seniors, children, health, and so on. Los Angeles book publisher and philanthropist Martin Early called his community foundation one morning and said, "I just sold my company to Scholastic Books. I want to give back something to my community. Can you find me a nonprofit board where I can really make a difference?" He was put in touch with Chrysalis, a job placement facility in skid row. After a few months of volunteering, he joined the board. Five years later, Chrysalis has opened four satellite offices, trebled its client load, and got its first Ford Foundation grant. It was also recognized in 1999 by Peter Drucker as the best-managed nonprofit in the country. Martin Early is now chairman of the Chrysalis board.

Whenever venture philanthropists demand board participation as a part of their grant partnership, they are actually being kinder than the traditional foundation officer who would never dream of "meddling" in a nonprofit board, but who is only too willing to reject a proposal because the agency's board is too weak. Unfortunately, however, the venture philanthropist may not have the connections to develop the board sufficiently. "Just because I'm rich doesn't mean I have a lot of rich friends," banking heir Howard Ahmanson once pled in an article in *Philanthropy* magazine.

Staff and personnel assistance can often be very basic at the nonprofit level. Organization charts, personnel and operations manuals, job descriptions, and salary comparability surveys are only a few important personnel matters the meta-foundation is prepared to offer. For years, the California Community Foundation actually maintained expenditure responsibility for a number of nonprofit start-up ventures, making payroll and paying bills. This proved so important to emerging nonprofits that a decade ago the community foundation joined with a few nonprofit attorneys and consultants to form a non-profit incubator, Community Partners, that now provides administrative support for almost 100 small organizations in Southern California.

2. *Asset development.* No entity in the nonprofit community is more capable of the whole panoply of development than the modern community foundation. From complicated estate gifts through gift annuities and unitrusts, from outright cash gifts to stocks, closely held businesses, works of art, and real estate, major community foundations handle them all. The Greater Kansas City Community Foundation, for example, is so skilled at real estate gifts it has created a separate corporation for their acquisition and disposition.

Most nonprofit organizations have absolutely no clue how to establish and maintain endowment funds, which are, of course, the bread and butter of community foundations. Many community foundations, notably San Diego and Seattle, have established agency endowment partnerships with nonprofit organizations. These partnerships provide training by community foundation staff to non-profit staffs and boards, often offer small seed grants to kick off the endowment campaign, and manage and invest the funds in a sophisticated and proven investment portfolio. The California Community Foundation has 20 such "endowment partners," which has resulted in more than $10 million in new funds for these partners in less than a decade.

3. *Communications and public relations.* Community foundations have no constituencies, no alumni, no grateful patients, and no season ticket holders. Virtually every contact with a prospective donor is a pioneering one. Community foundations have learned, therefore, market segmentation and relationship marketing. Brochures, booklets, seminars, and direct mail are community foundation stock in trade, and the desire to get a message across separates community foundations from the traditional foundation. Although representing less than 2 percent of total foundations, community foundations represent 25 percent of all foundations with Web sites, for example. Every major community foundation not only has a communications specialist, it has a communications department with three to five full-time employees.

Most nonprofits cannot afford any in-house communications staff, and those that do often see the position as an entry one. Their need for communications assistance is acute, but here the venture philanthropist is particularly at a loss to help. The small venture philanthropy staff cannot possibly provide enough communication support on its own, and often turns to the donor, who may indeed have an army of advertising and public relations departments at the ready. Unfortunately, most advertising agencies despise nonprofit clients, which seem too "soft" for modern advertising techniques. The ad agency usually throws up its hands and creates something called "We're here to help," with pictures of sunsets, seagulls, and earnest adults looking over the shoulders of earnest children. Good nonprofit marketing and communications bear no relationship to their corporate counterparts, a lesson that the United Way of America, with its hapless and often-satirized NFL spots, seems dead-set against learning.

4. *Legal services.* Nonprofits often have great difficulty obtaining proper legal counsel. Pro bono work by a board member is the kind of thing that keeps nonprofits small and is often ill advised. Community foundations know all the complex tax and estate rules and regulations as a part of their asset development work, and are competent in all aspects of nonprofit law, from expenditure responsibility to public charity status to restrictions on scholarships and self-dealing. The California Community Foundation has 150 scholarship funds and more than 1,000 donor-advised funds, owns two for-profit companies, and holds the majority stock interest in another. More than half our new funds come from referrals from lawyers who may not be as familiar with nonprofit or charity law as some other areas of expertise. It should come as no shock, therefore, that the community foundation has four full-time attorneys on staff.

5. *Finance and investment services.* Most nonprofit organizations have little or no endowments or reserve funds and have difficulty finding investment managers at an affordable price who can build a broad enough portfolio to ensure continued investment success. For years, some major community foundations have been offering to invest agency endowments for other nonprofits, greatly increasing the agency's total return on investment, while at the same time reducing

investment fees by pooling the agency funds with the hundreds of millions of dollars invested by the community foundation through its other funds.

Community foundations also are poised to provide sophisticated financial management assistance to nonprofits. There are no nonprofit organizations with more complicated financial dealing than a community foundation, with its thousands of funds, hundreds of scholarship programs and supporting organizations, reports to donors, and investment monitoring. It is little wonder, then, that modern community foundations have huge financial departments in comparison to traditional private foundations, and, as public charities, are more able to take on expenditure responsibility duties if a nonprofit is unable to handle its own finances in-house.
The meta-foundation must be prepared to grant funds, and manage them and disburse them as well, at least in the short run.

6. *Space and facilities.* The Columbus Foundation owns and operates the old Ohio governor's mansion, which it donates to other nonprofits for conferences, seminars, and fund-raising events. The Cincinnati Foundation owns a building downtown, where it serves as master tenant of its own nonprofit center, with dozens of other nonprofit occupants. The Arkansas Community Foundation owns an entire section of Little Rock, the Quapah Quarter, which it leases to other area nonprofits. The provision of adequate space to emerging nonprofits or nonprofits about to make the next step is important for success, and neither the traditional foundation nor the venture philanthropist is in a position to provide it. While this doesn't fall directly into the management areas listed above, adequate space at an adequate price can launch an organization and strengthen its capacity.

7. *Loans and other alternative funding.* It has been clear that foundations can provide much more than grants to accomplish their mission. The concept of program-related investments, which was pioneered by the Ford Foundation, has been demonstrated time and again as an effective method to get money into sensitive geographic and programmatic areas in a hurry. Most foundations, however, are not adequately staffed to deal with such loan or investment programs, and most nonprofit organizations seem befuddled in how to take ad-

vantage of them. Those nonprofits that know how to use program-related investments, such as the Manchester Guild in Pittsburgh and the Local Initiative Support Corporation (LISC), have seen some rather modest investments multiply dramatically. Venture philanthropists intuitively get this, perhaps more quickly than the nonprofits they join, but the nonprofit community is going to need constant training in ways to expand their funding horizons. This training can come from community foundations, which already know nonprofit accounting. Sometimes the alternative investment can be very far "outside the box." The Baton Rouge Community Foundation lent a private developer $3 million to buy and restore an old dead shopping center in the heart of the inner city. The developer secured an AT&T call center as the master tenant, and the community foundation provided grants and space to area nonprofits to establish complementary services such as day care, youth club, and community clinic. The community foundation is also working with local nonprofit housing agencies to build affordable housing around the revitalized center.

These seven areas cut across and go outside traditional management support, and are more a cafeteria of possible affiliations and assistance than a mandate for all. It is also clear that even with the greatly enhanced infrastructure of the modern community foundation, only a handful of meta-foundation grants can be attempted at any one time. But perhaps only a handful from each meta-foundation, working with existing traditional foundations and venture philanthropists, is all that is needed.

The nonprofit sector is the only area of American business to resist countrywide franchising and quality control. Whatever one may think of Starbucks or McDonald's, the harried mother who has just moved from Omaha to Phoenix can be assured of the same quality, pricing, and consistency of service from her new Starbucks in Scottsdale as she had from the one on River Road. She cannot be assured the same in day care, kindergarten, community clinics, or legal services. Traditional foundations, probably inadvertently, have prevented nonprofits going to scale through their grantmaking philosophy that punishes success. Venture philanthropists are dedicated to changing all that but need the delivery system of the meta-foundation to accomplish their mission.

The meta-foundation can help the strong organization to grow and can work with the weak, but essential, organization needing to be rescued.

And speaking of an organization needing to be rescued. . . .

I was the foundation executive who called Mollie Lowery down from the mountain. She and I first met with her board, which had dwindled from 10 to 5 members as the debts began to mount. I discovered that the board had not met at LAMP for more than a year, because "some board members felt uneasy down there," the LAMP chair told me.

Mollie and I outlined the partnership she and I had taken to my board for approval. It involved an immediate grant of $200,000 to hack away at the indebtedness, a promise of another $200,000 to get the laundry facility back up and running, the California Community Foundation's taking full charge of all financial matters of LAMP for three months or until a solid financial officer was in place, putting me on the board of directors and executive committee, and together seeking outside management consultants in asset development, residential use, and the LAMP industries. The board of LAMP agreed readily and asked if I would serve as board affairs chairman to reinvigorate the board.

My board also approved my spending 20 percent of my time for the six months considered necessary for the turnaround, which proved to be ample as a percentage of time, but less than half as long as proved needed.

Our legal staff worked with Mollie to renegotiate some service contracts, such as parking, security, and janitorial, getting better rates by using the community foundation's assets as collateral. Our chief financial officer set up a chart of accounts, paid bills (and haggled brilliantly in the process), and worked with Mollie to recruit and hire an in-house financial officer, then trained that person under Mollie's supervision.

It should be noted that at all times Mollie was in control of the partnership and could recommend to her board that the partnership be ended. If that unlikely event were to happen, the initial $200,000 grant would remain in place, but the subsequent grant would be reevaluated. Mollie's position in the agency was in fact strengthened, by changing her title to president and chief executive officer from executive director and spelling out her responsibilities and authority more clearly by the writing of bylaws, which had either been misplaced or never existed.

Together, we brought in three consultant firms, a fund-raising firm to do a development audit, Deloitte and Touche for the laundry service and convenience store, and the Executive Service Corps for the low occupancy rate. This freed Mollie up to devote herself to reestablishing an essential contract with the country department of mental health—a contract that had been more than halved the previous year because of the department's fears that the agency wouldn't survive to fulfill its end of the bargain.

When we agreed to hold monthly board meetings, and always at the LAMP facility, two of the remaining five board members resigned. Interestingly, a former board member, who had resigned in disgust two years before, came back and made a gift of $50,000 to hire a fund raiser. We put three more people on the board, two of whom were donor advisors at the community foundation and had a history of interest in the homeless and mentally ill.

At the end of a difficult board meeting when two members lamented that the term *skid row* seemed so negative, our communications director suggest we embrace the term instead, giving the area the same dignity Mollie and LAMP had given its residents. So a charitable golf tournament, the Skid Row Invitational, was born. With help from the Disney Company and a local television station, the first golf tournament netted more than $100,000, doubling the amount received from the public the year before.

The Executive Service Corps report found that although LAMP had been admitting women for years, other residential facilities on the row didn't know this and were not transferring clients when they were overbooked. The recommendation to hire a liaison to other skid row agencies, along with a scheduled maintenance to paint and refurbish rooms, increased bed occupancy from 60 percent to 85 percent in six months, and to 95 percent in less than a year.

The Deloitte study indicated that the laundry service should be reopened but the convenience store remain shut. The study also recommended that an entirely different method of payment and accountability be installed, which greatly reduced loss and slow payment. Three other skid row agencies signed contracts, and breakeven was anticipated within two years. The remaining $200,000 grant from the community foundation was made at that time to purchase inventory and add another dryer.

The mental health contract was restored, other foundations joined in supporting the innovative programs, the golf tournament continued, and the laundry service finally turned a profit, but in three years rather than two. All the time 30 people were employed at the service.

By 2000, LAMP had completely paid off all past debts and was running in the black. I resigned from the board that year, and Mollie found a chief operating officer, who would be trained to take Mollie's place in 2002, when she said she would again retire to her beloved mountains.

But fate had something else in store for Mollie. Thanks to an individual contributor and a new contract for rural mental health, LAMP bought a working farm in the hills near Bishop, California. In 2001, LAMP got all the licensing to open LAMP Ranch, a six-person residential facility. Soon Mollie will become a part-time LAMP employee, running and living at the LAMP Ranch, where she and her six guests will work together, take long hikes, and care for the llamas, which will no longer be only in her mind.

NOTES

1. Christine Letts, William Ryan, and Allen Grossman, *High Performance Nonprofits: Managing Upstream for Greater Impact.* New York: John Wiley & Sons, Inc., 1999.
2. Jed Emerson, "Venture Philanthropy 2001: The Changing Landscape." Reston, VA: *Morino Institute, 2001.*

CHAPTER 5

The New Gospel of Wealth

The Foundation as Communicator

An Interview with Hodding Carter III

PERSPECTIVES

Foundations have a legal mandate to communicate their activities through annual reports and other means. There are some foundations that espouse communication as essential to a civil society and integral to their mission. Whether by making grants to organizations to help them better communicate, by funding education programs to better inform the media, or by strengthening their communications and public relations infrastructure, foundations are growing more concerned about communications.

Hodding Carter, III, president of the John S. and James L. Knight Foundation, brings a special perspective to the issue of foundation communications. Most of the assets of the Knight Foundation originated from a bequests of Knight Ridder newspaper stock in 1981 and 1991. Over the course of a half-century, this foundation has supported community programs across the nation. More recently, it has targeted journalism as a grantmaking focus. A former journalist and son of a Pulitzer prize–winning author, Hodding brings to the philanthropic table many years of experience in media, education, and public affairs.

This interview took place several days after September 11. The impact of the tragedy echoes in professional issues and personal reflections discussed in this chapter.

FRANK ELLSWORTH: *I do have your resume and I know this puts you on the spot, but at this moment can give me two of the most interesting things that have happened in your life and career in the last—I won't say two weeks, I'll give you a couple months, what would they be?*

HODDING CARTER: Because of the events of September 11, it is almost impossible for me to answer that question in a way that is not distorted by them. Our board was meeting in executive session at the moment the first attack took place. We were interrupted by the vice president for programs who apologized, but suggested that we might want to know that there had been an explosion at the first tower. Of course, that then consumed us.

What has been, thereafter, central to my professional life has been trying to see clearly how we can go from being part of this massive outpouring of reactive relief and assistance to the victims toward something that might be more useful in the long term. To say that I'm looking for something—that we are looking for something more proactive or at any rate more built around the next step—is easy. To tell you what that will be turns out to be hard, and the search for that answer or answers has been probably the most pressing thing that I've been doing for the last couple of weeks.

In my private life, keeping in close touch with our 7 children and 11 grandchildren, and most particularly the ones in Washington and New York, has been my most continually consuming activity.

We have one assistant district attorney daughter in Brooklyn whose window looks straight across at the World Trade Center and for her, trauma is probably an understatement. Clearly, too, you know where I went to school (Princeton). It turns out I've got a couple of contemporaries who were there. I've got a number of folks that I knew directly or indirectly who were in the building, so following up on that has been hard.

FE: *It has been hard on all of us personally and as a nation. I am very grateful to work in a company and as a volunteer on projects that can help* *individuals and society deal with this tragedy. As we see in this tremendous outpouring of charity to New York and Washington D.C., the nonprofit world and philanthropy has an opportunity to participate in the short-term crisis needs of the victims and survivors but also local and global long-term programs and strategies. For example, my major passion at this point is the Japanese-American National Museum where I chair the executive committee. Due to this community's experience after discrimination and internment, we are currently devoting our efforts in cross-cultural communication and tolerance with the local Arab-American community. Joe, do you want to add anything to that?*

JOE LUMARDA: *In some ways, this has changed, and I hate to be repetitive with what the newscasters and commentators have said throughout the past two weeks, but this truly has changed the way we live and way we do business. I think the question we're encountering and asking ourselves is: If the world is changed, well then how do foundations change? And a follow-up question is, how can foundations react more quickly than foundations have traditionally reacted in the past and...*

HC: It's interesting that you put it that way. I guess because of a lifetime outside the foundation world and certainly because of my occasional forays in government and more frequent forays into politics, I am not in a great hurry. I think most of the mistakes that have been made have been made because of the urge to hurry up and do something as opposed to sit there and think through what you're doing. I think of that in relation to how we as a nation are going to deal with the immediate threat, however it is defined. I think almost everything that suggests that our first step should be to go toward "the center" is wrong. First, because we can't get to the center right away, second, because going to the center means that we have to do the kinds of damage to people and institutions which only prolong what is going to be a very long and difficult circumstance anyway. Admitting that you first have to do those things which are more on the periphery and then squeeze down to the center is the soul of wisdom for me.

JL: *Wisdom and foundations are two words not always associated with each other. I believe I know what you mean by rushing toward "the center," but please, go on . . .*

HC: I am really concerned that in the rush to do something about what many of us believe is a changed set of conditions, we will—and this is a classic foundation tendency—go rushing off after this newest scent when much of what we ought to do is to do better those things we claim to have been doing all along.

If there is any kind of rational explanation for what happened on September 11, much of it is going to be found in the vineyards that we claim to care most about: People deprived by circumstance, by history, by inadvertence, by government action of any reason to hope and given every reason to hate. Foundations anxious to go coursing off in new directions need to be really, really, really careful about jumping with their funds away from continuing work in areas that might deal with those circumstances at home and abroad.

I am particularly struck, in this respect, by the vast amount of money that was wasted by foundations in Central and Eastern Europe after the collapse of the Soviet Union and the Eastern Bloc. The felt necessity for everybody to immediately rush off to "do something" resulted in one of the biggest wastes of money that I ever saw. Indeed, the absolute insistence on everybody doing something separate guaranteed that there were any number of separate wastes of money. In this instance, I really hope to God we just slow down and think about it a great deal and work very, very hard at deciding whether sticking to our last is not the best way to go.

JL: *Following up on "Sticking to our last," are there any international programs that immediately come to mind in, for example, education or public policy programs, which represent areas foundations should stick to and do better? Moreover, does our world view need to change in order to serve the world better?*

HC: I can think of some things that we certainly must and should do better, and now I am going to be utterly simplistic. Here we are at the end of exactly 60 years at center stage in world affairs and our education system as a whole treats the rest of the world as terra incognita or as a sport for specialists to deal with seriously on the one hand or as a superficial diversion for everybody else. We must become better citizens in the sense of being better informed, better aware, less the self-righteous innocents abroad. That begins with trying to appreciate what other people understand the realities of their world to be. We absolutely have got to break out of our stubborn insistence after 60 years that our world view, inside out, is the only one that matters and that our prescriptions are the only ones that can possibly work. Even if they were, to not know enough about the cultures of the rest of the world to make the medicine go down easier is absurd. There is a lot of work that can be initiated—or work that can be returned to—by the foundation world. Many have been in and out of that field a number of times, found it boring, found it counterproductive, found it impossible, found whatever and left it, but it's an area that a lot of foundation folks actually know something about, having learned by trial and error over many years.

FE: Most of my background is in education and your referral to it piques my interest. Arguably, our public schools are in various stages of disarray. What strategies have you witnessed in order for us to reform the system or replicate the model districts?

HC: No. I mean, I do not know the answer to that. I do not have a prescription at hand. I would only guess a fairly informed guess, that there are out there some fairly successful ventures in this field waiting for adaptation. I spent several years on Ray Marshall's old quality minority education project. He was fond of reminding everyone periodically that the problem was not that we didn't know how to do some things, but that we didn't know how to do them in a big way, and that one of the reasons we didn't know how to do them in a big way is we hadn't tried them in a big way.

The second part is inherent in what you just said. A certain set of false assumptions about the public school system is one of the main problems in this country. It represents an intellectual and emotional abandonment of the public schools by much of the nation's elite. This involves not merely withdrawing their own children from the public schools, but also in abandoning the idea that they actually can and must work for the general benefit of all their students and society in general. Indeed, I would insist that if we are to have any hope at all, we have to adopt an attitude that is the opposite of giving up on the possibilities of the schools. That's not incantatory and rhetorical. Acting on this belief is essential to the future of this country, because public education has been the foundation stone of this democratic republic for a very long time and necessarily will remain the foundation stone.

Going through the specifics, however, I am reminded of the indictment constantly offered up of today's major media (i.e., newspapers and conventional television) that because they know so well how to make things interesting, they're inherently frivolous. But the fact is that they also know how to make the absolutely essential equally compelling. I do not think it is beyond the—no, let me put it the other way around. I know for a fact that you can make this kind of storytelling and this kind of information compelling to young children, to middle-school children, to high-school kids with most of the same skills that make music videos or breakfast foods compelling to them. That's part propaganda, it's part skillful packaging, but mainly it's imagination. Apply it to what has to be done. Of course, there's not much of a market for that kind of imagination today in the fields we're talking about. One of the things foundations could usefully do, for those interested in education, is to proceed on a systematic basis to create the environment that would reward such imaginative innovation through and by the media.

FE: *I know an example that comes to my mind that simply is a good footnote to your answer. A couple of small foundations here in Los Angeles have provided the Japanese-American National Museum thousands of dollars to support school buses to transport kids to the museum. Thousands of these kids coming from all kinds of urban backgrounds*

come and react to the story of the World War II Japanese-American in-
ternment camps. Listening to their depth and insight of their questions
and the power of the experience, it reminds me of your comments and
the potential of foundations.

HC: Let me point something out. In this weird world that I've come
into in which egos play a part that they shouldn't (as in all other
worlds) it can be argued that the Knight Foundation likely feels
it's in competition with the Freedom Forum, let us say. Wrong.
I wish to God that I had the imagination and the intelligent application of resources that went into their Newseum in Washington, which thrills more kids on a daily basis with the business
of current affairs and its presentation than anything else I know.

It uses virtually all the devices of show and tell taken up a
notch through communications technology to make the events
of the day and the communication of those events of real interest to kids for whom they are usually so much background clut-
ter. It offers something of value as opposed to the junk that they
watch on television and the games they play on the Internet and
on their computers. The Newseum proves it is not beyond our
capacity to do engaging things which will broaden and deepen
this oncoming generation's knowledge, understanding, and
sense of the world in all its great complexity.

JL: *Following along the theme of Foundation Communications intended*
for this chapter, you mentioned Freedom Forum's Newseum. The
Knight Foundation, following the family's roots in journalism, has fo-
cused on communications in its grantmaking. Are there any programs
the foundation has supported in communications or the media? I know
it's sensitive to place one grant made over others, but does any program
come to mind in the world of educating the media?

HC: That's a very interesting question, but I'm not going to answer
it directly. When asked who I think is doing the best job of covering the news, the honest answer is that I don't read all of them,
I don't see all of them, and I'm not equally familiar with all of
them, so it's not fair to play the invidious comparison game. But
let me tell you something that a couple of our grantees have

helped us to understand: It's all very well to make reporters better at their craft, but if they go back into newsrooms in which those who govern their daily activities find irrelevant what they have learned in those days, weeks, or months of seminars and classes and workshops, then they might as well never have had them except as an exercise in self-improvement. Useful as that is, it has nothing to do with the public interest. Thus, there is now considerable understanding that we have to work very hard at educating the gatekeepers, as well as the writers and presenters—so that the gatekeepers broaden and deepen their own understanding of the issues that the reporter is now better educated to be raising with them back in the newsroom. In practice, we're at the stage of tiny beginnings, but I think in the long run this approach can bear greater fruit than simply educating the reporters in these mid-career training programs and throwing them back into the pit of blank indifference.

JL: *Are there any methodologies that work better than others?*

HC: We have also begun to wonder whether it's not better to take training out to many small groups on a circuit-rider basis, as opposed to segregating out handfuls of people at distant centers of learning.

JL: *Now let me flip this—what about grants for the nonprofit community in order to support their communication efforts and work well with the media?*

HC: I was actually talking only about the former point, making the communicators better understand the issues they are communicating. As to the point that you are trying to extrapolate and which I, unfortunately, hadn't mentioned, it is extremely important to make better communicators out of those who have the program or the knowledge or the position to advance the kind of things that we think would be useful. In that respect, we are now wrestling in the second generation of the National Community Development Initiative with ways to better use the platform of our shared funding of community development efforts to improve, dramatically, the ability of those in the field to get their message out to the publics they not only serve, but also to the publics on whom they depend for support. That one is also harder to do than to say.

JL: What is the role of communications in a nonprofit?

HC: We are now trying to wrestle with what are the best ways to improve that process. The intermediaries in this particular effort have always done some training. The problem is that everybody inevitably spends most of their time doing that which is the most pressing, particularly in times of limited resources. The trick is to have people constantly go beyond lip service to mean it—to understand that an effective communications program would greatly enhance the reach and scope and future of what they do. But to repeat, knowing it, understanding it, and believing it is one thing. Having the time and the expertise and the money to do it is another. It is clear, the best way to get there is to add resources expressly for that purpose so that communication is not part of a zero sum game that takes away money from the fundamental mission. What we've got to be careful about (going back to the education thing) is that it's not simply the reallocation of limited resources, but additions to the existing pot. It was strange. I went to a segregated white public school in Greenville, Mississippi, in the immediate postwar period. In that school in 5th grade I learned Spanish—I was in a poverty-stricken place in Mississippi and I learned Spanish. I had Social Studies that taught me a great deal about the world. I was in a system that actually believed that our horizons ought to be extended beyond the Delta. My children never had any of that in the same public school system both before and after total integration. I expect their experience was and is a commonplace one. When you speak to educators as I did later as an editor and say, "Why don't we restore these kinds of fundamentals to the early education of our kids," they reply, "Why don't you find us the money, Mr. Editor? Right now we're scrambling to provide the basics with what you know full well is not enough money as it is."

In that respect, to go back to the question of what we ought to be doing, it's time to be a lot less skittish about advocacy. In the most crude as well as the most sophisticated sense, foundations must step up and say, loudly and collectively, that there are real deficiencies, real needs, and real opportunities which this society must meet for the sake of its long-term health. One of these is to create a wider and deeper group of citizens who understand the world in which they live and who are prepared to demand that the United States operate in ways that reflect its realities.

JL: *Let's take this microscope that we've been placing over the nonprofit sector and turn it back on the foundation world. Dot Ridings, a former Knight/Ridder publisher, is now the president of the Council on Foundations, the national trade associate. Her battle cry in her first few years was communication, communication, communication. In other words, the country doesn't know the good work of foundations. We need to get our message out and we need to get better at getting our message out. What is your response to this challenge in terms of a foundation's message, audience, all of the other classic aspects of communications?*

HC: You ask a number of pertinent questions, but I was somewhat surprised to learn when I got here that this foundation, which came out of communications money, had a very strong sense that it was wrong to spend a great deal of time trying to explain or to present what it was doing to the public; that it was for a number of reasons counterproductive and offensive. That has changed. It was changing before I got here, but it was very real and I discovered it was reflected in the attitude of any number of other foundations.

As to how you ought to communicate, you need first to ask for what purpose, and to what audience. Then it becomes a lot easier. If the purpose is to attempt to affect public policies that we think are necessary, arising from what has happened on September 11 or what September 11 represents or what it may come to mean, the target tends to be a fairly elite audience. If we're trying to communicate with a public looking for places that may offer services and information they don't have, well then the way we communicate and the approaches we take are going to be different and will be much longer term. That one is not susceptible to a campaign mode in which objective A will be taken by December 1 or legislation B will incorporate certain ideas by January 30. It's a much longer-term thing. I think Dot Ridings is thinking about that longer-term commitment to a sustained effort to disseminate the message that there are things that foundations can offer to society, do offer, which should be of great interest to a number of people who are currently ignorant of them.

Let me say, parenthetically, that I was once a consultant to the PR firm that Dot first used when she discovered that while foundations might be few in number, they had major enemies on Capitol Hill. What she was also aiming at was to take the sting out of the tail of that enemy with a strategy that was heavily focused on getting the message across up on the Hill. It is worth remembering that there's never any question but that a "message" is going to get out. Somebody else may paint you, you paint yourself or circumstances in the midst of pressure paint you, but painting there will be. If you really are concerned about what you understand to be accuracy and truth, then you better have a sustained campaign to paint your own picture and it better be a multifront campaign, and it ought to be offered without any reservation or embarrassment.

FE: One ongoing question in working with the media is their ongoing desire to embrace what is eye-catching, immediate, sexy. And what we're talking about is. . .

HC: Yes.

FE: What we're talking about is a steady long-term viewpoint and strategy. Any reflections on how we balance their needs and our strategy?

HC: Yes. It was always a matter of despair in the places of government and politics that I from time to time inhabited that it was so hard to build—to sustain—public support for long-term needs. An example: At the State Department there was a unit called Policy Planning, whose objective on paper was to do just that—long-term policy planning.

But the way it operated most of the time was as a crisis management center, a place for tomorrow's speeches in response to yesterday's headlines. Not surprisingly, it didn't do either job well enough. For any real management of the kind of issues we're talking about you have to take it as a given that short-term victories are going to be few and far between and that short-term distractions are going to be constant. You must simply decide on your objective and give it a minimum of three to five years of investment and time, constantly evaluating the need for tactical shifts but never abandoning the strategic objective.

FE: *Let me ask you a question about evaluating short-term wins versus long-term strategy. How do you know when you're hitting the bull's-eye this time or if you're even aiming at the right target?*

HC: It's a nice coincidence that you would ask me that. I was just reading a long memo from our director of planning and evaluation, John Bare, on the whole question of risk and results and definitions therein and how you're going to know when you get there and the like. The shorter-range thing is usually measured by such obvious factors as the number of hits that you're getting, by which I don't mean on the net but overall, the number of references, the number of times that a message you are trying to get across actually gains currency in the media, the number of times you see referrals to that message within the trade, the number of times in the general press, and the like, the number of times that you see a policy maker use it in a speech.

Conversely, you'll know you're not succeeding in the short term with any kind of communication strategy if you are forever in the penumbra of oblivion, public ignorance, indifference, simply not existing in terms of all the ways that we understand we communicate with each other.

In the long term, it's more that those with whom you are attempting to form partnerships, with whom you are attempting to reach objectives, automatically understand that you're a place to come, that you are about certain kinds of enterprises that are of interest to them, that your approach is one which is compatible with how they see themselves working in whatever area you would hope to be their partner. In the larger environment, it's having the public understand that what you do is in the public interest and is something which justifies the various legal and tax code protections philanthropy enjoys. At end of the day, you want the general public to have absorbed not a high number of specifics but a generally coherent sense of your mission, measurable by the difference between its understanding at the outset and at the end of a specific period envisaged in your communications strategy.

FE: *Let me ask a follow-up question to that. How do you set the right environment on a foundation board regarding the communications program? Certainly, I assume your board understands and appreciates the role of communications. But what if you're starting from square one with communications. Do you have any suggestions as to how to create an environment for board members to understand its role and also how it should be managed vis-à-vis the other departments or programs of a foundation?*

HC: Many boards have a very, very strong sense that they should not be in the publicity business, and I don't know precisely how to deal with this. I think that you must use a form of jujitsu, based on the assumption that all foundation boards want to have maximum effect with the dollars that they allocate, that they want them to be as beneficial to the communities they serve as they possibly can be, that they want those dollars to have real bounce and have real staying power. Assuming that's true, then I think that you can make a case, which, while not compelling on the first incarnation with a board that is reluctant to get into the muck and mire of public communication, will be over time. I think it is simply irrefutable on evidence that can be assembled that the reach and effectiveness of your money is magnified considerably by the awareness that it's there among organizations and individuals who might need it, and by the overall public's understanding that the money—the causes toward which your money is going—are causes which are, themselves, in the general public interest as well as the highly specific interest of individual recipients. You can't get either one of those effects without a major communication strategy.

There's not much to be done if board and staff in the end are content to say, "We know who our clients are, they are the ones we have always had. We know that what they do works. We wish to support them and they can handle the rest of it." But the fact is we can't possibly know that any of that is true unless we expand our reach and allow new people to ask questions about us and examine what we do. Communicating regularly and expansively allows foundations to not only better understand what it is their recipients are doing, but also to learn what others might be doing if they knew we existed, if they knew that there was the potential for new partnerships. Because it is, or should be, a two-way street, a vigorous communications program also enables us to learn the bad news faster when our programs are not working well.

I came into the foundation world in 1969 as a member of the Twentieth Century Fund board. It underwrote [Waldemar] Nielson's book, *The Big Foundations,* about the same time. That was also the year, of course, that our good friend Texas Representative Wright Portman was finally given the gift he had been looking for when the Ford Foundation used tax-exempt money to provide rest and recreation grants to some of Bobby Kennedy's people after his assassination. It was arguably the single act most responsible for the tax act clampdown on foundations in 1969.

Well, as Nielson discovered, the more general background was that most foundations at the time had little interest in public accountability and communication. There was a certain amount of arrogance in all this, and for those who for reasons of ideology ranging from right to left hated the tax-exempt accumulation of private money for unaccountable public purposes, it was an arrogance that worked to their advantage. They were able to draw extraordinarily distorted pictures of what foundations were about. 1969 to me is as good an argument in favor of communications and openness and candid public conversation as I can think of. We learned then that lecturing our auditors about our virtues was not going to work, that claiming saintliness simply because we were spending other people's money was not persuasive, and that we had better be doing a better job of defining who and what we were.

JL: *Our last few questions. I believe that leaders set the vision for an institution, but the vision muscle is not often exercised to see beyond the horizon in terms of communications. If you were to envision, whether it be the message, the quote, or the headline about foundations in this new world that we have what would that be? What do you see?*

HC: Foundations have discovered that beyond their inveterate rhetoric about their roles as venture capitalists, risk takers, and producers of significant innovation on the margins, they have embraced consistent truth-telling to power and consistent support of those things which they understand to be truly important to the health of the republic and the world. It would be wonderful if we were able to write that foundations finally learned that while public opinion may be a very shallow lake affected by each breeze that comes from East, West, North, and South, foundation policy ought to be set upon a much deeper bottom and with a much firmer anchor. It would be nice if in 5 years or 10 years it was discovered that foundations had responded to the changed world, or perhaps their changed understanding of the world after September 11, by applying their freedom from the bottom line and from each political wind to advocate and support programs, policies, and approaches that actually put the nation more in line with that world, with that new world or with that world revealed by the events of September 11.

FE: *Hodding, my final question is just an extension of what you were just addressing. In the early years of private foundations in our country,* *they did play a significant role with regard to public policy, as you know, in areas such as medicine and education.*

HC: Sure.

FE: And social issues. I think many of us perceive foundations today being more or less nonplayers with regard to affecting public policy. Do you agree with that perception? And how might a good communication plan or strategy allow foundations to speak more strongly as a group? Or is that wishful thinking?

HC: No, it's not wishful thinking. I spent a number of years on the board of an organization that ran political leadership exchanges around the world. Because it was a studiously bipartisan group, I got to know a lot of people across the political aisle. One of those Republican counterparts later became the founder and remains the founding president of an organization that uses tax-exempt money to accomplish precisely what I understand a lot of people think can't be done anymore. It's called the Heritage Foundation, of course. I remark on the Heritage Foundation because as the Reagan Administration was swept into power back in 1981, it used as background sheets and foreground justification massive amounts of policy advocacy paper turned out by Heritage. The same had happened in the 1930s when people at the Twentieth Century Fund were burning the midnight oil to write drafts for what became New Deal legislation, particularly in the economic area. The people who today usually say that it is no longer possible for foundations to do this kind of thing are not people who are on the political right. To put it more bluntly, there is a certain lack of appetite for risk taking among many mainstream foundations that is not matched by my old buddy over at Heritage and elsewhere among those who have had a significant say in what public policy has become over the last 20 or so years. I think that there is vast room out there for anyone willing to speak, to use the megaphone that goes with the ideas and programs that they support. What is required, and is too frequently lacking, is a certain amount of nerve—a willingness to risk sanctions and engage in public debate about public issues.

FE: Well, I think perhaps on that note, I hope the readers of this chapter will take heed and inspiration.

HC: Let me make two additional comments that have nothing to do with what we were talking about. When my father won the Pulitzer Prize for editorials in 1945, the editorial cited was titled "Go for Broke." It was the only editorial among the 12 submitted that didn't have something to do with Mississippi, but instead had to do with what was owed to Japanese-Americans for what had been done to them and what had been done for America by them as much-decorated soldiers in the 442nd Regiment. I mention this because we have at least two generations for whom it is truly new news that we ran concentration camps in this country within the lifetime of their parents and grandparents, the inhabitants of which were put there because of their ancestry and nothing else.

The second is a reminder that when Jack Kennedy was killed, I sent a reporter out into the streets of Greenville, Mississippi, to get the public reaction. He came back in—it was raining—crying and wet and said, "They're all happy. They're all cheering." My kid brother was then a member of our current president's fraternity, not at Yale but at Tulane. He was a Deke and fraternity mates organized a great celebratory party upon Kennedy's assassination.

Both stories are fervently denied even when remembered by Americans who profess themselves to be appalled that people could cheer elsewhere for what happened at the World Trade Center. But if we don't even understand our own past and its relevance to what is going on in the world, then I don't know how we're ever going to deal intelligently with that world.

FE: Your story about your father's origination of Go for Broke reminds me that the Go for Broke Memorial is part of the Japanese-American National Museum here in Los Angeles, and it's the first stop that these kids have when they get off of those buses I mentioned.

HC: That's wonderful, I hope to see it some day.

JL: On a personal note, Hodding, I can always remember how many years you've been president of the Knight Foundation because it coincides with the birth of my second son, Elias. Remember? Early in your tenure, you were visiting one of your grantmaking regions here in Long Beach. I helped to set up a day full of meetings with you and some local community leaders. The day of the meeting turned out to be the day after my son was born. I'll never forget—when I told you of his birth at the end of a long day of community meetings, you looked me straight in the eye and said, "Thank you for all you've done, but go home."

HC: My word, I almost forgot that.

JL: And to let you know, Elias is doing as well as you are at Knight— happy, energetic, and full of joy. Thank you again for sharing your thoughts today.

HC: Thank you both.

CHAPTER 6

A Foundation's Journey into Public Policy Engagement

by Emmett D. Carson

PERSPECTIVES

Much of foundation grantmaking treats the symptoms of social ills without addressing the root causes. For foundations that strive to influence public policy on community issues, what are some key concerns? What lessons have others learned when funding programs promising systemic change through advocacy?

The Minneapolis Foundation has experience in effecting public policy change at the local level. The Foundation's grant guidelines state that as a first priority among several, it will actively "pursue public policy change to solve critical needs and increase opportunities."

In this chapter, Emmett Carson, president of the Minneapolis Foundation, tells the story of his foundation's foray into the public policy arena. Carson, who has been president of the Minneapolis Foundation since 1994, was previously with the Ford Foundation in New York, where he was a program officer specializing in the areas of social justice, governance, and public policy.

INTRODUCTION

There is an old saying, "Follow where the path leads." The Minneapolis Foundation's involvement in public policy arose out of a commitment to improve the lives of children and families living in poverty in seven inner-city neighborhoods. The Foundation did not begin its effort with a primary focus on public policy, nor has public policy become the Foundation's exclusive focus. Rather, through careful and deliberate actions, the Foundation developed a comfort level with how and under what circumstances public policy engagement can be a useful additional tool in helping it to achieve its objectives for improving community.

As a general rule, foundations do not consider themselves active participants in the development and formulation of public policy, defined here as any effort (convening, public awareness, advocacy, and lobbying) to influence public decision making. This stance by foundations is both surprising and disappointing. It is surprising because most foundations see their role as improving some aspect of community life, and federal, state, and local governments directly or indirectly shape the quality of community life through either the establishment or failure to establish regulations and laws. The reluctance of foundations to engage in public policy is disappointing because it is often argued that a primary role of foundations is to provide the venture capital for important social projects and to build civil society.[1] By eschewing public policy engagement, foundations appear more interested in providing charity, treating the symptoms of injustice, rather than in promoting social justice to correct the causes of the injustice.

The purpose of this essay is to describe how the Foundation became engaged in public policy activities. By describing the Foundation's experiences, it is hoped that other foundations will consider the value of public policy engagement for achieving their grantmaking objectives. This chapter is divided into five sections. The next section describes how and why the Foundation arrived at a neighborhood-focused project. Section three examines how the Foundation's neighborhood focus led to a greater understanding of the complex challenges facing neighborhoods. Section four describes how a deeper appreciation of neighborhood challenges led the Foundation to recognize the need and value of a public policy approach for addressing these issues. Finally, the conclusion outlines the key elements that, in retrospect, helped to shape the Foundation's involvement in public policy.

Before proceeding, it should be noted that this case study has several significant limitations. As with all case studies, it is specific to the culture and social conditions in Minneapolis coupled with the Foundation's prior history and experiences. Further, because this case study is a retrospective based on events that began several years ago, it may inadvertently over- or underemphasize certain key events and omit some others altogether. It is also likely that the sequence of events appears to be more thoughtful, less chaotic, and having had greater board and staff consensus than what actually occurred. Perhaps the most significant limitation is that this is not an impartial case study conducted by an independent observer. The author was a key participant in the events that are described herein, and that likely introduces a number of biases in the recounting of the Foundation's activities.[2] Notwithstanding these and other limitations, it is hoped that this essay will stimulate discussion about the value of public policy engagement by foundations rather than be viewed as an all-purpose "how-to" primer on how to do it.

WHY A NEIGHBORHOOD-FOCUSED PROJECT?

The Foundation's interest in a neighborhood initiative began during a board retreat in 1992 in which the board and staff examined both trends in neighborhood poverty and its grantmaking strategies. The featured outside speaker was Sharon Sayles Belton, chair of the Minneapolis City Council, who would later become the city's first African-American mayor. Sayles Belton challenged the board about Minneapolis's rising neighborhood poverty and the Foundation's lack of grantmaking focus on this issue.

At least three disturbing trends were identified during the next nine months following the retreat. First, the Foundation was troubled by research that showed a widening gap between the rich and poor in Minneapolis. Second, there was concern generated by David Rusk's proactive article, "The Road to East St. Louis," that poverty was being concentrated in certain neighborhoods and that such a concentration would have a debilitating effect on both the neighborhoods and the larger city.[3] Third, it was felt that the concentration of poverty among children would likely lead to increased social ills as they became adults, including illegal activity, incarceration, and teenage pregnancy, all of which would be harmful to both the individuals involved and the larger community.

In addition to these observations about the neighborhoods, the Foundation reached several conclusions about its prior grantmaking experiences. In general, the Foundation's board felt that its past grantmaking had not made a substantial difference in affecting poverty at the neighborhood level. This acknowledgment was an important philosophical turning point for the trustees to assert that the Foundation's prior grantmaking wasn't accomplishing what it could and should to address neighborhood poverty. The question, then, was what should the Foundation do differently to significantly reduce neighborhood poverty?

After two separate efforts to survey the opinions of community leaders and nonprofit organizations, the Foundation began to develop a neighborhood strategy with three basic assumptions:

1. The Foundation's grantmaking needed more depth and less breadth.
2. The solutions to neighborhood poverty would be found in neighborhood leaders and neighborhood-based nonprofit organizations.
3. A substantial and sustained long-term commitment would be required to foster the level of changes in neighborhood poverty that it wanted to create.

Taken together, these assumptions led to the Foundation's Building Better Futures (BBF) initiative,[4] which was launched in 1995 to focus on Minneapolis's poorest neighborhoods where the poverty rates for children exceeded 60 percent. Predating a strategy that is now championed by venture philanthropists, the Foundation believed that a narrow focus, coupled with an unprecedented and sustained financial commitment ($20 million over 10 years), would yield measurable changes in the targeted neighborhoods.

Almost from the start, the Foundation was forced to reevaluate each of its initial assumptions. To meet the $20 million financial commitment within 10 years required the Foundation to direct nearly 100 percent of its grantmaking to the selected neighborhoods. The Foundation's grantmaking guidelines were revised to reflect this new focus, which created considerable dismay and anger by a wide array of nonprofit organizations throughout the city and suburbs that had previously relied on the Foundation for support. These nonprofit organizations felt that they and the causes that they advocated were being abandoned. The Foundation's board and staff spent considerable time addressing the concerns of these organizations to little or no avail and, only then, recognized the full significance of its new strategy.

Using the geography of the neighborhoods also proved to be problematic. The social relationships of people in the neighborhoods and the program reach of nonprofit organizations did not correspond to the official geographical neighborhood boundaries. The Foundation also quickly recognized that many of the nonprofit organizations did not exclusively work in a single neighborhood and so additional exceptions had to be made to the seven neighborhood focus. In addition, "border" projects that served both the target BBF neighborhoods and equally poor adjacent neighborhoods also were allowed to receive grants.

Another complication was that in several of the neighborhoods, neither the political nor the school boundaries overlapped with the geographical neighborhood boundaries. Having more than one elected city council member speaking on behalf of different parts of the same neighborhood or parts of different neighborhoods posed a variety of problems. It meant that various political interests would need to be considered by different political and neighborhood leaders and the Foundation in determining strategy and who would get credit or blame. The Foundation had hoped to elicit the active involvement and support of the Minneapolis Public Schools, primarily in providing space for after school mentoring and enrichment activities. Unfortunately, for the Foundation's purposes, the Minneapolis public school system is not neighborhood based, meaning that students from any neighborhood can enroll in any public school. As a consequence, it was impossible to use the school system as a primary vehicle for reaching youth in the target neighborhoods. These geographical issues were minor compared to what the Foundation would learn as it began its neighborhood work in earnest.

UNLEARNING WHAT THE FOUNDATION KNEW

While the Foundation had extensive prior grantmaking experience in the BBF neighborhoods, its new neighborhood focus enabled it to see new things that it had either ignored or was unable to see in the past. Without the intensive neighborhood focus, it is highly unlikely that the Foundation would have gained these insights. The four primary insights were related to neighborhood differences, building neighborhood assets, economic development and the primacy of affordable housing. Together, these insights on neighborhood dynamics directly led to the Foundation's interest and comfort in pursuing public policy. Each of these insights is described in further detail below.

Neighborhood Differences

When the Foundation began its work, an underlying assumption was that because the seven neighborhoods had nearly identical levels of poverty, they would have similar strengths and weaknesses. This assumption turned out to be completely false. With the exception of widespread poverty, we learned that the neighborhoods shared little in common. To better understand the differences across neighborhoods, the Foundation contracted with the University of Minnesota's Institute on Race and Poverty to develop an innovative and never-tried approach of mapping the assets and weaknesses of the neighborhoods at the block level. As the Foundation stated in its report, *Measuring Neighborhood Health:*

> Through BBF, we have developed a new diagnostic tool to assess the health of a neighborhood. In the past, we were

like early 20th-century medical doctors asking a patient where it hurt and prescribing an all-purpose pain reliever. Sometimes it worked; most times it didn't. For the first time, we now have the equivalent of an x-ray or MRI (magnetic resonance imaging) to show all concerned precisely what and where the problems and opportunities are in a neighborhood. We can now pinpoint where resources should be directed and measure whether our efforts have been successful.[5]

The mapping research documented neighborhood health using multiple variables including day care, number of school children whose native language is not English, crime reports, toxic waste sites, new construction, ratio of renters to homeowners, and abandoned buildings, among other measures. A major success of the effort was in getting the county government (which provides all social services) and the police department to release the block-level raw data to the Foundation. Because this data could be directly linked to individuals, both agencies had significant concerns about maintaining the privacy of the raw data. The Foundation's direct engagement was key in the legal agreements obtaining release of the data as well as the interest of these agencies in using the findings of the mapping research for their purposes. By examining how the socioeconomic variables listed above related to each other within a neighborhood revealed important information and helped the Foundation to recognize that each neighborhood needed different things and, as a result, its grantmaking in each neighborhood had to be different.

For example, one neighborhood had a high percentage of renters. This insight led the Foundation and the neighborhood to recognize that it was a community in constant transition as renters of low-income apartments had or wanted little long-term attachment to the neighborhood in which they lived. Similarly, we found that some neighborhoods had growing numbers of young children but had few day care centers. In other neighborhoods, there were an adequate number of day care centers; however, they were situated near high-crime areas or near toxic waste sites.

This information not only guided the Foundation's work but also became an important tool for neighborhood leaders, nonprofit organizations, foundations, the county government and elected officials. In numerous cases, these other stakeholders were unaware of the trends within neighborhoods, and the maps became a way of creating a shared view of the facts. Foundation staff accepted a variety of invitations to present the results of the mapping work to various groups including the Minneapolis City Council, the state legislature's Subcommittee on Children and the office of the Vice President of the United States. An unanticipated consequence of the popularity of the mapping approach was that other neighborhoods throughout the city and state wanted similar information. This need was largely met when the McKnight Foundation made a major grant to extend this research to include all Minneapolis neighborhoods and the twin city of St. Paul.

The Foundation also hoped the mapping approach would allow it to measure its impact. The issue of measuring and evaluating outcomes was a challenging methodological question. Each neighborhood had multiple actors including other foundations, corporations, city and county government, and nonprofit organizations, all engaged in efforts to improve the local neighborhood. Moreover, as stated above, each neighborhood required a different set of strategies tailored to meet its needs. The idea that the Foundation could isolate its unique contribution within the context of neighborhoods in which multiple entities were providing funding to the same groups or projects was impossible—the research methodology simply does not exist. Second, because the Foundation was interested in improving the overall health of a neighborhood by alleviating poverty and was not specifically interested in the effectiveness of a particular grant to a specific nonprofit organization, it needed a different methodological approach and the neighborhood mapping provided it.

Building Neighborhood Assets

The Foundation strongly believed that an asset approach rather than a deficit model approach was both the preferred philosophical and strategic starting point. By asset approach, the Foundation hoped to build on neighborhood strengths rather than focus on neighborhood weaknesses. It firmly believed that there were neighborhood-based nonprofit institutions that, if empowered, would be an important element in making a positive difference in improving the quality of life in the neighborhoods. What the Foundation found was that the neighborhood residents were resilient people with remarkable character who possessed extraordinary survival skills. Unfortunately, the neighborhood nonprofit organizations that served neighborhood residents had limited organizational capacity.

To its dismay, the Foundation came to the conclusion that most of the neighborhood nonprofit organizations would require significant technical assistance, financial resources, and staff development to appreciably expand their ability and capacity to provide additional community leadership or services. These concerns were described in detail in an interim report to the community, *Building Better Futures: Community Report.*

> The asset-building perspective is fundamental. But it's also fundamental to recognize the stress that poverty imposes on organizations. Often, churches cannot afford to support a pastor who has time to be a leader beyond his or her flock. Businesses are small, without the capital or human reserves to do more than survive, and often without owners in the neighborhood at all. Home ownership is likewise weak, making it difficult for block clubs and neighborhood associations to organize on the basis of protecting asset values. Schools are rarely rooted in the neighborhoods they serve.
>
> Paradoxically, then, in high poverty areas there are likely to be numerous strong individuals, but also numerous stressed institutions. So much energy goes toward survival and making ends meet that little time is left for the organizing work, inspiration of others, consensus building and sheer hours of volunteer leadership that help hold communities together and foster a sense of empowerment.[6]

Even more disconcerting was that the Foundation's interest in forming partnerships with neighborhood organizations was, in some cases, causing them additional stress. The Foundation's renewed appreciation for the technical assistance and capacity building needs of stressed neighborhood organizations directly led to the expansion of the number of nonprofit organizations that received operating support and increasing the size of such grants. The Foundation was faced with the sobering reality that strengthening neighborhood organizations would be a long-term and expensive effort. Further, prior experience had shown that raising the skill level of specific individuals within an organization without raising their salaries to the prevailing market rate, more often than not, led the individuals to move to better paying jobs at other organizations. While this was certainly beneficial to the individual and of short-term value to the neighborhood organization, this did not appear to be a viable, cost-effective, long-term approach for building the capacity of neighborhood organizations.

Economic Development

Not surprisingly, economic development emerged as a central strategy for the Foundation's neighborhood poverty alleviation efforts. If businesses could be developed in poor neighborhoods that employed neighborhood residents, the process would simultaneously help to revitalize the community and increase the personal income of residents. Due to limited transportation options to enable neighborhood residents to commute to the suburban communities with the fastest job growth and the lack of affordable housing in suburban communities, economic development within the targeted neighborhoods became a high priority. The question was how could the Foundation effectively engage in neighborhood economic development?

The answer came when the State of Minnesota established the Urban Initiatives Fund. The Fund provided matching funds to approved economic development organizations to make micro-development loans to neighborhood businesses. While the Foundation is not a bank, it has one of the oldest nonprofit lending programs (Minnesota Nonprofits Assistance Fund) in the United States, having started making loans to nonprofit organizations throughout the state in 1980. With this experience, the Foundation successfully applied to become a partner in the state program committing $1 million from its endowment to be matched by the state program. In addition to developing sound business plans, loan applicants had to be located in one of the seven BBF neighborhoods, demonstrate how the business would be a value added to the community, and indicate their willingness to hire neighborhood residents.

During its existence, 1995 to 2002, the Entrepreneur's Fund made 56 loans totaling $2.06 million. The Fund wrote off 10 non-performing loans totaling $357,000. Over time, the loan program has evolved to be a primary lender to newer immigrant groups in the BBF neighborhoods, particularly in the Somali and Ethiopian communities, and works closely with commercial banks that would otherwise not make these "character" loans.

In addition to the loan fund, the Foundation supported a number of more traditional grantmaking strategies to spur economic development in the neighborhoods. In particular, the Foundation supported job training programs, community economic development projects and the development and implementation of state-backed individual development accounts (IDAs). IDAs allow qualified residents to have their savings matched so that they can be used for education, home purchase, or starting a business. The Foundation's public support of this strategy provided some early experience in the importance of public policy in impacting local neighborhoods. While the Foundation's primary interest in IDAs was limited to the BBF neighborhoods, the resulting state policy benefited all qualified individuals throughout the state.

The Primacy of Affordable Housing

More than any other learning, the Foundation's deeper understanding of the affordable housing crisis led it to recognize the value of public policy engagement. *Affordable housing* is defined as housing that requires no more than 30 percent of an individual's income. The Foundation had long been aware that affordable housing was a problem for low-income people and had supported traditional housing development projects. However, the Foundation was unprepared for what it would learn. It was estimated that there was a need for over 230,000 units of affordable housing in Minneapolis and its suburbs. In addition to affecting people under or near the poverty level, people working full-time jobs as salesclerks, bus drivers, and others could not find affordable housing. Even more shocking was that the shelters for the homeless were overflowing. The majority of shelter residents were children and over two thirds of the shelters' adult residents (80 percent were women) worked full or part time.[7]

As the Foundation interacted more intensively with neighborhood organizations, it found that the lack of stable, safe, affordable housing was a major contributing factor for a host of other problems. For example, neighborhoods had little stability because residents were constantly moving from place to place in a fruitless search to find safe and affordable housing. As a result, it was difficult for neighborhood organizations to develop long-term strategies with the support of residents who had no long-term interest in remaining in the community. Parents, moving from place to place, moved their children from school to school. The Foundation would later discover that the children attending Minneapolis Public Schools had a mobility rate of 46 percent, compared to the statewide public school mobility rate of 18 percent.[8] The mobility of these students is a significant contributor to their poor academic performance.

How had the lack of affordable housing become so severe, and what could the Foundation do that would have significance? Further investigation revealed that the housing crisis was largely the result of property owners paying off 30-year low-interest development loans from the state and federal governments that had required them to provide below-market rental rates. As the low-interest development loans were paid off, owners of the apartments were free, per the terms of the original loan agreements, to charge market rates. The lack of new subsidies over the last 30 years meant that there were no new affordable housing units to replace the older units as they became market rate.

The Foundation confronted an enormous dilemma. It was committed to improving the quality of life in the poorest neighborhoods. The lack of affordable housing was a major impediment to the stability of poor neighborhoods. And this was not a problem that could be solved using the assets of the neighborhoods or through the Foundation's traditional grantmaking strategies—the scope of the problem was too big. To exclusively rely on the Foundation's traditional grantmaking strategies would result in only a limited number of new affordable housing units being developed and would be woefully inadequate to what the neighborhoods and the city as a whole needed. Another approach would be required if the Foundation was to fulfill its commitment to improving the quality of life in the neighborhoods. The Foundation decided that it would have to try to broaden Minnesota's awareness of the affordable housing shortage and influence the state's housing policy if it was going to make a significant difference in this area.

PUBLIC POLICY AND HOUSINGMINNESOTA

At least one reason why foundations do not engage in public policy is the perception that such activity requires political partisanship and lobbying or, in some way, jeopardizes the foundation's neutrality. It does not. Political partisanship is ill advised for any foundation, especially community foundations that are to represent broad community interests. Community foundations can, by law, engage in direct lobbying activities and should examine whether this is a worthwhile activity to meet its objectives.[9] Finally, while foundations—especially community foundations—perceive themselves as neutral, they should not be neutered. Every grant reflects a social value about what a foundation believes and how it would like to improve the community in which it works.

After considering a range of options, the Foundation made three observations that would guide its public policy work on affordable housing. First, the affordable housing advocates across the state had little interaction with each other and few common themes in describing the importance of their work. Second, the larger public, as well as their elected representatives, was largely unaware of the affordable housing crisis, its cause, and the collateral problems it was causing. Finally, no advocacy organization had the requisite statewide credibility or public relations expertise to engage in a prolonged effort aimed at changing public opinion and creating a favorable climate at the statehouse around affordable housing issues.

To meet these challenges, in 1999 the Foundation issued an initial $250,000 request for proposals (RFP) to housing advocacy organizations. The RFP was sent to housing advocates who were required to establish a statewide coalition and to partner with a professional advertising or public relations firm. The purpose of the coalition would be to develop a coordinated effort to raise public awareness on affordable housing as a precursor to lobbying state officials to increase state funding for affordable housing. The requirement to develop a coalition required housing advocates who had relatively minor differences to have extensive conversations with each other and recognize their common interests. None of the housing advocacy organizations had ever interacted with a professional public relations firm about how to systematically shape public opinion on affordable housing and what themes to use. They were advocates without access to the resources and skills to market social ideas.

HousingMinnesota was selected as having the most comprehensive proposal by a review group consisting of Foundation staff, housing experts, and public relations representatives, none of whom were connected to the proposals that were received. The impact of HousingMinnesota has been tremendous. Over 70 organizations are part of the coalition, and many are making financial contributions to its work. All of the coalition's members have agreed to use common themes and share a common Web site (*www.HousingMinnesota.org*) and have overseen a statewide public information campaign on affordable housing. Minnesota's Governor, Jesse Ventura, participated in the public launch of the campaign and has participated in subsequent radio ads promoting affordable housing as impacting the economic competitiveness of the state. Representatives of HousingMinnesota are routinely asked to comment on legislative proposals by the print and broadcast media and is credited with helping to create a better climate for state funding of affordable housing. Other foundations are beginning to provide support for HousingMinnesota as they recognize the enormity of the affordable housing problem and the viability of the HousingMinnesota's approach. HousingMinnesota has hired a lobbyist to track and advocate for specific state legislation on affordable housing.

Affordable housing is still at a crisis level in Minnesota and in the BBF neighborhoods. There is still significant progress to be made. The Foundation's initial grant of $250,000 and subsequent grant of $250,000 would have done little if directed to building new units of affordable housing. However, these grants have aided in raising public awareness of the housing issue and coordinating the efforts of housing advocacy organizations in lobbying for increased state funding for affordable housing. HousingMinnesota has become a national model for housing advocates across the country, having received recognition from the national Low-Income Housing Coalition.

CONCLUSION

Although the Minneapolis Foundation completed its $20 million financial commitment to the BBF neighborhoods three years earlier than planned, the neighborhoods remain disproportionately poor.[10] The Foundation's commitment to these neighborhoods remains strong as it furthers its experience and comfort in pursuing public policy initiatives. For example, the Foundation has again revised its grantmaking guidelines to specifically identify its preference for public policy systems change projects. Research from the Foundation's housing and public school education efforts led to new initiatives around the growing numbers of homeless children. More specifically, elected officials, business leaders and nonprofit organizations have been brought together to discuss what public policy changes can be advanced, including: increased state appropriations for affordable housing, changes in municipal zoning ordinances, and reciprocal access across counties in referring and placing homeless people in shelters.[11] Of course, HousingMinnesota has been an important partner in each of these efforts.

The Foundation's most significant public policy engagement was a $100,000 grant to the Minneapolis Public Schools. This grant enabled the Minneapolis Public Schools to advocate their position in support of a public referendum on whether to continue a property tax levy. Failure to pass the referendum would have resulted in the dismissal of 600 teachers, and the school system was prohibited from using public funds to advocate the merits of its position. The referendum overwhelmingly passed, and while the Foundation's grant did receive some public mention, there was no negative press coverage.

There are at least three components that have enabled the Foundation to increase its understanding and appreciation for public policy engagement: board leadership, a culture of learning, and time and experience.

1. *Board leadership.* The Foundation's board has been and remains committed to making a tangible difference in the quality of life in Minneapolis' poorest neighborhoods. This belief led to the creation of the BBF initiative and to the resolve to follow the path that led to public policy. These decisions were not always easy. The discussions between the board and senior staff were greatly facilitated by a shared sense of values and open communications about the risks beforehand and continued communications and feedback throughout each initiative.

2. *A culture of learning.* The Foundation has made an intensive effort to fully understand the issues it is interested in. No matter how knowledgeable the individual staff person, the acquisition and dissemination of good information to the broader public is critical. While research and data alone will never solve a problem, it can tell you who is affected trends and, over time, reveal patterns and nuances for Foundation engagement that will often escape the casual observer. The

dissemination of the material in a user-friendly format helps to publicly establish the Foundation's interest and legitimacy on a topic, informs other interested parties, and allows for the possibility of dissent if the underlying hypotheses of the research are inaccurate. This latter point is essential if foundations are to avoid acting in a vacuum. Everyone may not agree on the direction, but everyone should know what the direction is and why it was set.

3. *Time and experience.* As with most things, start small and keep practicing has been the experience of The Minneapolis Foundation in public policy engagement. The Foundation's comfort with public policy engagement emerged over a period of several years and continues to evolve. Public policy work is no panacea and should be viewed as one tool that is available to use as circumstances warrant. Engagement in public policy should not be held to higher standards of success than foundations apply to their traditional grantmaking. Unless foundations are willing to selectively engage in public policy and accept the risks inherent in failure, they are likely to be in the business of charity, maintaining the existence of the poor, rather than trying to prevent the causes of poverty and injustice.

NOTES

1. As developed by Brian O'Connell, the definition of civil society used here is to refer to activities that engage individuals in recognizing their rights and responsibilities as citizens within a democracy. Brian O'Connell, *Civil Society: The Underpinnings of American Democracy.* New Hampshire: University Press of England, 1999, pp. 10–11.
2. Council on Foundations, *Community Foundations on Public Policy.* Washington, DC: Council on Foundations, 2000, pp. 32–25.
3. David Rusk, "The Road to East St. Louis," *The Monthly Memo,* Minnesota Center for Corporate Responsibility, January 1994, p. 6.
4. The Minneapolis Foundation, *Building Better Futures for Youth and Families in Poverty through Neighborhood and Community Partnerships,* June 10, 1994.

5. The Minneapolis Foundation, *Measuring Neighborhood Health: Baseline Indicators for Seven Minneapolis Neighborhoods,* November 1998, p. 1.

6. The Minneapolis Foundation, *Building Better Futures: Community Report,* November 1998, p. 6.

7. The Minneapolis Foundation, *Let's Fix This,* January 2001.

8. The Minneapolis Foundation, The Minneapolis Public Schools and the Greater Minneapolis Chamber of Commerce, *Measuring Up: A Report on the Minneapolis Public Schools 2000,* February 2000, p. 5.

9. Thomas R. Asher, *Myth v. Fact: Foundation Support of Advocacy.* Washington, DC: The Alliance for Justice, 1995.

10. The Minneapolis Foundation, *Building Better Futures: Changing Neighborhoods, Changing Lives,* 2001.

11. The Minneapolis Foundation, *Troubled Waters: Growing Up Homeless in Minnesota.* Summary Report, May 2001.

Section Three

Building the Foundation Board of the Twenty-First Century: Diversity and Strategic Planning

CHAPTER 7

The Foundation Board for the Twenty-First Century

by Stewart Kwoh and Bonnie Tang

PERSPECTIVES

Often, foundations are created from the vision and wealth of one individual or family. For the purposes of succession and continuity, it is often seen as desirable that those individuals are represented on the foundation's board. Thus, while the 2000 census reflects an increasingly diverse country, many foundation boards are comparatively homogeneous. Since any foundation's mandate includes serving the needs of charitable organizations and the community, does community representation and broad ethnic, racial and gender, and other diversity add value to the governing board?

This chapter explores the historical aspects of foundation boards and the potential value of diversity. Authors Stewart Kwoh and Bonnie Tang weave fact and opinion into a compelling argument for the diversity of foundation boards. Kwoh, president and executive director of the Asian Pacific American Legal Center, and has chaired the board of the California Endowment and is a member of the boards of the California Wellness Foundation, the Fannie Mae Foundation, and the Los Angeles United Urban Methodist Foundation. He received a MacArthur Fellowship in 1998. Bonnie Tang is a staff attorney for the Asian Pacific American Legal Center.

INTRODUCTION

At the start of the twenty-first century, foundations are faced with a host of complex challenges in responding to public need and in shaping public policy. The gap between the haves and have nots widens at an alarming rate; people dependent on governmental social services find their much-needed benefits dwindling; innovative solutions to educational inequities are sorely needed; health service and medical problems plague both the rich and poor. These and a multitude of perplexing problems persist in the context of huge demographic changes in the U.S. population that include growing pockets of immigrant communities, increases in both the aged and infant populations, a growing disabled population, and substantial gay and lesbian populations. These challenges have huge implications for the governance of foundations.

As policy makers for the foundation, board members have tremendous responsibilities to ensure that the foundation's vision and policies are responsive as well as proactive in addressing societal challenges. This makes it imperative that foundation boards are composed of skilled, resourceful members who are knowledgeable about diverse populations and their pressing issues.

"It is necessary to have diverse voices within the philanthropic community. A foundation needs to create a board that has a collective lens of many viewpoints because it will make the ultimate decisions as to where investments should be made that benefit all sectors of society," states Peggy Saika, executive director of Asian American/Pacific Islanders in Philanthropy and board member of the California Wellness Foundation and the Joyce-Mertz Gilmore Foundation. Adds Jim Crouch of the California Rural Indian Health Board and board member of the California Endowment, "Foundations in America regardless of their mission are engines of change, which operate as public trusts for the ultimate benefit of the general populace. Diversity among the board membership is essential to the maintenance of public good will as it assures that a multiplicity of voices are engaged in the governance process concerning the allocation of resources and the selection of operating methods."

Introduction

In the last decade, some foundation boards have made concerted efforts to increase their board diversity. While some progress has been made in diversifying board membership, the progress is uneven. In 1988, 29.2 percent of foundation board members were women, 93.8 percent were white, and 6.2 percent were persons of color.[1] In 1996, 33.6 percent of foundation board members were women, 89.9 percent were white, and 10.1 percent were persons of color, according to the Council on Foundations—a membership organization of foundations and corporations. (See Exhibit 7.1.) By 2000, 34.4 percent of foundation board members were women, 89.5 percent were white, and 10.5 percent were persons of color.[2]

The statistics speak for themselves. Some increase in diverse board membership occurred in the late 1980s and early 1990s, but extremely limited growth occurred between 1996 and 2000. Diana Campamour, president of Hispanics in Philanthropy, comments: "[T]here has been some anecdotal evidence of progress, [but] this progress has not been proportional to the population, the opportunities, the needs, or any other criteria that one might use." Stacey Davis, president and chief executive officer of the FannieMae Foun-

	1996	*1998*	*2000*
Gender			
Male	66.4%	69.2%	65.6%
Female	33.6	30.8	34.4
Race/Ethnicity			
Whites	89.9	90.2	89.5
Persons of color	10.1	9.8	10.5
Asians/Pacific Islanders	1.2	1.3	1.3
African-Americans	6.1	6.1	6.3
Hispanics	2.3	1.7	2.5
Native Americans	0.3	0.4	0.3
Other	0.2	0.4	0.1

Exhibit 7.1 Foundation/giving program boards—gender and race: 1996, 1998, and 2000.

Table from the December 2000 Inclusive Practices Program Report, Special Insert to *Council Columns*, February 2001, "2000 Progress Report on Inclusive Practices Diversity in All That We Do." Reprinted with permission from Council Columns, *www.cof.org*.

dation adds: "At the board level, white males still dominate the field. This is shocking especially because foundation play a huge role in benefiting society."

Indeed, as institutions providing service and benefit to millions of diverse constituents, foundations require leadership from board members with a wide range of backgrounds and experiences. "Diversity on foundation boards is important—it can lead to better decisions on needs and opportunities. Without these voices from diverse board members, foundations miss information on societal needs and changes," asserts Monica Lozano, former board member of the FannieMae Foundation and president of *La Opinion*.

Clearly, with the number of different types of foundations, including family, community, corporate, private and public, and with the variations in emphases and size, each foundation is uniquely situated to meet the challenge of diversifying its board. Different solutions and varying timelines will undoubtedly be needed. But the compelling reasons for diversification cannot be ignored. "Board diversity is not about 'political correctness': it is an essential component of a forward-thinking, effective governing body of the twenty-first century," asserts Bob Ross, president and chief executive officer of the California Endowment.

WHY SHOULD FOUNDATION BOARDS DIVERSIFY THEIR MEMBERSHIP?

First and foremost, foundations should view diversification as an opportunity to be more effective. Foundations with inclusive board membership increase their ability to make significant and positive impacts on grantmaking and foundation practices such as investments and the evaluation of programs. Gary Yates, president and chief executive officer of the California Wellness Foundation, comments: "At the California Wellness Foundation the focus is on improving the health of the people of California, particularly underserved populations. So we need a board that is in part reflective of the state population. Not to have this is to lose perspective of the different groups the foundation is working with and to lose a stronger grantmaking program."

In a survey conducted by the Joint Affinity Groups in their study on the impact of board and staff diversity, it was found that "more board diversity" was the answer receiving the highest "votes" by foundation employees to the question of what would make their organization more effective. This answer ranked above all other answers including more risk taking by the organization, more staff diversity, more accountability to communities served and more staff discretion.[3]

Secondarily, as institutions serving the public good and upholding the public's trust, foundations are also obligated to have leaders from diverse backgrounds who reflect the changing demographics in society, and have depth of knowledge about constituencies.

As beneficiaries of nonprofit tax laws, foundations have even more responsibility to be accountable to the larger public which includes people of all backgrounds. With sheltered tax protection, foundations must act in the public's interest. It is therefore imperative that foundation leadership is truly representative of its diverse constituents.

On a personal level, Stewart Kwoh has seen that board members from diverse communities have helped their foundations make a significant impact for their constituents because of their unique contributions. He has had the opportunity to serve on a variety of boards, from small to large foundations, and has served as the first, or among the first, Asian Pacific–American member of several boards (the FannieMae Foundation, California Wellness Foundation, California Endowment, California Consumer Protection Board, Los Angeles United Methodist Urban Foundation) and the only Asian Pacific–American board member serving at the time for Liberty Hill Foundation. Stewart has also been a board member of a family foundation, The Chung Ying Tang Foundation. During his tenure as chair of the board of the California Endowment, the board formalized their commitment to diverse boards with a "Philosophy on Board Composition" (discussed later in this chapter).

Through his years of board service, he has observed firsthand that boards that diversify their membership benefit in numerous ways and ultimately increase their impact on their constituent communities. The following is a summary of the key benefits; these points are elaborated later in the chapter.

The inclusive board has the advantage of broad and in-depth knowledge because of the range of experience the board members bring to the table. A diverse board also benefits from the multiple perspectives and insight shared from each board member. Essentially, the foundation board becomes a learning institution where sources of knowledge and experience are shared in lively discussions and board members process that information to make informed decisions about how best to strategically address community needs.

By maintaining a diverse board, a foundation is signaling its endorsement of inclusiveness. This support has positive implications at all levels, from foundation staff to grantee boards and staff to constituent communities.

Finally, a diverse board serves as a vehicle to include voices from diverse communities and opportunities for shared decision making with individuals from those communities.

As Stacey Davis of the FannieMae Foundation states, "Foundations need a high level of guidance from people who have a fundamental understanding of the parts of society that the foundation serves. Foundations contribute huge societal benefits. If foundations are not in sync with the communities they intend to serve, there are missed opportunities to make an impact."

Peter Pennekamp, executive director of the Humboldt Area Foundation and board member of the California Endowment, adds: "With diversification, everyone will benefit. There is no downside. Foundations caring about impact should be rushing towards diversification of their boards and organizations." In sum, foundations that fail to diversify their boards abandon the opportunities to make the most significant and strategic impacts on their constituent communities.

WHAT IS ACTUAL DIVERSITY?

Diversity is often used as a one-dimensional term focusing on racial or ethnic inclusiveness. While racial and ethnic diversity are critical, diversity must also encompass inclusiveness in categories like gender, sexual orientation, geography, religion, age, socioeconomic status, and disability.

Beyond demographic diversity, however, a board must include members who meaningfully represent the foundation's constituency. The myth that demographic diversity ensures broad representation must be dispelled. As Diana Campamour of Hispanics in Philanthropy states: "Inclusiveness doesn't just mean having more of one group or another; it means revamping the whole process. Because it is so small, the foundation world has a tendency to recycle the same ideas."[4] "When you look for inclusiveness, you must bring in perspectives that are truly different. We need to say and mean that it's okay for people with real differences to be a part of our institutions."

Peggy Saika of Asian American/Pacific Islanders in Philanthropy adds: "True progress in diversification encompasses more than superficial numerical goals. We need to look for board members who contribute a multicultural point of view and a vision of inclusion rather than positioning of self."

Effective, diverse representation may mean targeting board membership. "If the foundation intends to have a positive effect on certain populations, for instance, the disabled population, or the gay and lesbian populations, then it needs perspective from those populations on staff and on the board. [You need meaningful representation] not tokenism," according to Gary Yates of The California Wellness Foundation.

WHAT ARE THE SPECIFIC BENEFITS OF HAVING A DIVERSE FOUNDATION BOARD?

Multiple Perspectives

Perhaps the most significant opportunity in having a more inclusive board is to receive leadership input from individuals who each have unique perspectives and experiences that shape board discussions and critical decisions.

"Diversity is important for all important foundation decisions. People of diverse backgrounds bring different sets of realities to the table when the board makes an overall assessment of an issue. For example, they can determine which are the relevant organizations to be brought in and how will an issue be perceived by the community. When there is more breadth of experience, ultimately there will be richer discussion around the table, which will lead to better decisions," according to Joanne Scanlan, senior vice president for professional development at the Council on Foundations.

When multiple perspectives brought to the table, individuals are challenged to think differently and consider new ideas and approaches. This spawns an environment of creativity and innovation for the foundation board.

One example of how diverse board perspectives can add to a foundation's understanding of its constituent communities and grantees is from the California Wellness Foundation. Through insight from board members with nonprofit experience, the board recognized the challenges nonprofit organizations faced when they received restricted program funding without sufficient funds for general operations. Acting on this information, the foundation began giving core operating support to nonprofits, which allowed them to pay for administrative costs, leadership development, strategic planning, and other nonprogram costs.

"I've found that having a diverse board of directors expands the knowledge base of the governing body, brings the richness of different perspectives into the boardroom, and stimulates creativity in problem solving and planning in ways I could not have anticipated," asserts Bob Ross of the California Endowment. He continues, "Diversity at the board level is integral to the evolution of any organization. Through a push-and-pull process, it can drive the conversation to new levels and ultimately bring the board to a strong consensus, having fully reviewed an issue from many different vantage points."

Indeed, . . . "[D]iversity may be related to overall organizational effectiveness in several ways. Among them are . . . the creative problem solving that results when minority group members offer alternatives to standard approaches that come out of a difference experience;

a higher level of critical analysis as diverse perspectives and varied approaches are considered; and a reduced emphasis on conformity to norms of the past, which frees the group to think more creatively."[5]

As Peter Pennekamp of the Humboldt Area Foundation adeptly states: "The very notion that a board is homogenous is a capitulation to be less farsighted, less creative, less innovative. We want different backgrounds, cultures, among people committed to working together to be most far reaching . . . If board members all have the same point of view, there is a high comfort level because they all know the same thing. They become very blinded to information that could be brought in and could change policy. [It is critical that the board have diverse sources of information] because the board members are the policy developers."

Knowledge

With diverse sources of knowledge at the table, a more inclusive board makes informed decisions that lead to significant impact on the foundation's constituencies. For pragmatic reasons, board members are often recruited from the ranks of those in the legal, financial, and management fields. Naturally, expertise from professionals is valued and important, but boards that have attempted to diversify by selecting only people with specific professional backgrounds from diverse communities have found that these individuals often lack knowledge about the those communities. For example, an Asian Pacific–American investment broker has valuable knowledge but not necessarily about the Asian Pacific–American community.

Therefore, foundation boards must include members from the community sector who have firsthand perspectives about the populations the foundation serves. These individuals bring community-based experience to the table as well as a community-minded sensitivity. "I was once on a board that was composed of white, wealthy members. They couldn't understand the issue of seniors on a fixed income. Unless there is community perspective based in experience, you can't shape a responsive program," comments Luz Vega Marquis, president of the Cosey Family Grants Program and former executive director of the Community Technology Foundation of California and 2002 chair of the California Wellness Foundation.

One philanthropic leader speaks of another board of a foundation in which a sizeable population of its constituents was Native American. While the foundation's staff tried to dispel the prevailing misconception that federal funding was adequate for the Native American population, it was not until a Native American joined the board that that the board finally understood the foundation's niche in reaching out to that community. Needless to say, perspectives borne out of direct experience in the community are imperative.

One frequent objection to including community organization leaders on foundation boards has been the potential for conflicts of interest. Because these leaders are often from nonprofit organizations that are potential recipients of foundation funds, foundations sometimes preemptively exclude considering these leaders as board candidates. However, as long as clear conflict-of-interest policies are established, conflicts should not arise. For instance, a policy can state that a board member must recuse herself from a board decision pertaining to funding her organization.

In addition to their extensive knowledge about issues and concerns of the grassroots populations, nonprofit group leaders possess strong networks and contacts in the communities. These contacts are essential as the foundation may see them as new, potential grantees or call upon them as advisors. Furthermore, with board members with ties to particular community groups, credibility for the foundation comes far easier and the potential for foundation partnership is all the more great.

Jim Crouch of the California Rural Indian Health Board warns: "Change that is perceived to be elitist in its origin and intent is frequently either resisted by the community that it is presumed to assist or is simply ineffective. This lack of effectiveness could be due to a lack of rigor in the analytical phase of program development at the board level that is directly related to a lack of diversity at the board level. In short, diversity can create a form of connectivity that can help assure program success."

Signal for Overall Inclusiveness

A diverse board is also a signal to all that a foundation is committed to inclusiveness. This publicly known conviction will have a positive ripple effect. The executive staff within the foundation knows that diversifying her staff will be supported; nontraditional grantseekers will become more apparent on the radar screen; and grantee organizations will be challenged to be more inclusive in their hiring practices.

Besides the ripple effect, a board's diversification has an impact on public perceptions of the foundation. ". . . The concept of diversity is closely related to community perceptions of a nonprofit organization's egalitarian image and the ideals of fairness. There is an implicit assumption that board composition makes a difference in terms of accountability and accessibility; for an organization to be responsive to a diverse constituency, its board must comprise a diverse membership."[6] Irene Lee of Asian in Philanthropy, Senior Program Associate of the Annie E. Casey Foundation, and member of the Asian American/Pacific Islanders in Philanthropy, states: "If there were diversified boards, it would be an important message to the community." "The message is, who is the money for? Is it for the use of an exclusive group? Or, is it to be used to improved the quality of the community?"[7] Clearly, the foundation's profile in the public can only be enhanced as its composition reflects that of the larger community.

Shared Decision Making

"If building a multicultural democracy is our vision as a society, then philanthropy must reflect that vision. If you look at a board as having leadership and decision making power within an organization, communities cannot be empowered unless its members can be in those decision-making positions," asserts Peggy Saika of Asian Americans/Pacific Islanders in Philanthropy. Indeed, as institutions creating public benefit, foundations must embody our country's ideals of democracy and empowerment.

Therefore, underrepresented groups must have the opportunity to share in the influence that foundation boards yield in society because they have been traditionally excluded. "The heart of inclusiveness is equality, based not simply on goodwill, but on shared power in the circles of influences and decision making."[8]

Moreover, including traditionally underrepresented communities at the board table can have larger positive implications for those communities. Diana Campamour of Hispanics in Philanthropy speaks of the potential for creating a culture of engaged citizenship by involving everyone—including the poor and working class—in nontraditional philanthropy. Board diversity can be one step in paving the way for a movement to mobilize our communities to proactively participate in philanthropy.

Increased Value on Diversity in New Circles

Individuals who are not from diverse communities often become proponents of inclusive boards from first hand experiences with board colleagues of different backgrounds. Upon witnessing the multiple benefits of a diverse board, these members become important advocates for inclusive practices as they can tout the benefits to their corporate, philanthropic, and other circles that have not embraced diversity.

WHAT ARE THE CHALLENGES IN DIVERSIFYING FOUNDATION BOARDS?

Nomination Process

In their landmark study on diversity, Women & Foundations/Corporate Philanthropy found that: "The affinity groups all agreed that the major barrier to board diversity has been the selection process.

There are three routes to board membership: designation by the donor, appointment by an outside agency, and selection by other board members. These methods of selection tend to reinforce the status quo and promote self-perpetuation because of the tendency to choose among the 'good ol'boy network.'"

Indeed, no matter which nomination process is used, those in a position to select have traditionally drawn upon narrow networks of contacts. Instead of taking advantage of opportunities to meet diverse candidates, many involved in the selection process have remained isolated and self-contained. "Recruitment of multicultural decisionmakers may require cultivating and identifying different networks of candidates from outside a foundation's economic and social circles."[9]

Resistance to Change

Resistance to change—whether based in fear, a reluctance to secede power, or inertia—also prevents board diversification. Luz Vega Marquis of the Casey Family Grants Program comments: "Board members are fearful of change. Power sharing must be prodded if necessary. Foundations that have changed and diversified willingly have [benefited enormously.]" Peter Pennekamp of Humboldt Area Foundation adds: "Most boards have not diversified because of the comfort factor. Members have a need to stay on top and it's hard to break that cycle."

Family Foundations

Family foundations are particularly challenged to diversify their membership. Given that family foundations are often focused on specific issues that the family is concerned with, attention is sometimes not given to increasing its familiarity with diverse community needs and issues. Moreover, because board membership is often family based, there is a high level of comfort in the status quo and no perceived need to broaden the scope and contacts of board members.

Many family foundations are relatively small, and founders are hesitant to expend resources for additional board members, even for costs associated with attending meetings. Others may not even have regular meetings, and their decision making is an informal family affair.

Despite these general trends, some family foundations have made extensive inroads to diversification. For example, the Hyams Foundation has made diversification a top priority within its own organization and with its grantees. The Diversity Initiative that it funds specifically provides technical assistance and funding to nonprofit human service and cultural organizations committed to creating greater racial, ethnic, and cultural diversity within their staff and boards.

There may be no easy solution to the challenges to diversify family foundations. The evolution and growth of an individual foundation may allow for more diversity. Having advisory groups, even though informal, may be an interim step. Additionally, family foundation affinity groups may be an important source of discussion and a place to link with minority and other diverse affinity groups for recruitment.

Corporate Foundations

Like the boards of family foundations, corporate foundation boards often draw from select groups for membership. Diversity in background is often lacking, with a substantial number if not all board members possessing corporate backgrounds. Many corporations have foundations in which only corporate staff are involved in the decision making. It is essential to diversify corporate boards as well as management itself in order to have diverse foundation decision makers.

The lack of diversity in these top corporate levels is a continuing challenge. However, foundations like the FannieMae Foundation are leading the way in implementing inclusive practices in their board membership recruitment. Some corporations have made a commitment to diversity as expressed in their giving. Some corporations have contributed funds to establish new foundations that advance diversity. For instance, SBC contributed $50 million to the new Community Technology Foundation of California. Some have enabled existing foundations to expand their giving programs. For instance, Verizon contributed $25 million to the California Consumer Protection Foundation to improve efforts to lessen the digital divide.

Attrition of Diverse Board Members

Even when foundation boards have diversified, their attempts at inclusion have not always met with success because of the attrition of minority board members.

"Some members of minority groups are uncomfortable with their roles on the boards or staffs of mainstream institutions, feeling that their presence is barely more than a gesture and that they wield little real influence. Some have departed out of frustration. Some long-time board and staff members say they feel threatened by the arrival of non-whites and that they have seen their own influencing waning."[10]

Peggy Saika of Asian American/Pacific Islanders in Philanthropy points out: "To sustain diversity, organizations need to think about their internal processes. It's not just a matter of bringing diverse people together. It's necessary to build understanding and awareness at all levels of the organization. You must look at the organization with a holistic approach."

Joanne Scanlan of the Council on Foundations remarks: "There have been cases where boards have diversified, but members didn't stay. It's dismissed as 'that person didn't fit in.'" But it needs to be two ways. Foundations don't always realize they have culture of their own—a formal, hierarchical culture and style. They must be sensitized to the fact they have a culture, and that may need to change."

WHAT CAN BE DONE BY THE PHILANTHROPIC COMMUNITY NATIONALLY?

Education and Discourse

National education and discourse on the need to diversify is the first step toward seeing inclusiveness in foundation boards. The Council on Foundations (COF) has taken the lead in this area since the mid-1990s when its board of directors made a public commitment to inform the philanthropic community about its efforts to build more inclusive practices in its own operations and throughout the philanthropic community. In its educational campaign, COF has developed resource materials highlighting the benefits of diversity, developed trainings around diversity and communication, and actively researched the issue in the philanthropic community.[11]

COF's work has been groundbreaking and far-reaching, yet more needs to be done by foundations and those committed to diversity about the need to diversify board membership. First, the educational campaign must focus on existing board members. Presentations to board members from constituent communities, grantees, and applicants can be made part of the board meeting agenda. Dialogue on demographic changes and pressing community issues should also be integrated into meetings. Visits to grantees or other community sites can also prove to be informative. With the information flow coming from these various sectors, board members have in-depth knowledge on the diverse communities and see firsthand the need for inclusiveness in foundation leadership.

Vision and Leadership

As Miyoko Oshima, president of the Southern California Association for Philanthropy, states: "What is really needed at this time is clear vision. What does a vision of diversity look like in the field of philanthropy? What do all of us want to see? This vision needs to be grounded in conviction, so there is commitment and strategy to implement change. Who will lead the process to widen the circle and include different people? Where would the most effective leadership come from? We need to know where is leadership coming from?"

The vision and leadership to diversify foundation boards should come primarily from foundations themselves, from their internal introspection, and desire to improve their functioning. While racial minorities, women, and others will have a strong role to play in this endeavor, it is white male leadership that can be decisive. On several boards these voices have made an impact. For example, Gary Yates, president and chief executive officer of the California Wellness Foundation, not only led efforts to diversify his foundation board (over 50% racial minority membership), but has advocated for greater diversity on foundation groups like Grantmakers in Health.

Promote and Position Qualified, Diverse Individuals

The obligation to promote and train potential candidates falls on those committed to seeing more diverse boards not the foundations alone. Board members, executive staff, community leaders, and others committed to diversity must promote and position people of diverse backgrounds for nomination to foundation boards. For example, untapped, qualified individuals should be initially recruited for nonprofit boards and smaller foundations. There, they can receive learn the ropes about board member responsibilities, acquire and refine the skills required to execute the responsibilities, and develop networks with the philanthropic community. This can better position them for board membership of larger foundations.

Affinity groups play a key role in acting as a reference for qualified individuals with diverse backgrounds. Gary Yates of the California Wellness Foundation comments: "Affinity groups can publish a list of qualified individuals, or at least let foundations know about their availability to give suggestions. They can be proactive and positive in availing themselves as resources for diverse, qualified board candidates."

Affinity groups also can train individuals for board membership. A chapter of the Asian American Pacific Islanders in Philanthropy has developed quarterly sessions for trustees and foundation executives to discuss how to assist foundations wanting to identify new board candidates, how to train potential candidates to successfully serve on a board, and how to make individuals aware of board openings when foundations appreciate the assistance. Activities such as these should be broadly replicated so that identification and training of individuals is an ongoing process.

WHAT CAN BE DONE BY FOUNDATIONS INTERNALLY?

Mission Development

First, a foundation must embody a commitment to inclusiveness. Leroy Barnes, vice president and treasurer of PG & E Corporation and board member of the California Endowment remarks: "We need awareness that diverse communities are underrepresented on boards and that's not sustainable. Foundations need to start with the conviction that a diverse board is a better board."

With an underlying commitment, the foundation must express its endorsement of diversity. "The values of diversity must be expressed in the mission because the mission is the framework for the operation of a foundation. When a value in diversity [is expressed] then the values will be carried out by the staff," states Luz Vega Marquis of the Casey Family Grants Program. She continues, "Diversity must be a mandate from the board. The board must reflect that diversity, and live it out. [This will inevitably] lead to better outcomes."

The Joint Affinity Groups study recommends that a commitment to diversity should be included in key statements. "Statements and organizational policies that reflect the centrality of diversity formalize institutional commitment and establish a standard of accountability."[12]

**THE CALIFORNIA ENDOWMENT
DIVERSITY AND INCLUSIVENESS STATEMENT FOR
GRANT-MAKING ACTIVITIES**

Since its inception, the California Endowment has placed a high value on diversity and inclusion. We define diversity in broad terms to include ethnicity, race, age, physical ability, gender, socioeconomic status, and sexual orientation. We believe that diversity and inclusion add to organizational effectiveness and excellence and that services are enhanced when organizations are reflective of communities being served.

Our commitment to diversity is reflected in the composition of our staff, management, and Board of Directors. As such, the Endowment will continue to raise issues of inclusion and promote diversity in our grant-making activities.

To that end, this policy is intended to further guide staff in its grant-making efforts.

Statement of Policy

Because of the Endowment's commitment to diversity in California, staff will pursue opportunities to discuss issues related to diversity and inclusion with grantees and applicants.

Staff will take every opportunity to constructively engage in efforts to assist grantees and applicants better serve the needs of California's diverse communities. As appropriate, applicants seeking funds from the California Endowment will be asked to provide information related to governance, management, staff, and volunteer composition in the interest of encouraging diversity and inclusion whenever possible.

An example of a foundation that has embraced diversity at all levels of the organization is the California Endowment. Its diversity is reflected throughout the organization, including the composition of staff, management, and the board of directors. (See Sidebar "Diversity and Inclusiveness Statement for Grant-Making Activities.") In its "Philosophy on Board Composition," the California Endowment states:

A healthy community has many different faces and voices. Accordingly, the California Endowment embraces "diversity" as an important value in our work to expand access to health care and improve the health status of Californians. The Endowment Board of Directors should reflect a diverse cross-section of California's people and communities, and Board composition should reflect our core values:

- The importance of diversity and multiculturalism to improving health
- Addressing the health needs of both rural and urban underserved populations
- Recognition of the critical role of community in health improvements

The Board should specifically maintain diversity in the following areas: ethnicity, gender, community-based experience, region, professional expertise.

The California Endowment's stated mission and philosophy are models for other foundations seeking to increase diversity. For all foundations, this mission must truly be embraced at all levels. Where some organizations with a diversity mission have failed is in neglecting to integrate the mission into every aspect of administration, programming, and staffing. Without comprehensive strategic planning on implementing the mission, the diversity mission becomes an external mandate void of understanding or meaning.

Improve Recruitment Practices

Once a conviction to an inclusive board is established, foundations must improve recruitment practices to ensure quality, diverse board membership. Jim Crouch of the California Rural Indian Health Board states: "In general diversity must be achieved through an incremental process. This makes it important for the sitting board to clearly define the elements of diversity that they believe would have utility to their governance process. Once these are established a review of existing skill sets and orientations can provide a guide for focused recruitment."

The first challenge then is to come to consensus about the profile of skills, knowledge, and background that the board seeks in board members. Sherry Hirota, executive director of Asian Health Services of Alameda County and board member of the California Endowment, comments: "The composition of foundation boards would become more diverse when we create new criteria for board nomination and selection that weights knowledge of different cultures and subcultures as important."

Other qualities like sensitivity, openness, and a shared vision must also be considered. Of course, the quality of the candidate's contributions along with specific demographic attributes like gender, ethnicity, race, geographic locale, sexual orientation, disability and age must be taken into account.

Once agreement on the profile is reached, a number of recruitment practices can be implemented to tap into the pool of diverse board candidates.

Networking

When nominating committees from boards are used to recruit new members, these committees can be effective only if their networking is extensive. "Nominating committees need a charge to do year-round outreach to meet potential board members. They need to search for candidates in all kinds of environments and be forced to go out of their comfort zones. They should attend grantee functions and meet community members," states Joanne Scanlan of the Council on Foundations.

Whatever nomination system is operative, every board member and each executive director of a foundation has a responsibility to expand their networks to meet and know individuals from diverse backgrounds. Diana Campamour of Hispanics in Philanthropy emphasizes: "Foundations tend to have an individualistic culture, and as most institutions, they tend to select staff, boards and grantees from their networks. We need concerted strategies to tap other networks and, in effect, to democratize, as well as diversify the field."

Luz Vega Marquis of the Casey Family Grants Program also believes that networking among board members from different foundations who are committed to inclusiveness is important. She stresses that these individuals should form strong relationships and collaborate in strategies to diversify foundations. "When positive change in diversification has occurred, it happened because of either individual board members or an executive director who has a commitment to diversity. Board members need to encourage their colleagues to be active in the process of change."

Leroy Barnes, board member of the California Endowment, adds: "Foundation boards should energetically court and solicit diverse candidates for their boards and value their unique contributions."

Through extensive networking, the goal is to have a rich pool of potential candidates from which to choose a quality, inclusive board.

Other Recruitment Methods

Other specific recruitment methods that aid in building a diverse pool of board candidates include the use of program staff and grantee recommendations and search firms. These recruitment tools provide valuable sources of information from groups and individuals often most knowledgeable about diverse, community leaders and can greatly assist in focusing the search appropriately.

A particularly useful tool is the community advisory board. When constituent community members are able to have ongoing dialogue and relationships with board members, their input at the time of board membership selection is respected and valued. Family foundations that tend to be more isolated particularly benefit from community advisory boards. As Miyoko Oshima of the Southern California Association for Philanthropy notes, "If family foundations want to establish closer relations with the community, forming an advisory board is a good way to establish an open line of communication. The information and dialogue that ensues will be helpful in shaping the foundations thinking and giving."

Diversifying is An Ongoing Process

The process of diversifying must be intentional and continual. Having committed itself to a process of building internal diversity, the Tides Foundation created a "Diversity Approach" which states: "Creating inclusive organizations demands changes in the way we operate and the way we make decisions. The process is an ongoing one, which may, at times, feel uncomfortable. It calls for our willingness and commitment to adapt organizational culture. Gradually, diversity transforms organizations."[13] As the JAG study recommends: "Anticipate some failures, internal resistance and departures. A willingness to change systems to remove institutional barriers is a must. More consideration needs to be given to sustained diversity efforts over time."[14]

Other Considerations

"The struggle . . . does not end with selection of a new and more diverse board. Tolerance must be practiced if new and unusual voices are to join the table of decision makers. New board members may need to learn how to operate in a board context not as mere representatives of a group. At the same time, the board must develop ways of mining the new prospective without condescension or ghettoization of the new decision makers. In the end, diversity in foundation board governance is a goal which requires continual effort," states Jim Crouch of the California Rural Indian Health Board.

Clearly, ongoing work to make a diverse board successful must be pursued. Once new board members join, a thorough orientation must take place so that members understand the shared vision, mission, expectations, and responsibilities of the board. Equally important must be the evaluation of the board and foundation culture itself to ensure that a diverse board can operate effectively. (See the section "Attrition of Diverse Board Members earlier in the chapter.)

Decisions must be made as to whether changes need to be made to accommodate and integrate the new voices into the board's work.

Education and reexamination may be difficult to approach but may be necessary. As Bob Ross of the California Endowment states: "Diversity among board members can be difficult to manage—different reference points, experiences, values, and priorities can draw out decision making. But, once agreements are struck and decisions are made, they are lasting—members have invested too much time and effort in them for anything else to happen."

CONCLUSION

Diversification is inevitably an ongoing process, and each foundation must carve its unique path to develop and implement diversification plans. "Inclusion is never really done. It should be one of the wheels of democracy because we will always have new communities. Inclusive practices need to be embedded in all sectors that society does business," reflects Peggy Saika of Asian Americans/Pacific Islanders in Philanthropy.

While the challenge is great, the world of philanthropy must recognize that the foundation board of the twenty-first century must be inclusive of diverse members in order to effect significant change. Leaders in the philanthropy field state it best: "Why diverse boards? There is no stronger source of perspective than that fueled by one's ethnic and cultural heritage. Though subliminal at times, this heritage impacts the way we see the world. With public benefit as an outcome of philanthropy, who can better contribute to decision making around such benefit than those who see the world through the many lenses of the diverse public," states Laura Wiltz, Ph.D., 2002 chair of the California Endowment.

"The greatest untapped potential to add value to foundation boards is to increase its diversity. Efficacious policy making and strategic grantmaking will become increasingly dependent on a board's ability to understand multicultural views and issues," comments Sherry Hirota, board member of the California Endowment.

The tragic events of September 11 and the economic downturn in 2001 and 2002 have put philanthropic and giving in general in the spotlight. There is a new urgency to make sure that foundations and charitable institutions are responsive and effective for their constituents. Many lives depend on this. Ensuring that the policymakers of foundations have the perspectives, knowledge, insight and wisdom to make the best decisions can only happen if there are diverse and cohesive boards. This drive to diversify should be a top priority for all foundations as we begin the twenty-first century.

NOTES

1. Council on Foundations, *Foundation Management Series,* 9th ed. vol. 2, *Governing Boards* (Washington, DC: Council on Foundations), pp. 11–12.
2. Figures are stated to show general trends. Direct comparisons between the 1988 figures and the 1996, 1998, and 2000 data should be approached with caution as differing response rates from year to year must be considered.
3. Joint Affinity Groups, Lynn C. Burdridge, William A. Diaz, Teresa Odendahl, Aileen Shaw, Emmett D. Carson, and the University of Minnesota, *The Meaning and Impact of Borad and Staff Diversity in the Philanthropic Field: Findings from a National Study* (Joint Affinity Groups, 2002), 70 (hereinafter, "The JAG Study").
4. Council on Foundations, *The Value of Difference: Enhancing Philanthropy Through Inclusiveness in Governance, Staff & Grantmaking* (Washington, DC: Council on Foundations, 1993), 3.
5. Judith Miller, Kathleen Fletcher, and Rikki Abzug, *Perspectives on Nonprofit Board Diversity* (Washington, DC: National Center for Nonprofit Boards, 1999), 4.
6. Id, 3.
7. Women and Foundations/Corporate Philanthropy, *Far From Done* (New York: Women and Foundations/Corporate Philanthropy, 1990), 11.
8. Council on Foundations, *The Value of Difference: Enhancing Philanthropy through Inclusiveness in Governance, Staff & Grantmaking* (Washington DC: Council on Foundations, 1993).
9. JAG Study, p. 137.
10. Judith Miller, Kathleen Fletcher, and Rikki Abzug, "The Non-Profit World's Diversity Dilemma," *The Chronicle of Philanthropy,* September 20, 1994, pp. 25–26.
11. "2000 Progress Report on Inclusive Practices, *Diversity in All That We Do,*" Special insert to *Council Columns* (Washington, DC: Council on Foundations, 2001).

12. JAG Study, p. 137.
13. JAG Study, p. 116.
14. JAG Study, p. 138.

RESOURCES

Council on Foundations. *Foundation Management Series*. 9th ed. Vol. II. Governing Boards. Washington, DC: Council on Foundations, 1998.

Council on Foundations. *The Value of Difference: Enhancing Philanthropy Through Inclusiveness in Governance, Staff & Grantmaking*. Washington, DC: Council on Foundations, 1993.

Joint Affinity Groups, Lynn C. Burbridge, William A. Diaz, Teresa Odendahl, Aileen Shaw, Emmett D. Carson, and the University of Minnesota. *The Meaning and Impact of Board and Staff Diversity in the Philanthropic Field: Findings from a National Study*. Joint Affinity Groups, 2002.

Miller, Judith, Kathleen Fletcher, and Rikki Abzug. *Perspectives on Nonprofit Board Diversity*. Washington, DC: National Center for Nonprofit Boards, 1999.

"The Non-Profit World's Diversity Dilemma," *The Chronicle of Philanthropy* (September 20, 1994): 25–26.

Rutledge, Jennifer M. *Building Board Diversity*. Washington, DC: National Center for Nonprofit Boards, 1994.

"2000 Progress Report on Inclusive Practices: *Diversity in All that We Do*." Special insert to *Council Columns*. Washington, DC: Council on Foundations, 2001.

Women and Foundations/Corporate Philanthropy. *Far From Done*. New York: Women and Foundations/Corporate Philanthropy, 1990.

CHAPTER 8

Issues in Foundation Planning

by Joe Breiteneicher and Leslie Pine

PERSPECTIVES

Do foundations need to plan? Most answer yes but don't always know the key issues to address. This chapter outlines a systematic process for foundation leadership to ask: What are we doing? How are we doing? And what can we be doing better or more in line with our mission?

Joe Breiteneicher is president of The Philanthropic Initiative, Inc. (TPI), a nonprofit organization formed in 1989 to help donors increase their impact through the development of innovative and strategic approaches to philanthropy. Breiteneicher has been with the firm since 1990 and has crafted and facilitated planning initiatives for donors who are initially developing or revitalizing the mission, focus, and approach of their philanthropic pursuits. While his work has concentrated on family philanthropies, Breiteneicher has also helped a number of community foundations and corporate giving programs redesign their structures.

Leslie Pine, TPI's Vice President for Program, participated in the start-up of TPI in 1989. She manages and coordinates TPI's efforts to help funders develop new and more effective approaches to the issues that concern them. In addition to programmatic planning, research, design, implementation, and evaluation, Leslie oversees TPI's ongoing assistance to a number of foundations and corporations.

INTRODUCTION

"Dream no little dreams, for they have no magic to move men's souls."

The above words of the philosopher Jeremy Bentham serve as a guide and reminder of the continued power and potential of philanthropy in the twenty-first century. Crafting the path to the "long view" of making change is integral to what is best about the visions, aspirations, and impacts of philanthropy. It is about understanding and refining past and present goals and objectives and creating an effective roadmap for the future. It is about looking at the future as practical visionaries to create a plan of action that is of our choosing and that focuses on what we aim to accomplish. It is about finding the paths and leverage points with the greatest potential for long-term impact. Finally, it is about setting in motion a consciously chosen process that transforms planning information into knowledge and learning.

We have had the extraordinary good fortune to assist all manner of philanthropies—family, private, community, and corporate foundations—in the intelligence gathering and thoughtful plotting out that serve as the basis for deliberate implementation strategies that seek to extend the reach and scope of their charitable assets—human and financial. We have been fortunate to be part of diverse planning processes that have always been an integral part of the whole of the philanthropic organization, never separate nor on the periphery.

What follows is a distillation of the best and most promising practices that have been drawn from those experiences and that have been recurring effective elements in the planning quest philanthropies undertake to ensure that they are trying to make the most significant difference with the resources under their stewardship care. Because there are numerous books and workbooks on approaches to strategic and long-range planning, we have sought in this essay to provide readers, assuming that their foundations represent the full and growing range of diverse philanthropic institutions, with a straightforward framework that all can use—identifying basic issues and core components common to effective strategic planning. In addition to the basics that many in this field employ, we have included not-so-typical ingredients that our colleagues and we have used to ensure that the planning process is as full and complete an experience as possible in helping foundations take advantage of the opportunity "to make no small plans."

THE POTENTIAL OF STRATEGIC PHILANTHROPY

Can strategic philanthropic efforts truly have a long-term impact on the social issues that concern them? We think so. Based on our experience over many years with individual donors, families, companies, and other foundations, we believe that smart and creative strategic planning can enhance the impact of philanthropy on society.

We do not, however, suggest that the planning process is necessarily simple or straightforward. It is often time consuming and non-linear, with no easy answers. Indeed, the idea of promoting social change through philanthropy can sound positively daunting. In the United States alone, there are over 600,000 nonprofit organizations and over $200 billion of annual private contributions that support philanthropic causes. How can a single philanthropic entity—even a large one—have a broad impact on a social issue or field?

Virtually every philanthropic gift, no matter how large or small, that goes to support an effective organization or program is making a difference in some way. There are certainly many foundations that are content to publish grant guidelines, screen and assess funding requests, and make grants within their areas of interest.

Some foundations want to go beyond making some good grants. They may reach a point where they start to view their giving is "an inch deep and a mile wide." Others feel dissatisfied that they are not fully realizing the potential impact of their philanthropic resources. Still others want to be more fully engaged in the process of learning about issues and collaborating on potential solutions. For these funders, the challenge is how to have an impact that ripples out far beyond the life of a few grants.

This notion of leveraging long-term social change is at the heart of TPI's notion of "strategic philanthropy." In the words of Paul Ylvsaker, one of the wise teachers of philanthropy in the twentieth century, strategic philanthropy is about "finding systemic solutions to underlying causes of poverty and other social ills." In line with this concept, some of us like to think of philanthropy as "society's risk capital" and believe that the best use of philanthropy may well be in supporting high-risk social ventures with the promise of producing a significant "return on investment."

Definitions of strategic philanthropy can include an emphasis on addressing the root causes of social problems, rather than treating their symptoms; building the capacity of communities and organizations, rather than artificially or temporarily propping them up; and, of course, teaching people to fish so they'll have food for a lifetime, rather than giving them a fish so they can eat for a day. Another way to think about strategic philanthropy is to ask whether a foundation is helping to make something important happen that would be unlikely to happen without that funder's intervention. In a recent paper, our colleague Ellen Remmer said, "Strategic philanthropy refers to funding based on a knowledgeable examination of social needs and best practices that address them and executed through the creation and follow-through of carefully planned strategies (and good instincts sprinkled with an entrepreneurial spirit)." It is the model of the donor as smart investor!

In the for-profit world, strategy is the deliberate search for a plan of action that will give a business a competitive edge that can be grown into an enduring advantage. For foundations, it is the organized process of determining what an institution wants to be in the future and what it does to achieve that end. Further, it is about a process of dialogue and discovery—both internal and external—that leads to a set of decisions regarding what is seen as the best path to accomplish the most important things. It involves making choices that focus on long-term goals, programmatic initiatives to achieve them, and the allocation and integration of resources to support this priority work.

Some philanthropies allow their planning to be driven by what great things the institution wants to do next (playing to organizational strengths and passions); others opt first to investigate where the greatest needs are and then seek to mobilize the organization to address them effectively. In a number of situations in which we have worked, funders also employ a "scenarios" approach in which they envision what may come of their journey down a strategically chosen path. We believe that most planning processes end up as a blend of these approaches.

Further, although some definitions separate out strategic and long-range planning, we believe they are two sides of the same coin and use them interchangeably. Strategic planning, though, is definitely not the same as yearly or operational planning that focuses on short-term business or organizational objectives. For most institutions, the long-range plan involves a futures horizon of three to five years.

Guiding Principles

There is a set of core principles (and some prejudices!) that has informed our planning work with various large and small, staffed and unstaffed, established and emerging philanthropies. It is a relatively short but powerful docket of beliefs and prejudices—the "what" to us that planning work is all about:

- The absence of a deliberate plan—a focus—often leads to funding decisions by default or to others' setting the foundation's agenda.
- The whole planning process is about effectively informing and guiding the difficult but absolutely necessary long-term choice making that philanthropies must commit to in order to have a chance to contribute to making real differences.
- No strategic plan means that there is no "glue" to bind together individual funding decisions, however meritorious each may be.

- The most effective philanthropic strategies emerge from iterative, research-based, and creative processes.
- There are few good excuses for not doing a planning exercise.
- The best planning is highly participatory and seeks to have widely held ownership of its results.
- Make use of the process to think the unthinkable—pose critical "what ifs" in thinking about future scenarios for the foundation.
- Great planning is driven by a "gap" mentality that seeks to identify the underfunded critical areas in society's funding grid that represent real opportunities for powerful impacts to be generated.
- The most effective processes are those that lead to workable action agendas that are aimed at focusing resources where need, opportunity, issues passions, and a foundation's collective resources intersect.
- Successful plans are flexible road maps, not something requiring lock-step thinking for years to come.
- Strategic planning should provide the impetus for ongoing strategic learning. Good plans create deliberate strategies to achieve long-term goals; plans with great potential allow room for strategies to emerge as the plans evolve over time. This is accomplished most effectively when the foundation builds into its planning and plan implementation an ongoing learning system.
- The planning process should be an opportunity for serious reflection and for celebration of past accomplishments.
- Foundations are organisms whose environments and capacities change. Critical review, analysis, and dialogue and mid-course corrections are part of the life cycle of the responsible philanthropy.

Why?

While a cliché, the axiom that if you don't know where you're headed any path will suffice offers wise counsel to those in the philanthropic community who would ignore the opportunity to make informed choices about paths. From our perspective, there are a number of key reasons why foundations should undertake strategic planning work. Strategic planning

- Is a fulfillment of a basic requirement of philanthropic stewardship
- Improves overall performance
- Stimulates forward, more creative "big picture" thinking among foundation staff and trustees
- May begin to address big challenges and get at solutions to those pressing problems
- Identifies where the philanthropy ought to be positioned to do great things and leverage its resources
- Provides a proactive context to make the most of scarce resources
- Builds teamwork and organizational capacity and offers the chance to get everyone on the same page
- Creates a window for serious dialogue—a free space within the foundation for critical thinking outside the press of quotidian matters
- Provides overt evidence to public and community sector stakeholders that the philanthropy is acting in a highly responsible manner
- Shows leadership

Why Not?

Having argued that there are few legitimate reasons for not having a strategic planning process, we feel compelled to identify (and respond to) recurring excuses:

- *We're too small.* It would seem to us that the smaller the size of the foundation, the greater the need to seek to leverage impacts.

- *We're too new.* What better time to set in place a discovery and planning process to fix on a course of action?
- *We just finished a process.* Then, rather than a new process, it may be useful to assess what types of early or midcourse corrections would enhance impact.
- *The results of the last planning process went unheeded—the report sits on a shelf somewhere!* So what? Revisit the work product and the process to see why there was no action agenda and determine whether the prior plan is a useful template for the future.
- *No one was pleased with the last planning process.* Find out why and build the antidote into the next planning round.
- *The task is too overwhelming.* Although there are core elements of successful planning efforts, there certainly is no "one-size-fits-all" approach to planning. Each foundation should be able to craft or tailor-make a planning process that suits its special resources and requirements.

When Not to Plan

We do believe there are several situations in which foundations may want to defer decisions regarding the launch of a strategic planning initiative. Examples include:

- There is not sufficient critical mass in the foundation's leadership (e.g., key board positions are vacant or there is an interregnum between CEOs).
- The dynamics within the organization are wildly dysfunctional.
- The foundation is dealing with a major crisis that must be resolved before its leadership can focus effectively on longer-term issues.

When to Plan

There are a number of conditions that serve as useful indicators that it is an appropriate time to consider initiating a strategic planning process. Among those that have triggered planning processes in which we have participated are the following:

- At least three years have passed since the last planning/review process was completed.
- There is new executive leadership at the foundation.
- There has been major turnover in the board.
- There has been a significant shift in the size of the foundation's asset base.
- A major programmatic initiative is coming to an end or to a juncture that presents new opportunities.
- Foundation leaders reach a point where they are frustrated or dissatisfied with the impact of their efforts, or with some critical aspect (e.g., a dearth of funding proposals that reflect research-based solutions to critical issues).
- There have been dramatic changes in the public policy context that surrounds the foundation's funding priorities.

Who Gets Involved in Strategic Planning?

Regarding who should participate in the ongoing work of the planning process, our experience suggests that an inclusive process works best in many, if not most, situations. A "big tent" approach that engages the foundation's leadership—trustees and staff—often produces cohesion around vision and goals, along with powerful strategies. For the sake of efficiency, this type of inclusive process can be structured to involve a division of labor among participants in conducting various discovery tasks. Planning processes may also provide an opportunity for the foundation to engage past or emeriti leadership whose guidance or input may prove invaluable.

When we consider the personal characteristics that, in the composite, help to make the planning process enjoyable and successful for all, there are a number of key qualities that make a positive difference in the group's dynamics and outcomes. If possible, we seek a mix of participants who are

- Good at building concepts out of data and comfortable with the chaos and ambiguity of big picture thinking
- Holistic in their thinking and fearlessly imaginative
- Interested in contemplating the future, and in reflecting on the past
- Committed to the organization
- Team players
- Passionate to see ideas turned into action

A PLANNING FRAMEWORK

For any funder, whether public or private, needs and opportunities are virtually infinite, and resources are always limited. Thus, foundations with ambitious goals recognize the critical need to engage in effective and proactive strategic planning. Stages of the planning process can include

- *Early-stage* planning, which can be critical to defining an ambitious vision, realistic goals, and creation of a strong but flexible framework
- Ongoing *programmatic* or issue-focused planning, focusing on how to address the social issue or set of issues of concern to the foundation—the goal of this planning is to determine how best to target resources in ways that could produce long-term social impact
- Planning for *effective execution* of programmatic strategies, including organizational structure, staffing, budgeting, and other implementation issues
- A process of ongoing *reflection, revision, and renewal*—an essential element for foundations that strive to continually do more and better with the resources available to them

In this section, we outline some of the basic elements of foundation planning, offer thoughts on key issues and challenges, and share some stories to illustrate what can result from such efforts.

Early-Stage Strategic Planning

For foundations that are getting off the ground or want to rethink their philanthropic efforts, there are some basic steps that can help to build the framework for a more strategic approach to philanthropy. We refer to this process here as *early-stage strategic planning.* The outcome is a preliminary strategic plan that outlines the foundation's vision, mission, goals, focus areas, and guiding principles.

This process also addresses governance issues. These issues often include determining who should be involved in foundation planning and decision making; how often the board will meet, how meetings will be structured, and how decisions will be made; how trustees will be trained; and how new members will be identified and added to the board over time.

The values, interests, personal experiences, and styles of the trustees will provide the starting point for developing a foundation's overall mission, focus, and strategic framework. An effective process, therefore, offers opportunities for trustees to share and explore their values and philanthropic passions. While the process should always be tailored to each foundation's specific needs, objectives, and style, it often includes the following steps:

1. *Determining who will participate in the planning process.* Key stakeholders typically consist of foundation trustees and may include other trusted advisors. In the case of corporate foundations, stakeholders generally include senior executives of the company, and may involve outreach to a broader cross-section of employees.

2. *Preplanning.* Define overall goals, scope, and timeline for the planning process.
3. *Opportunities for reflection and articulation of values and passions.* A good planning process gives each stakeholder a chance to reflect on key planning questions and express their individual views. For many foundations, it can be helpful for an outside facilitator or objective staff person to conduct individual interviews with each stakeholder, using a set of questions tailored to the foundation's specific situation.
4. *Summary and synthesis of stakeholder views.* To help move the process forward, it is often helpful for the facilitator to prepare a summary of interviews or discussions with key stakeholders, including an analysis of where there seems to be consensus and what issues require further discussion.
5. *Facilitated planning retreat or working sessions.* The purpose of a planning retreat or series of working sessions is to enable foundation trustees to reach consensus on key elements of the preliminary plan and more fully articulate their thinking that will guide the foundation. This process may result in the crafting of a vision and mission statement; development of focus areas, goals, and guiding principles; and clarification of various governance issues.
6. *Appropriate follow-up to keep the momentum going.* Follow-up documents might include meeting notes, a draft mission statement, a preliminary strategic plan, and a workplan outlining next steps along with a timeline. For foundations run by Board members, the workplan might include creation of board committees that will take responsibility for moving forward with specific tasks. For staffed foundations, senior staff might be asked to take the lead on next steps in the planning process.

Other core elements of early-stage strategic planning follow.

Getting Ready

There are key threshold steps that each planning process seems to go through to prepare for the work. Basic questions for the foundation's leadership to answer include:

- What are the expectations of the process? What issues are driving it? What purposes will it serve? What outcomes are central to the effort's success?
- How will the process be managed? Who will be the internal driver, the logistician, who will coordinate work and ensure that information/data are in all participants' hands in advance of discussions? What might be an appropriate division of labor within the foundation's leadership team regarding who will take responsibility for key elements of the process?
- If there has been a strategic planning process in the foundation before, are all the present participants knowledgeable of its work and results? Is there a record of the process that can be shared with participants?
- If the process is a first-time experience for the foundation, do its leaders know of other similarly situated foundations that have been through the process and might share their experiences to help craft an approach?
- Is there a need for outside technical assistance in the process? Would the process be best served with support from an outside facilitator?
- What is a realistic timeline for the overall process? For key individual elements? Is the foundation working against any deadlines?

Values and Vision Identification/Affirmation

Central to the first measures to take in the strategic planning process is a renewal of the foundation's vows. We believe that before a foundation starts to look at its past performance and future goals and objectives, it needs to ask itself several very basic questions about the shared vision and common values that drive the organization. Such an early-on step in the process serves as a touchstone for the work of the planning effort and as a key reinforcement regarding why the planning work is so very relevant to the foundation's mission. Queries for the group of key internal stakeholders are:

- What is the vision each has for the foundation's work and desired long-term outcomes?
- Ten years from now, what would those in the foundation like to be able to say about their experiences and accomplishments? What would make their work in service to the foundation's aims most satisfying?
- What are people in the foundation most passionate about in its work?
- What values are central to the foundation's work? What should the foundation stand for? What would go on its philanthropic shield?
- Has the foundation been true to itself and its core values in all aspects of its work?

Core Elements for Family Foundations

An important overall question for family philanthropies to document is what role the foundation plays in adding value to the family:

- How does the foundation contribute to centripetal forces within the family? How can the foundation help to bind the family together around common values and goals?
- How does it abet positive dynamics in the family?
- In extended families, does the foundation create "connective tissue" across branches of the family?
- Does it serve as a counterweight to the diaspora that many families undergo?
- Does it offer support for intergenerational connections within the family?

- Does it provide a focal point for the family's ongoing growth and learning?
- Is it the "elevated common ground" in the family?

Stakeholders' Voices

The planning process is an extraordinary opportunity to connect with the foundation's key external constituencies and to gather their insights and guidance. It is a vehicle for the foundation to be as inclusive as possible in the search for information and knowledge that can inform the strategic plan. It is also an effective way for the foundation to "throw open the window" on its work to as broad a public as is possible and practical.

Who are those constituents whose voices would add so much to the planning and crafting of strategies? Among those whose voices have been productively added to planning work with which we have been affiliated, consider:

- Grantees—past and present
- Representatives of those populations that foundation seeks to serve
- Practitioners, other than grantees, in the foundation's fields of interest
- Civic and community activists and leaders (including business leaders)
- Academicians and other researchers active and expert within the foundation's focus areas
- Key political figures and public policy officials
- Other funders and their intermediaries

Once stakeholders have been identified, the foundation needs to determine how it wishes to include their voices most effectively and efficiently. Foundations have employed all manner of methods, often in tandem:

- Written questionnaires developed by the foundation's leadership seeking responses to a set of core questions

- Individual, face-to-face, interviews with key influencers
- Focus groups of colleagues convened by the foundation or a third-party consultant
- Brainstorming sessions that focus on creative approaches to a key challenge or opportunity facing the foundation

The outreach process often sets in motion an ongoing dialogue between the foundation and its stakeholders. It raises the level of discussion to the level of the seriousness of the strategic planning process. It also often reaffirms or helps to build out the important concept of the foundation's stakeholders as part of the funder's extended family network, whose insights may serve to provide ongoing guidance for the foundation and enduring value-added connections as it plays out its strategic action agenda.

Programmatic Strategic Planning

Over the years, TPI has had the good fortune to work with a number of foundations and donors who want to tackle important social issues in ways that will have a lasting impact. These include foundation trustees who are passionate about a cause and believe in the power of philanthropy to serve as a catalyst for social change.

Foundations with ambitious goals, regardless of the focus, ask critical and challenging questions:

- How can we be strategic and proactive in working to foster long-term social change?
- What are the key leverage points?
- What are the potential roles, strategies, and tools that might enhance our impact over time on a particular issue?
- How do we move forward in developing or finding promising strategies or opportunities?
- What kinds of partnerships would help us to effectively work toward our goals?

Once a foundation has determined what social issue (or set of issues) it wants to address, how does it move toward development of promising philanthropic strategies? In our experience, the best strategies are developed through a constantly evolving process that places great emphasis on research, ongoing learning, reflection, analysis, and creative conceptualization of strategies. While this process is often nonlinear, it relies on some basic building blocks.

- *Define goals and desired outcomes.* In some cases, foundation trustees may start out with a vague sense of what social issue, problem, or opportunity they want to address. A good planning process will push trustees to articulate their goals and interests more clearly.

  As an illustration, after several years of responding to unsolicited funding requests focusing on early childhood development, youth development, and violence prevention, the trustees of a small family foundation decided to rethink their overall strategy. They came together for a two-day planning retreat and spent time redefining their focus. On the first day of the retreat, they agreed to focus on youth development in underserved communities. By the end of the second day, based on research combined with their own experiences, they developed the more targeted goal of creating or expanding youth mentoring programs in two disadvantaged communities of concern to the trustees.

- *Gain an in-depth understanding of the issue.* The research process can be structured in a variety of ways, depending on the learning styles of the foundation trustees and/or staff. In this context, the term *research* refers to a learning process that relies and builds on the research, thinking, and ideas of others. Components can include review of relevant reports, studies, articles, and other written materials; discussions (by phone or in person) with a wide range of people with different perspectives on the issue; and site visits or other opportunities to see and learn through firsthand experiences. Depending on the foundation's goals and interests, the leaders of this process might reach out to community leaders, practitioners, researchers, policymakers, government officials, and other funders.

This learning process is critical to the development of effective strategies. As illustrated by the following example, research findings can in some cases result in a significant shift in the foundation's thinking and approach. Following the death of the family's patriarch, a new foundation was created. The trustees, who had lost their mother to breast cancer, decided to start out with the goal of finding a cure for breast cancer. The research process involved discussions with scientists and medical researchers, funders (both public and private), and breast cancer advocacy groups, as well as a review of various books, articles, studies, and other written materials on the state of the art of breast cancer research. Based on the report summarizing this research, along with a series of meetings with various experts, the trustees were surprised to learn about the phenomenal increase in federal funding for breast cancer research, from an estimated $93 million in 1991 to over $500 million five years later, resulting from the successful efforts of the breast cancer advocacy community. Given the magnitude of federal research dollars, combined with the challenge of how a private foundation could identify the most promising research proposals, this foundation decided against the idea of funding breast cancer research directly. It has instead adopted the strategy of supporting advocacy efforts that are working to leverage even greater federal resources for breast cancer research.

- *Identify potential financial and nonfinancial resources.* Foundations that deliberately think through what resources and assets might be available—both financial and nonfinancial— often begin to develop creative ideas for mobilizing these resources to leverage long-term change. Foundations with powerful strategies tend to view grants as only one piece of an integrated strategy. Corporate foundations, in particular, can tap into significant nonfinancial resources that can greatly increase their philanthropic impact, including the skills, talents, and interests of employee volunteers; in-kind contributions; and corporate capabilities such as marketing, media outreach, and human resource development. Private foundations can also harness a variety of nonfinancial resources and strengths, including the ability to convene and mobilize people around an issue; disseminate reports and thought pieces that can influence other funders and policymakers; and gain access to thought leaders, journalists, and others who can influence public opinion.

- *Develop and assess ideas and options for specific strategies.* Building on the programmatic research and analysis of what approaches might be feasible with available resources, this part of the process involves creative conceptualization of ideas for tackling an issue. Foundations often explore a range of options and ideas, and then decide which strategies are most promising from their perspective.

  As part of this process, many strategic givers find it useful to articulate the theory of change or logic model that drives their decisions. By identifying and analyzing the link, or potential link, between programmatic strategies and desired outcomes, this analysis can help sort out which strategies are likely to be most effective in achieving the desired results. Is there existing research that supports the premise that a particular strategy will produce the desired outcome? If not, a donor may want to build in a strong research and evaluation component that could enhance knowledge within a particular field. Within a particular issue area, there are usually a wide range of approaches that a foundation could support. Careful thinking about theories of change can help a foundation to assess which options have the greatest promise.

The basic elements of this process can help foundations develop effective strategies, regardless of whether their goal is to improve educational opportunity so all students can achieve their full potential; bridge the digital divide; prevent homelessness; foster the development of a more tolerant and civic-minded society; find a cure for a particular disease; promote behavior changes that will produce a healthier, happier society; build the capacity of communities to promote locally driven economic development; or address any number of other critical issues facing society in the twenty-first century. Foundations that want to be proactive, entrepreneurial, and innovative in their approach to philanthropy incorporate and interweave ongoing research and analysis, conceptualization and design of programmatic strategies and initiatives, communications and other leveraging strategies, and continuous evaluation and adjustments to the overall strategy.

Following are a number of other elements, adapted from the for-profit sector, that can help to strengthen the programmatic strategic planning process.

SWOT Exercises

Taking stock of the foundation's internal and external environments is a critical contextual element in the planning process. It is partner to the identification and inclusion process for key stakeholders. It seeks to gather, understand, and apply data on what the foundation has accomplished vis-à-vis its programmatic priorities and how it has been structured to carry out those priorities and to produce a scan of the environments in which it works.

The assessment—honest and candid, with no finger-pointing—looks at:

S   Both programmatically and organizationally, what are the foundation's core strengths? Its measurable accomplishments? What have been the keys those achievements? Are any of these strong points at risk?

W   Programmatically and structurally, where has the foundation been weakest? Are any of these deficiencies critical obstacles to carrying out the foundation's vision or its present funding thrust?

O   What opportunities are out there that represent serious chances for the foundation to move its agenda significantly ahead? What would be required to take advantage of the situation? Is the foundation equipped to do so?

T   What real threats are on the horizon that may frustrate or negate the foundation's agenda? Are any of these matters that the foundation can address? Or are they givens that may determine the degree of difficulty the foundation faces in carrying out its aims? What are the key public policy issues within the foundation's funding focus? Do these or would these policies abet or hinder the foundation's strategies? What would it take to change them? How likely could that change be?

In identifying and taking the full measure of the opportunities and threats, the foundation may wish to engage outside assistance to produce a scan of the field or generate relevant research. The process need not be complex or enormous, but foundations need to be constantly cognizant of their environments, most especially as they craft strategy. Integrating a SWOT scan into all of the foundation's long-range thinking builds a certain level of due diligence discipline and rigor into all strategy building and makes for a significantly better action agenda.

Risk Analysis

A key question for foundations to consider in the planning process is what level of risk they wish to take. As with financial investments, philanthropic investments can be relatively risk free (e.g., supporting a higher education institution's capital campaign) or high risk (e.g., working with a social entrepreneur to develop a new nonprofit organization). The SWOT analysis can be easily modified to provide a useful risk analysis tool. We work with one family foundation that calls this modified tool an SOR analysis—strengths, opportunities, and risks.

Competitive Analysis

Although the competitive analysis process (scrutinizing and analyzing the strengths and market advantages of competitors) is seen as a business-sector planning tool, it has its value for a foundation's own crafting of strategy, albeit in a more collegial way. In the planning process a foundation should ask itself whether there are other funders who do what it does as effectively or better. Some basic questions among collegial foundations are:

- How does a sister foundation build its capacity to implement strategy? Is it structured differently?
- Does it play roles in carrying out its plans that the foundation does not?
- Does it work differently? Does it apply its resources differently?
- How does it keep current with information on real opportunities and threats in its marketplace?
- Could other, possibly more experienced, foundations play a mentor role for the foundation through its strategic planning work and subsequent implementation efforts?

Planning for Effective Execution

Once a foundation has designed an overall programmatic strategy, the next step is to develop an implementation plan. This plan typically defines each element of the strategy in considerable detail and how each element will be operationalized. Elements include:

- The overall goals driving the philanthropic strategy
- Specific initiatives that comprise the strategy and how these initiatives fit together and support one another
- How initiatives will be implemented and over what timeline
- Organizational structure and staffing

- Resources needed for effective implementation, including annual and multiyear budgets (Resource needs might include grants, management and coordination, technical assistance, grantee convenings, evaluation, communications [e.g., media outreach, dissemination of reports and white papers, convenings of funders with shared goals and interests, etc.], and administrative costs.).

The implementation plan guides how resources will be allocated and mobilized, as well as the structure, workplan, and timeline for executing philanthropic strategies. In terms of structure, there are a wide range of models, including operating foundations, partnerships with intermediary organizations, outsourcing of the design and management of strategic initiatives, and various hybrid models.

Other elements that are often built into ongoing implementation planning include:

- *Identification of leveraging strategies.* Through smart and creative leveraging opportunities, foundations can build on their initial strategies in important ways. These opportunities could include innovative communication approaches, efforts to ensure sustainability, scale-up of effective approaches, or strategies to engage the public and influence public policy.
- *Evaluation to assess impact over time and revise strategies as needed.* In line with the development of a theory of change, measures of success and evaluation plans should be built into the design of a strategic initiative as early in the planning process as possible. Early development of the evaluation component can help to fine-tune or improve the strategy before moving into implementation, and ensure that evaluation resources are in place. It can also prompt the collection of important baseline data that could be critical to evaluating an initiative's impact.
- *Troubleshooting.* Despite the best planning, unanticipated challenges and barriers are likely to arise. A flexible implementation process expects the unexpected and builds in contingency planning as needed.

Reflection, Revision, Renewal

Effective foundations systematically institute a process for revisiting their fundamental building blocks periodically. This ongoing assessment, reflection, and revisiting of strategies is certainly an important part of the planning process.

"More and more I've come to realize that regularly examining what you do and worrying about it, about how to do it better, is more important than almost anything else we do in this work." These words of our colleague and TPI trustee Melinda Marble, executive director of the Paul and Phyllis Fireman Family Foundation, remind us that reflection and planning should be infused at every stage and level.

An important planning and management tool, evaluation can help foundations to obtain feedback to improve programmatic initiatives and stimulate good planning for the future. Depending on the size and type of a foundation, there are many structures and processes that can help to ensure ongoing reflection and renewal, including:

- *Periodic planning retreats.* Useful planning retreats often include board members as well as staff. Foundations of all sizes and types often find it useful to build in time for regular planning retreats, which may be semiannual, annual, or less frequent. Such retreats might be facilitated by the board chair or an outside facilitator.
- *Meta-evaluations.* In addition to evaluation efforts focusing on grantees, we encourage foundations to undergo "meta-evaluations" periodically, involving a comprehensive assessment of effectiveness in achieving stated goals. Going beyond looking at the impact of individual grants, foundations conduct meta-evaluations to assess the impact of their overall efforts.
- *Internal evaluation units.* Some large foundations create evaluation units or other internal procedures that systematize ongoing evaluation, knowledge management, and reflection and sharing of lessons learned among foundation staff.

- *Peer mentoring/coaching models.* Models that rely on peer mentoring and coaching among foundation trustees and/or staff members are uncommon, but we believe they deserve more attention. These types of models are gaining popularity in some fields, including the teaching profession, and some foundations are beginning to experiment with these approaches.

Regardless of the process, key questions can include the following:

- Have we defined our philanthropic goals clearly enough to achieve a measurable long-term impact?
- Do our strategies for soliciting proposals uncover the most innovative or promising funding opportunities?
- Are there ways to enhance the overall impact of our philanthropic strategies?
- How do we build on successful efforts, as well as lessons learned?
- How can we more effectively leverage our resources?

KEY CHALLENGES FOR FOUNDATIONS IN THE TWENTY-FIRST CENTURY

Foundations can face a wide range of challenges and barriers in developing and implementing effective philanthropic strategies, including:

- *Finding time, staff, and other resources needed to develop and build on promising strategies.* Some foundation boards prefer to put resources into direct grants rather than development of philanthropic strategies and leveraging opportunities. In our experience, foundations that are serious about developing creative strategies with potential for high impact need some combination of talented staff, highly engaged trustees, and/or outside consulting to assist with programmatic research and strategic design.

- *Insufficient resources for technical assistance and capacity building of grantees.* Another question is the extent to which foundations choose to put resources into technical assistance and other types of support for grantees, to help them assess, reflect, and adapt their approaches over time so as to increase their impact. Related to this issue is the challenge of developing a more partnership-oriented relationship with grantees, rather than the traditional grantor–grantee relationship. Foundations that view their grantees as true partners encourage them to experiment with new ideas, learn from what works and what does not work well, and make changes where needed. Funders seeking to develop this type of relationship work to actively engage with grantees as co-learners.

- *Limited attention spans.* There is often a tendency among policymakers, the media, and others to focus on the "hot issue" of the day and seek quick fixes, rather than efforts that could produce lasting positive change over a long-term horizon. A key challenge for strategic funders is how to disseminate best practices and effective models in ways that will attract broader attention, and lead to expansion of effective models or other leveraging opportunities.

- *Evaluation limitations.* The difficulty of evaluating the impact of foundation efforts in concrete terms has always been, and will continue to be, a major challenge.

- *Inertia.* Due to evaluation limitations, foundation board pressures, and other reasons, it is often easier for foundations to stay locked into strategies with limited impact, rather than openly exploring opportunities to enhance impact or even shift strategic direction. The most effective foundations will be those that are good listeners, open to learning and developing new ideas, and compelled to continually do more and better with available resources.

Other challenges include knowledge management (how to effectively document and manage information in ways that lead to improved strategies); effective use of new information and communications technologies; and effective collaboration with other funders, nonprofit organizations, and other sectors including government and business. While there are no easy ways to overcome these challenges, first steps include a willingness to openly acknowledge and discuss barriers that stand in the way of greater impact and a desire to explore and invest in creative solutions.

CONCLUSION

Foundation planning, at its best, is intellectually challenging, innovative, constantly evolving, and above all, full of hope and possibility. It is not ever a picture-perfect model of precision. The process often produces the humbling realities of how difficult even modest change may be, but planning gives foundations a fair chance to make a sustained and sustainable difference. We firmly believe that great planning, like great funding decisions, is a synergistic blend of art and science. It is as much driven by intuitiveness, values, instincts, and passions as it is by knowledge and experience and by the lessons learned from the promising practices of other funders. It is the merger of the art and the science of philanthropy that makes for the "informed leaps of faith" that characterize the very best of philanthropic practice in the United States and beyond. Through good planning, philanthropic entities of all types—staffed and unstaffed, large and small, family, community, and corporate—can craft and undertake creative strategies and play an increasingly important role in society. The previously described approaches to strategic planning seek to answer basic questions:

- Where is the foundation now in its work? What are its core strengths? Are there serious organizational weaknesses? Could those deficits get in the way of effectuating a new course of action?
- On the basis of what has been accomplished and learned, where does the philanthropy want to go? What are the great opportunities and challenges in these areas? What are the

stark realities of what the foundation would face if it set out in pursuit of these funding goals? What harm could the foundation's funding enthusiasms cause if not carefully thought out and carried out?

- With the knowledge gained from answers to the first and second queries and a keen appreciation of the "degree of difficulty" associated with achieving critical aims in mind, what path to effective action does the foundation wish to craft for itself?

- How will the foundation's leadership know it is on course? Or how to adjust the course? What are useful milestones? And what will tell them they have reached their destination?

- Who else might accompany the foundation on the journey as supportive fellow travelers?

Final Words

What do we see (and wish for) on the philanthropic horizon? More and more, foundations will experiment with new collegial and collaborative approaches, learn from and interact with the for-profit sector in innovative ways, and develop more sophisticated strategies to communicate with and engage the public around social issues of concern. In a time when new challenges are facing the world, public/private partnerships will continue to evolve in interesting ways. Foundations will increasingly seek out opportunities to integrate lessons from relevant social experiments, and apply research findings in ways that will enhance their effectiveness.

Foundation leaders will seek out a greater understanding of social movements, and "tipping points" that bring issues to the public's attention and even change behavior—and perhaps public policy. Without any doubt, the potential for philanthropy to stretch in new directions, and to serve as a change agent and leader in promoting positive social change, is limitless.

Section Four

Building Foundation Wisdom: The Challenge of Accumulating, Synthesizing, and Sharing Knowledge

Spending Smarter: Knowledge as a Philanthropic Resource

The Project on Foundations in the Knowledge Economy with the support of The David and Lucile Packard Foundation

by Lucy Bernholz

INTRODUCTION

Imagine an organization that routinely gathers data, systematically derives new learning from it, makes decisions based on those lessons, invests both dollars and the expertise that is gathered from the organizations it supports, and you have a new institution: the knowledge foundation. Such an organization relies on a revaluing of foundation assets to include not only their financial resources, but also their information technologies, knowledge bases, and organizational learning systems.

The thesis of the Project on Foundations in the Knowledge Economy is that the strategic use of information assets, supported by new structural incentives and the judicious application of information technologies, offers foundations an opportunity to significantly increase the impact of their grantmaking.

As foundations recognize the value of their information assets—timely knowledge about social trends, community change, and organizational behavior—they will place the kind of emphasis on

233

knowledge development, management and dissemination as they now do on grant processing. Understanding the role of information assets will benefit from and contribute to current discussions on the added value of philanthropic grantmaking.[1]

This paper is a first attempt to redefine institutional philanthropy in this way. We seek to add to the recognized definition of foundations' resources in ways that can unleash more of their potential as change agents. Knowledge fits in at many levels and places in the organization. By better understanding the roles of information and knowledge, foundations can augment their resource base and add to their set of available tools.

One caveat about knowledge as a resource: valuing foundation knowledge neither subtracts from the importance of financial resources nor is it meant to distract foundations from thinking strategically about those resources. Rather, knowledge assets add to the foundation's resources, as they become strategic guides in deploying financial resources, as well as one of the desired returns on those investments.

The development of new ways of using and sharing knowledge will improve the ability of individual foundations to accomplish their missions. It also will improve the ability of the industry as a whole to calculate the overall contributions it makes to society in return for the public trust it holds. Foundations that can manage knowledge and apply it strategically will leverage other private and public funds to their issues and initiatives, and manage more effective partnerships. They also should be able to measure improvements in their internal efficiency and the effectiveness of their staff and board decisions.

This paper considers the current context of institutional philanthropy as both a reason and an opportunity for this redefinition. It also looks at knowledge management in the commercial sector, and considers what those lessons offer in the field of philanthropy and where they fall short. To avoid putting a square peg in a round hole, we adapt what we know about knowledge management to what we know about philanthropy and not vice versa. It has been said that foundations have only the "blunt instrument of money" to bring to the public problem-solving arena. We would propose that the deliberate use of knowledge sharpens that instrument.[2]

THE OPPORTUNITY

Foundations are institutions of time and place. The momentous economic and social changes of the early twenty-first century are having as great an impact on philanthropy as they are on Americans' sense of identity, the pace of modern life, community and family values, and how Americans' view national and global affairs. Foundations are beginning to feel the effects of new information technologies, new wealth creation, growing disparities between rich and poor, an increasingly diverse American populace, and new ways of doing business. Indeed, they are experiencing profound changes as a result of these broad societal shifts.

Three things define philanthropy at the dawn of the twenty-first century: the rate of growth of and the bifurcation in the industry, a rapid diversification of participating institutions, and the development of ancillary industries.

The recent growth of foundations and philanthropic assets is unprecedented. In the last 20 years, the number of U.S. foundations has more than doubled to over 55,000, which as a group managed endowments worth more than $448 billion.[3] Concurrent with this growth in assets, the independent sector is preparing for an unprecedented intergenerational transfer of wealth. Some estimate this transfer will reach more than $100 trillion over the next fifty years, with estimates of charitable contributions in the range of $6 to $25 trillion.[4] The near-term decline in assets and growth rates will eclipsed by the long-term increases.

The industry is bifurcated and dispersed. The majority of U.S. foundations (62.5%) have assets of one million dollars or less. At the other end of the spectrum, the 190 largest foundations (.4% of the whole) manage more than 50% of all foundation assets. Their grants account for more than 37% of the industry total.[5] At the large end of the spectrum, forty-five foundations manage more than one billion dollars in assets. At the other end, almost 30,000 foundations manage assets of a million dollars or less.

The second defining characteristic of philanthropy is the diversification of structures within it. In the past decade several new organizational hybrids have been created that pull from both the commercial and nonprofit sectors and have rapidly amassed enormous financial resources. The industry includes a variety of structures, all of which operate within the same sections of the tax code, but which are otherwise distinct. The mix includes foundations (public, private, corporate, and community), bank trusts, financial service firms' charitable fund products, giving circles, donor advised funds, public grantmaking charities, and e-philanthropy firms.[6] This is much different from a few decades ago when the major philanthropic categories were only bank trusts and foundations.

Third, the industry has given rise to a significant number of secondary vendors including consulting firms, research institutions, and product firms. The industry is developing both watchdogs and infrastructure support. Some of these organizations represent an increasing lobbying, communications, and advocacy role for philanthropy. Others are dedicated to staff and board development. Some focus on ethical management, and many simply sell customized products or services for which institutional philanthropy is their target market. These developments are important for the culture of philanthropy, as well as for the role that networks and relationships begin to play.

Other important developments in the last decade include:

- Increased public scrutiny of and academic research about the independent sector;
- The proliferation of new philanthropic communities of interest and professional alliances (such as geographic and issue-based networks); and
- The increasing diversity of foundation staff and founders.

In addition, both established and emerging philanthropic institutions are seeking ways to measure their impact, leverage their financial resources, and capitalize on select business practices to improve their work.

This moment presents an important opportunity for foundations. For all their growth and changes, and their newfound place in the public view, foundations continue to struggle to show the effect of their work, the impact of their investments, and the justification for their tax-exempt status. The coming years will see increased public scrutiny of philanthropy and calls to account for its privileged place in the tax code.

While some view foundations as money-printing machines, all foundations have limited financial resources, most of which pale in comparison to the size of the problems they wish to alleviate and even the size of the public budgets dedicated to the same issues. No single foundation has the resources to solve any problem. Increasingly, major foundations are looking for funding partners or ways to leverage other financial resources. It is here that we find a compelling incentive for organizational change. To attract other resources to their issues, to their partnerships, and to their nonprofit partners, foundations must establish themselves as savvy, smart, effective organizations. They must be able to show results. And they will do so by the effective use of *all* of their resources: financial and knowledge. In short, they must spend smarter.

Change in philanthropy will happen within a unique framework of human networks, competition and collaboration, rapid growth and diversification, and the challenges of measuring social change. What this will take is not change on a one-by-one basis, but the deliberate evolution of an industry. Networks of foundations in cities and regions around the country can adopt deliberate, collective, knowledge-based, networked strategies to achieve shared goals.[7]

KNOWLEDGE AS A PHILANTHROPIC RESOURCE

Foundation knowledge assets take many forms and are found in many places. They include community data on key issues, staff knowledge of effective strategies, experience-based information on community leaders, public sector issue data, research reports and analysis, evaluation data, the skills and resources of their reference librarians, and the institutional memories of their long-term administrative staff people. The assets also include community relationships, their convening skills, and their abilities to draw together disparate information and people to address complicated issues. Given the variation in these assets, finding, cataloguing, deploying, and valuing them is only possible if the purpose for doing so is clear.

Foundations, of course, have fundamentally different bottom lines than commercial entities. For philanthropy, the meaningful bottom line is mission accomplishment—which usually is linked to social change.

The only way to know if a foundation has accomplished its mission is to know how well its nonprofit partners have achieved their goals. Since nonprofit mission accomplishment does not generate a financial return to the foundation, the currency of this exchange cannot be measured in dollar values. Instead, the appropriate currency to assess this return is knowledge creation and application.[8]

Both the key sources and users of information and knowledge are external to the foundation—other grantmakers, policymakers, and nonprofit organizations. As such, foundations trying to find and use knowledge as a resource need to rethink where the borders of their organizations are, where they get knowledge from and how they use it, and, most important of all, how using information and knowledge aligns with and can accelerate progress toward the foundation's mission.

A *knowledge foundation* is a philanthropic institution that views knowledge as a distinct asset and strategically develops, captures, uses, and shares knowledge to achieve its mission. The foundation recognizes that it relies on both external and internal knowledge, and develops strategies that are appropriate to both sources. There are several strategies currently being tried to connect knowledge capture and use with mission accomplishment.

PHILANTHROPIC KNOWLEDGE STRATEGIES: AN EARLY INVENTORY

Examples of knowledge management strategies abound in the philanthropic industry. Most of these are quite new, and long-term assessments of their impact on the financial bottom line or the mission achievement of their host organizations are not yet available. They are useful to consider, taking into account that they are currently underway as separate business models within the industry. The challenge will be to develop a means for the industry and its analysts to understand which models provide which benefits and at what costs.[9]

Managerial Approaches

Several foundations have designated chief knowledge officers to oversee all knowledge management functions in the organization. The Charles and Helen Schwab Foundation, for example, recently restructured. In doing so it brought into one organization the grantmaking functions and operating programs of what previously had been two separate family funds. The chief knowledge officer (CKO) will have primary responsibility for developing and implementing ways that this new enlarged grantmaking entity can capitalize on the issue-specific expertise from the former operating fund.

Cross-Program Initiatives

A number of foundations are trying to encourage and institutionalize cross-program learning and exchange. The Fannie Mae Foundation, which has a considerable library of resources on housing issues and policy, launched a knowledge initiative in 2000 to help program staff who worked on the Foundation's national and local programs use the information the foundation was generating.[10] In another example, The James Irvine Foundation has scheduled regular organizational learning days managed by the evaluation department and linked these to foundation-wide priorities. These will promote knowledge exchange across all foundation staff, not just program staff. The Foundation is building an intranet that will first host internal management-related documents as an enticement to get people to use it (expense reimbursement and vacation request forms are likely to draw staff to the system, for example). The goal is to start small, change the culture of where staff members look for information, and then begin using the intranet to facilitate organizational learning across programs as well.

Institution-Wide

The Northwest Area Foundation restructured itself to focus exclusively on efforts to alleviate poverty in its eight state area. The Foundation has abandoned the strategy of funding models and trying to get the government to take them to scale. Its new focus is on "producing knowledge that customers and allies can use to reduce poverty."[11] The Foundation dedicated $150 million over ten years to 16 communities working on poverty reduction. It has allocated $25 million over ten years to "facilitating access to information, knowledge, services, and other resources that will help communities as they plan and implement strategies to reduce poverty."[12] A third initiative, budgeted at $25 million over ten years, will focus on developing leadership on these issues in the region.

The Foundation started this work in 1998, and has focused primarily on the first program, community ventures. The foundation has been consistent in setting its structure to match its mission, developing strategies for capturing, using and sharing knowledge, and for driving all of the efforts from a new focus on its mission, "help(ing) communities in our eight-state region reduce poverty."[13] The Foundation has identified knowledge as one of four core resources it can bring to this effort: financial resources, knowledge, products and services. Northwest Area Foundation provides a useful case study for the investing of knowledge as a philanthropic asset.

Cohort Learning

Foundations have been funding initiatives for years. As part of these proactive efforts they often identify opportunities for collaboration among nonprofit partners. Supporting these clusters of grantees, paying for and arranging time for them to share ideas, and providing them with technical assistance support are frequent foundation activities.

More and more, foundations are taking a deliberate look at these clusters as learning opportunities and seeking to support the group work as a substantial funding strategy in and of itself. Some such efforts have yielded the development of common outcomes and joint strategies. Some, such as the Community Clinics Initiative of the Tides Foundation and the California Endowment, have explored their potential as joint purchasers of customized commercial software, and even as investors in the creation of such products. This initiative is also building evaluation tools online so that each of the nonprofit partners will be able to learn from its peers, instead of having the evaluation information simply directed to the foundation.[14]

Web-Based Knowledge Exchange

Several foundations and groups of foundations are experimenting with shared databases of information. These groups are designing and paying for internet-based shared databases of grantmaking and issue interests. For example, several health care foundations in California created the *healthfunders@work* extranet. The Funders Network for Smart Growth and Sustainable Communities recently launched an extranet of shared databases on funding interests, community partners doing this work across the country, and policy snapshots (*www.fundersnetwork.org*).[15] Even as they have invested in these tools key questions remain regarding how they are to be used, where they might inform action (in the individual foundation users? In the affinity groups themselves?), and whether or not the nonprofit organizations with whom the foundations work should have access to these tools.

Foundation Peer-to-Peer Learning

Some of the most deliberate efforts to share information about philanthropy are the direct results of the growth of the industry. Many new donors have been quite willing to say, "teach us.'" Social Venture Partners (SVP), a giving circle approach to philanthropy founded by Paul Brainerd in Seattle in 1995, expanded to include 18 regional spin-offs by 2001. In many of those the SVP affiliates, the partners quickly identified their need for a semi-formal curriculum to learn about philanthropy and the issues they intended to address with their giving.

In San Francisco, for example, the SVP chapter signed up 60 partners in a matter of months. These partners organized themselves into committees. Two of the committees are explicitly focused on learning and knowledge sharing: a curriculum committee which sponsors monthly meetings with local issue experts, as well as with local philanthropic thought leaders, and an information-exchange committee which is charged with developing strategies and tools (online and offline) for sharing information within SVP, with their grantees, the community, and other philanthropists. This last audience is seen as critical, as SVP Bay Area identified the need to leverage other philanthropic resources as a key criteria for its grantmaking. It is, therefore, developing mechanisms to share what it learns "even before we learn anything," as one partner noted.[16] SVP Bay Area also launched in partnership with the region's oldest community foundation, recognizing both the cost savings and knowledge gain of doing so.[17]

Knowledge Marquees

Several foundations have taken steps to make explicit and public the lessons they have learned from various grants. The Robert Wood Johnson Foundation hosts a publicly accessible, searchable database of grant evaluation syntheses.[18] These are structured in a uniform way, written by a dedicated paid staff, and made available through the Foundation's web site.

The Annie E. Casey Foundation has funded the KIDSCOUNT project for years, which works with organizations in 50 states to collect and disseminate standardized data on the health and well being of children.[19] These are two of the strongest examples of investing in the development of knowledge and then sharing it with the public. These models have the opportunity to move to the next level, which is to develop metrics for assessing how their information is being used (citations indices are an easy example), working with change organizations and their partners to collectively analyze the data and information, and strengthening the feedback loops to the foundation on the leveraging impact of these sites.

Many large foundations are beginning to use their websites to make selected research reports public as well. Examples include the Surdna Foundation, the David and Lucile Packard Foundation, the Ford Foundation, The Charles Stewart Mott Foundation, and The W.K. Kellogg Foundation. Sharing this information is a useful first step. Moving beyond static brochures to structures that can help potential partners use the information and then feed back information to the foundation are ways to take advantage of the interactive qualities of the web.

Information Communities

The Donors Forum of Chicago is a regional association of grantmakers (RAG), one of more than 30 nationwide. It is one-year into a strategic planning process that includes a core knowledge management component. The Donor's Forum has been working with consultants from IBM to help them identify, prioritize, deploy and assess their knowledge assets. Sample knowledge assets for an association such as the Donors Forum include explicit information on the number of foundations, size of assets, employment opportunities, joint funder partnerships, and state regulations that are of use to their members and the public.

The organization and its staff also know a good deal about the political culture of public-private partnerships in the region, the pressures and key challenges of the local nonprofit community, and other more tacit information about their local constituencies. The association currently dedicates significant human capital to sharing information with its members through a staffed library, as well as online, while also assessing the knowledge generating and sharing roles of its management, communications, and member/program services staff. It is in the process of considering information technology options to help it achieve its newly stated objective of becoming an "information community."

One of the key challenges for a membership association such as the Donor's Forum is to distinguish between the knowledge assets of its own organization and those of its members, to which the association has temporal access by virtue of a committee position, a board seat or a joint partnership.

Another example of an information community is the Los Angeles Urban Funders (LAUF). Founded in response to the Los Angeles riots in 1992, LAUF represents an intentional community for foundation learning, or as it calls itself, "a living laboratory for innovative grantmaking."

From its start with seven foundations, LAUF has grown to include more than two dozen funders. The foundations jointly identified a problem, developed a strategy working closely with three communities, and have sought new foundation members according to the needs determined by the strategy. Each foundation member dedicates funds to LAUF directly, and then also makes grants from its own resources to organizations and issues in the three communities.

The structure is deliberately set up and staffed so that foundations focused on economic development can do what they do best, while also learning from their arts or education funding peers from LAUF. Staff and board briefings, technical assistance opportunities with nonprofits, and the human and information systems to share lessons learned have helped LAUF document its own work as well as changes in the way some of its member foundations operate. LAUF also recognizes the value of its members' knowledge and connections, and counts these into its investment strategies.[20]

FOUNDATIONS AND KNOWLEDGE STRATEGIES

Until recently, the ability to capture and use this knowledge has been somewhat under exercised. Nonprofits, of course, have tried to capture 'best practices,' as have many foundations. There have been too few deliberate connections and incentives between knowing what work needs to be done, using that knowledge to develop and imple-

ment foundation funding strategies, capturing that knowledge as the work progresses, and reconsidering and reapplying the new knowledge through the grantmaking cycle.

"Any company that depends on smart people and the flow of ideas must choose a knowledge management strategy."[21] Certainly this applies to foundations. They rely on smart staff and board and the judicious gathering and application of information to guide their program strategies and to assess their impact. How then do they choose a knowledge management strategy?

There are several strategies for knowledge management that have particular benefits for foundations. In one widely regarded review of management consulting firms, two categories of strategies emerged: codification and personalization.[22] Choices between the two were driven by whether the firm focused on solving multiple variations of the same types of problem, or whether they tended to work on many different types of problems that required a core set of analytic skills.

For those who work on the same kinds of problems, the best firms could invest heavily in solving a problem once, and then build ways to codify the solutions for quick, reliable, re-use. For the firms that worked on highly differentiated problems, the most effective strategy was to develop ways to learn from each engagement, codify who knew what, and then build a system to find the right colleagues at the right time to address new situations. The first strategy, codification, relies on an economic model of re-using knowledge for multiple projects. The second strategy, personalization, uses a model of assembling expertise appropriate to each situation.

This example is important for foundations. They must determine whether or not they know enough from their past work to codify solutions, or if the more appropriate strategy will be to codify "who knows what." They must consider how many "problems" they are working on, how useful is the current state of information on what works, and whether or not they can identify "re-usable" strategies for each new grant opportunity.

Given the need for foundations to leverage other resources, the catalogue of effective solutions is best not held within an individual foundation but should be an industry resource that would be freely shared with nonprofit and government partners. At this time, no such resource exists, although much of the raw data may be locked within foundations in reports, research, evaluation studies, and other internal sources. At the same time, personal relationships and experience clearly matter a great deal in philanthropy. Some industry associations have made concerted attempts to catalogue philanthropy's "human knowledge."[23] Given this, the personalization strategy augmented by codification efforts seem to fit best with philanthropic culture and existing resources.

FACTORS IN SELECTING A STRATEGY

Knowledge management strategies in the corporate sector are linked to efficiency and profits. In the nonprofit sector they must be linked to mission accomplishment. What foundations need to consider is how the various tools for knowledge management apply to their organizations.

Several factors will influence these decisions. Many are internal to the foundation–how many staff people work for the foundation? What types of information do they use? Where do they get this information? How does the staff use technology? How does the foundation currently measure its success?

Several important factors in choosing a knowledge management strategy are external to the foundation—how does it communicate with the public? With whom does it partner? How does it work with nonprofits?

QUESTIONS TO ASK IN DEVELOPING A FOUNDATION KNOWLEDGE STRATEGY

- How will knowledge help accomplish our mission?
- What types of problems is the foundation trying to solve?
- What information and knowledge sources does the foundation use?
- How does the foundation use information and knowledge?
- What are the organizational barriers and facilitators to changing?

Determining how knowledge fits into a foundation's mission requires at least two preconditions:

1. A clear mission with articulated outcomes
2. Knowledge application opportunities that are explicit enough to be considered as factors in success or failure

The first and last question foundation executives or board members should ask themselves about using knowledge is: toward what end? How will creating or fostering an emphasis on the use of knowledge improve our work help us achieve our mission. All decisions should be made with clear answers to this question in mind.

TOWARD A KNOWLEDGE FOUNDATION

Here is an example. The K Foundation is committed to helping children learn and develop into healthy adults. It funds afterschool programs as part of this mission. In addition to research and advocacy, it funds several local programs. In each of these proposals, it notices a budget item for transportation.

After several years, the foundation staff realizes that they have been spending tens of thousands of dollars every year on bus insurance. They know from research on afterschool programs that transportation is key to success. They also know from informal conversations that their peer foundations are effectively funding the bus and insurance companies as well. They also know that the local city government spends millions on public transportation. They decide to see if there isn't a more efficient and effective approach.

The K Foundation's evaluation staff review five years worth of grant proposals and develops a standard means of calculating transportation expenditures. A graduate student researcher is hired to gather the same data from as many of their local foundation peers as possible, and they assemble historical data from twenty foundations, totaling several million dollars annually.

The K Foundation convenes its peer foundations and the non-profit organizations that were being funded by most of the foundations to run these programs. They share the data analysis and ask the group, "Isn't there a better way?"

After several discussions, the group decides to jointly investigate pooled transportation opportunities. It also proposes several ideas for working with the city to make better use of public transportation facilities. One of the foundations has its research staff analyze the local public transportation system and budget on behalf of the group, while another foundation's reference librarian identifies model transportation partnerships. The researcher contacts the local newspaper's transportation and city desk reporters for data and past analysis, and to let them know the work is happening. A report is developed and the foundations and nonprofits invite several department heads from the city and school district to review the study and help them develop alternative, cost-effective solutions for transporting the city's children to afterschool programs.

The joint group of foundations, nonprofits, and city leaders identify numerous short and long-term options. They include a private bus pool, safety monitors on public bus lines so parents will allow children to ride by themselves, new public bus routes, reduced bus rates for program staff so they will ride with the children, a public awareness campaign, parent information workshops, and coordinated schedules and locations for afterschool programs.

Some of the short-term solutions are implemented, work begins on the longer-term strategies, the media covers the story, and other cities begin to seek out the lead nonprofit, foundation, and department heads for advice.

Over the years, the individual foundations see a decrease in expenditures for transportation and bus insurance. The programs track improved attendance rates, and the city sees an increased use of its public transit without an increase in safety violations. The foundations share their analyses of the joint work with the nonprofits and the public, and new opportunities for helping young people learn and develop are identified.

The simplicity of the example above is intentional. Many foundations executives will read this and say, "Of course, we are already doing this." But the subtleties are important. How often do foundations actually do the syntheses and analyses of grant reports and share that back with a group of nonprofits? How often do they work with community agencies to identify the next round of community education goals to pursue? How often do they tap journalists as data resources? How often do they work to publicly demonstrate how what they are learning is informing their next round of decision-making, or actively seek ways to help nonprofit partners demonstrate the same thing?

Acting the way the example describes would require new types of behavior by most foundations. It would involve a level of participation in the problem definition stage that few foundations open up to the nonprofits. It would require a willingness to reveal what sources and research are being used to inform strategy development. It also would involve foundation staff (or board) sitting at the table, learning from and with nonprofits, local government and journalists, doing some of the heavy lifting (synthesis and analysis), while acknowledging that the nonprofits themselves are the source of the data, the information and much of the knowledge about what families need to access high quality afterschool programs. In this example, the foundation is developing, using and sharing this knowledge.

Such changes require new staff structures and responsibilities. They need new definitions of communications and evaluation. They call for a different role and emphasis in the work of program staff. Many foundations are, in fact, moving on some of these tracks. But the example above requires that these changes be made simultaneously and strategically within each organization.

BUILDING KNOWLEDGE FOUNDATIONS: INTERNAL CHANGES

Using knowledge more effectively in foundations requires reimagining key elements of philanthropic structures. This paper is an open call to think differently about the structure of philanthropic foundations. This must be done in ways that recognize the value of the staff and board of foundations in new ways. Indeed, these individuals and their knowledge and relationships are the fundamental difference between foundations and other charitable giving vehicles. Unlocking their potential to put their knowledge to work is the goal of the knowledge foundation.

However, this paper does not profess to have a "one-size-fits-all" blueprint for what the resulting organizations might look like. Experts on organizational restructuring are quick to point out that there is no "design machine" that can select the best option for any given organization. The key for any organizational restructuring is to know why and how undertaking such an effort will achieve better results.[24] Knowledge foundations are evolved versions of existing philanthropic institutions; they are neither separate nor wholly new.

Staffing and Performance Measures

Foundations come in many sizes, but they fall largely into two shapes: staffed and unstaffed. Foundations with few or no staff are the majority of the industry, accounting for about 47,000 of the 50,000+ U.S. foundations. Two-thirds of American foundations with staff have two or fewer employees, and the average staff size of foundations with more than one million dollars in assets is 5.1 people.[25] They are heavy users of consultant support, specifically with regard to investment, legal and tax advice. Eighty percent of the members of the Association of Small Foundations use investment, legal or tax consultants. Nine percent of the consultants hired are used for proposal review or evaluation purposes related to grant making.[26] For these foundations, the ability to think across functions is eased by the small number of people involved. It is limited by the overwhelming number of things these people need to do.

As foundations add staff, they tend to develop an organizational structure that uses the same functional divisions described above—management, investment, finance, legal, program. How foundations "grow" over time is an unstudied phenomenon. We do know that in large staffed foundations—those with 10 or more staff people—these functional divisions become quite pronounced. Program staffs dominate in number. Certain functions, especially legal and investment departments, remain heavy consumers of outsourced expertise even at the largest staffed foundations. Foundations seem to be using grant making and program consultants in increasing numbers, although data on this are hard to find. Several newly large foundations (Gates, Hewlett, Barr) have publicly stated their commitments to manage large giving programs with the fewest possible staff. Even as the overall number of foundations with paid staff increases, the size of these staffs remain small. As of 2000, only 26 foundations in the United States reported employing more than 50 staff people.[27]

What is often lost in the growth process is the organization's ability to think across functions. Foundation grantmaking decisions are not only made in isolation from many of the legal and investment choices, they are often made in isolation from program to program. As it now stands for many staffed foundations, the work is dominated by the processing of proposals. This can be thoughtful work. But the pressure to meet payout requirements, stay ahead of the "inbox" curve of proposal, review, report, proposal, often predominates over all else.

The cumulative effect of this current business process is "that wisdom is lost in knowledge, and knowledge is lost in information."[28] Efforts to assist foundations with more effective application of knowledge, therefore, must start from the big—how will it improve opportunities to accomplish our goals?—and the small—how do the internal business processes of the organization have to change? Such change calls for deliberate, sustained evolutionary action.

The opportunity that faces foundations, both emerging and established, is to consider their structures in light of the ways they think knowledge relates to their mission. Some foundations have in-house libraries. Others are hiring chief knowledge officers. Some focus on team learning, cross-program initiatives, and shared budgets.

Many look to their communications departments as the grease that can unlock knowledge from internal departments, make it widely available internally, and share it with the public. Several foundations have turned to their information technology departments or consultants and said, "Build tools that can help us learn from one another."

All of these are crucial pieces of the puzzle. Knowledge foundations need systems and processes for sharing information internally and externally that take advantage of the skills and capacities of all these functions: program, technology, communications, investment, evaluation, management and finance. In order to do this, foundations need to rethink their organizational charts, job descriptions, personnel performance measures and incentive structures. As one organizational guru puts it, the question to ask is:

> Are the organization's policies for recruiting, selecting, paying, training and developing, and organizing its workforce consistent with the core capabilities it needs to succeed. . .? In many organizations. . .the answer is no. Policies have built up like deposits in cages, and the alignment with what the organization needs to do is poor.[29]

Foundations that are turning to one of their departments, evaluation or communications, or developing individual positions to manage knowledge across the organization, are taking partial steps. Given the networked and public nature of what foundations need to know and use, all foundation staff that interact with the public need to be responsible for knowledge gathering. Since organizations pay for what matters to them, performance measures and job descriptions need to prioritize knowledge development and exchange. The ripple effects of these changes should be considered in the beginning of a knowledge management planning process. Adding work to job descriptions without the right incentives (time, money, and promotions) is a set up for failure.

While staff structures and performance matter considerably to placing an emphasis on knowledge, a real challenge lies outside the staff and rests with the board.

Governance and Accountability

Foundations are established in the public trust. They derive from and are shaped by tax law, and are regulated with regard to their expenditures of funds and their public reporting. The first of these regulations, the so-called "payout" requirement, is the subject of much debate.[30] It serves as an industry stick and standard for establishing budgets and grantmaking appropriations. The second of these, the public reporting requirement, is the analogous, though much weaker, regulatory tool that guides public reporting of foundation activities.[31] Although much debated in its early days, it now causes considerably less concern than the payout requirement. This is important, for as the economic landscape has contributed to the attention on the payout requirement, the rapidly shifting world of communications and information may be useful in directing attention to public reporting by foundations. This reporting now focuses on the financial assets. What if it could be a stronger tool for thinking about knowledge assets?

Foundation boards are ultimately responsible for governing the organizations and meeting these two public requirements: payout and reporting. They are the entities granted power and responsibility to manage the public trust of both the foundation's financial resources and knowledge assets. The priorities they set drive the actions of staff.

This is true to a greater degree than in commercial corporations. The structures appear the same—both types of boards of directors are charged with fiscal and legal responsibility and usually claim the role of strategy and policy setters. However, foundation boards (90% of which choose to hire no staff at all) tend to be much more closely involved in the actual work of the professional staff than are corporate boards. In general, their meeting schedules (usually quarterly) drive grantmaking cycles and they require a significant amount of staff time to support. The result is often a staff emphasis on "managing up," leaving little time for managing knowledge.

If, then, foundations are to consider new ways of operating, their work will have to start with their boards. The regulatory environment in which foundations operate really only serves to shape the board's attention to financial accountability and the stewardship of endowments. The opportunity being missed in this is especially ironic, given the growth in charitable alternatives to foundations. The true differentiating potential of foundations when compared to these alternatives is the opportunity to actively develop, apply, and generate knowledge as part of the work of grantmaking. The current priorities and structures are formidable obstacles to capitalizing on that differentiating advantage.

The opportunity to change this lies both inside and outside the foundations. Certainly, new regulatory measures are one option. More amenable, no doubt, would be the use of the industry's own value on "spending smart" and its focus on mission accomplishment. Some boards also may be amenable to knowledge strategies that can lower costs or leverage other resources to their causes.

Inventories

Foundations need to inventory the knowledge they have and that which they need. Not all of the information and skills for assessing proposals may live, or need to live, in program staff or board members. For example, as foundations see an increasing number of proposals for nonprofit investments in information technology, it may make sense to involve their own IT staff in assessing those proposals. Some foundations have developed consulting relationships with IT specialists to assist with this work.[32] Melding their technical expertise with an experienced program staff's perspectives would surely yield stronger analysis of viability, fit and costs of technology-related proposals.

Once this door is open, it also raises the question of where else within a standard staffed foundation does useful program expertise live? Are there legal documents to be produced as part of a proposal, land trust deeds for example? Is the foundation's legal counsel useful here? Can the finance and accounting staffs develop tools that could help program experts assess financial viability? Unstaffed foundations know which board member to turn to for legal, tax, financial and business planning insights regarding certain proposals. This same type of "knowledge inventory" can be done with foundation staffs of any size—the challenge is to open the box as to whom and what should be included in such an inventory.[33]

A foundation's knowledge base includes technical know-how of process and outcomes, as well as its understanding of its issues and the markets of potential grant recipients and other resource providers. Knowledge sources include the proprietary grant reviews, research reports, public opinion surveys, meeting minutes, and evaluation analyses that they conduct. It is the sum of their individual grant analyses, taken in the context of the larger research reports they commission or to which they have access, and filtered through their experiential knowledge of working on certain issues over time.

Knowledge inventories identify what knowledge the foundation uses and where it resides. It will exist in many forms: prior staff experience, reports, videos, interview transcripts, Internet links, internal forms and external professional networks. Such an inventory process immediately reveals the different types of information (both tacit and explicit) that are of value. Strategic analysis of these types— taking into consideration the culture and budget of the organization—should consider how the different resources in the inventory are currently shared internally and externally. These steps need to occur across the foundation, even if the intention is to pilot some new strategies within a certain program or department.

BUILDING KNOWLEDGE FOUNDATIONS: EXTERNAL CHANGES

While much of the work that foundations undertake in designing and implementing knowledge strategies will happen at first within individual organizations, we begin with a consideration of external forces that shape those strategies. Two of these forces—networks and outcomes—are critical to helping foundations be effective users and distributors of knowledge.

Networks

Foundations are only one part of a networked industry of public problem solving. Others in the network include nonprofit organizations, public agencies, community groups, activists, researchers, and the media. The knowledge of social change lives within these networks and generally outside the actual walls of the foundations. Foundations are neither the creators of most knowledge about social change nor the only beneficiaries of it. Foundations do create important knowledge, through research and evaluation, and in the development of strategies and their own analysis of society's problems and opportunities. All of these knowledge products have value outside of the foundation.

Grantmaking foundations often sit at the intersections of what is known and what needs to be known. Foundation knowledge management strategies therefore should take advantage of the networked nature of the work. This is understood by nonprofits, which have emphasized the value that foundations could play in providing synthesis, analysis, and distribution roles.[34]

Foundations can do more than this. They can develop grant procedures that provide incentives for knowledge sharing among grant recipients. They can provide the forums and tools for nonprofits to do this. They can capitalize on all of their resources and help build powerful knowledge exchanges from within and beyond their existing partnerships that will help achieve the missions they share with nonprofits, concerned citizens and other emerging partners in solving social problems.

Outcomes

First and foremost, knowing what is to be achieved will influence what kinds of knowledge and knowledge sharing are valuable. Second, knowing the desired outcomes of grantmaking will shape the networks within which a foundation situates itself. And, finally, new knowledge itself may be a meaningful outcome of some grantmaking strategies.

Because missions and outcomes drive the development of knowledge management strategies, powerful strategies for foundations need to transcend the walls of individual institutions. They need to include methods of capturing and categorizing knowledge from external research, evaluations, policy analyses, media reports, community activities, polling data, focus groups and other survey research, and grant proposals and reports. There needs to be an internal process for cataloguing what is known (and/or who knows what) and time and systems to allow it to be used. And there needs to be a means of connecting this internal work to the outward activity of the foundation, including grantmaking, convening, public awareness, and public education, and public reporting. The feedback loops from external to internal are critically important.

The Currency of Change

Changing the way foundations interact with their networks will be no small feat. Foundations have been trying to develop meaningful ways to partner with nonprofits for years. In most cases, the power imbalance between those with financial resources and those who need them has hindered these efforts. What is needed is a means of shifting from the sense of nonprofits as "sellers" in a foundation "buyer's" market. Recognizing the value of nonprofit knowledge to a foundation's attempts to achieve its mission helps set in motion both a new dynamic between the two and viable new ways of collaboration. The currency in such a shift is knowledge.

Using knowledge as a currency of exchange within philanthropy stands to strengthen the power of the networks while also serving as both a measure of outcomes and an outcome in itself. Sharing knowledge begets new knowledge. The real value of knowledge in the philanthropic industry is that if it is used successfully to accomplish the missions of individual organizations it will advance the entire social change process.

CHALLENGES OF USING KNOWLEDGE RESOURCES

Developing and implementing deliberate strategies to use knowledge is neither revolutionary, nor is it likely to vault foundations into a new stratosphere of effectiveness or positive public perceptions. What it can do is position philanthropists to leverage other resources, strengthen their ties to their community partners, and make them more internally effective. It also will contribute to the definition of value that distinguishes foundations from other charitable giving structures that enjoy the same tax benefits. This value definition will benefit the entire foundation community in subsequent upcoming regulatory reviews and economic downturns.

To avoid jumping into knowledge management without truly considering its limits as well as its potential, it is worth looking at several common mistakes.

If You Build It, Will They Come?

One of the great failures of knowledge management has been the mistaken belief that it starts with technology. Knowledge management efforts that begin with building new intranets, extranets, email systems, library catalogues, databases, or other technological wonders, will fail. People will not change how they work just because they are told to, or because a new set of computer-enabled tools is dropped on their desks. The first steps must be setting clear goals and building staff and board support toward a shared vision of the value and purpose of the change effort. Planning for new uses of knowledge must start with the people involved, not with the power of technology.

Silos of Knowledge

Foundations often organize themselves into program categories that align with the various interests of the board and the functions of running the operation. These program areas often develop into silos—

separated by individual budgets, individual strategies, and individual outcomes. Knowledge gets trapped in these silos. In the worst cases, the education program officer has no opportunity or incentive to share ideas with the environmental program, even though the foundation has an interest in environmental education.

Breaking down these silos is both a challenge for philanthropic knowledge management and an opportunity. Sharing knowledge can be the means of building connections across programs. Doing so in meaningful ways requires joint accountability across programs (mutual outcomes, for example) and valid incentives.

Add Without Subtracting

The nonprofit sector has been a late adopter of almost every management fad to ever hit corporate America. Often these management tools and theories, which meet with mixed success in the corporate sector, fail miserably in the nonprofit sector. One reason for this is the temptation to overlay the new thinking and approaches onto existing structures, without taking anything off of anyone's plate. Knowledge management will meet the same fate if capturing and sharing knowledge simply get added to foundation job descriptions without meaningful restructuring of those jobs, the development of new incentives and performance criteria, and the removal of existing requirements.

Knowledge for the Sake of Knowledge

Effective knowledge strategies derive from and lead toward the foundation's mission. Restructuring staff and organizations and dedicating resources to knowledge for knowledge's sake is a temptation for foundations to avoid. Including key partners at the table as advisers, design consultants, or intentional users of the knowledge is critical for developing foundation knowledge practices that are meaningful. While many such strategies focus on changing the internal behavior and structure of foundations as organizations, they are important insofar as they facilitate changing the ways in which philanthropic organizations interact with their partners in pursuit of their missions.

THE LONG VIEW

The potential for using knowledge as a deliberate element in philanthropic activity must be tied to what is one defining characteristic of (most) foundation philanthropy. Almost all endowed foundations are established in perpetuity. They are here for the long haul. What is often held up as an example of the lack of foundation accountability—they can neither be voted out of office and they won't go broke—instead makes them a good fit for learning from their work (and that of their peers) over time. They can, and should, be taking the long view. This perspective calls for learning from what you do, sharing those lessons, and seeking new information, free from the short-term pressures of shareholders or voters.

We are only starting to understand how deliberate knowledge management and application principles can work in the philanthropic sector. But we have an imperative to learn how to do this work better—for even as philanthropic assets have exploded in size in recent years, the social challenges they seek to redress have grown faster and bigger. If we compare foundation grantmaking to energy production (an apt metaphor for California in 2001), knowledge is akin to sustainable, renewable resources. Knowledge is generated from grantmaking as heat is generated from energy production. As we seek to not waste—but instead harness—that heat, we should seek to use that knowledge. Doing so will require new ways of working with partners, new means of distributing what is learned, new ways of structuring organizations and new methods of measuring value and outcomes.

The relationship between knowledge foundations and their nonprofit partners is, effectively, a two-way distribution system. Nonprofits provide foundations with a distribution system for applying their financial resources to social improvement efforts. In return, foundations must become conduits of the nonprofits' knowledge.

NOTES

1. Michael E. Porter and Mark R. Kramer, "Philanthropy's New Agenda: Adding Value," *Harvard Business Review*, November 1999.
2. Craig McGarvey, Program Director, The James Irvine Foundation, upon receiving the 2001 Robert Scrivner Award for Creative Grantmaking from the Council on Foundations.
3. Foundation Center, *Guide to US Foundations* (New York: The Foundation Center, 2000).
4. John J Havens and Paul Shervish, "Millionaires and the Millennium: New Estimates of the Forthcoming Wealth Transfer and a Coming Golden Age of Philanthropy" (Boston: Boston College Social Welfare Research Institute, October 1999).
5. Ibid.
6. See "E-philanthropy v2.001: From Entrepreneurial Adventure to an Online Community" *www.actknowledgeworks.org/ephil* for 2001 review of e-philanthropy efforts. Also see "High Tech Hopes Meet Reality," *The Chronicle of Philanthropy* (June 14, 2001), 1, 8–23.
7. See Lucy Bernholz, *The Deliberate Evolution*, paper prepared for the Marco Polo Project, October 2000. Available at *www.blueprintrd.com/publications*.
8. A great deal of work is now underway regarding metrics of social return on investment. See the Roberts Enterprise Development Fund (*www.redf.org*) and The Morino Institute (*www.morino.org*).
9. Kristin Lindsley, External Relations Manager of the Donors Forum of Chicago, developed a useful brief compendium of knowledge management strategies at several foundations for a panel session at the 2001 Council on Foundations Annual Conference, Philadelphia, PA, May 2001. See *www.donorsforum.org*.
10. The foundation also sought to define ways that it could make this information useful to its grant partners and act in a more externally focused direction as well. At the time of this writing those strategies were not yet clearly defined.
11. Karl Stauber, "Mission Driven Philanthropy: What do we want to accomplish and how do we do it?" *Nonprofit and Voluntary Sector Quarterly*, 30:2 (June 2001), 396.
12. Ibid, 397.
13. *www.nwaf.org*
14. Etienne Wagner and William Snyder, *Communities of Practice: The Organizational Frontier* (Harvard Business Review, January–February 2000), 139–145.
15. Other affinity groups are considering such shared databases. An informal survey by the author identified at least early interest among at least four additional formal affinity groups of the Council on Foundations.
16. Marc Lohrmer, Founding Partner, SVP Bay Area. Author interview.

17. See for example, "The New Philanthropy," *Time Magazine*, July 23, 2000.
18. See *www.rwjf.org/app/rw_about_our_grantees/rw_gra_grantees.html*
19. See *www.aecf.org/kidscount/*. Also see efforts of the John and James L. Knight Foundation, which makes evaluations, literature reviews and data on children available through its websites, *www.knightfdn.org* and *www.childtrends.org*.)
20. Elwood Hopkins, LAUF Executive Director, Author interview, LAUF program materials, and *www.scap.org/lafunders.html*.
21. Morton T. Hansen, Nitin Nohria, and Thomas Tierney, "What's Your Strategy for Managing Knowledge?" *Harvard Business Review* (March–April 1999), 111.
22. Id., 106–116.
23. The Association of Small Foundation's "Peer Exchange" is a classic example.
24. Orit Gadeish and Scott Olivet, "Designing for Implementability," in Frances Hesselbein, Marshall Goldsmith, and Richard Beckhard, eds., *The Organization of the Future* (New York: The Peter F. Drucker Foundation for Nonprofit Management, 1997), 55.
25. Highlights of the Foundation Center's "Foundation Staffing" Report. New York, NY: The Foundation Center, 2000. *http://fdncenter.org/research/trends_analysis/pdf/found_staff_hi.pdf*. While a small number, this is more than double that of 1991. This seems in line with general trends showing increasing staff levels during the 1990s, a decade that saw more than a doubling of professional foundations staff.
26. *Membership Survey Report, 2000*, (Bethesda, MD: Association of Small Foundations, 2000), 7.
27. *Foundation Staffing Report, 2000* (New York: The Foundation Center, 2000).
28. See T. S. Eliot, "The Rock," 1934.
29. Jeffrey Pfeffer, "Will the Organization of the Future Make the Mistakes of the Past?" in Hesselbein, et al., 51.
30. The Tax Reform Act of 1969 requires that foundations payout at least 5 percent of the value of their endowment, on average, each year. This requirement, while set as a *de jure* minimum, has become a *de facto* industry maximum.
31. The Tax Reform Act of 1969 also required foundations to file annual records of their grantmaking (forms 990 and 990 PF for private foundations) with the IRS and to make available public reports of their activities, which has generally evolved into the practice of publishing annual reports.
32. For example, The W. K. Kellogg Foundation works closely with the Alliance for Community Technology at the University of Michigan.
33. See Andrew Blau, "More than Bit Players," a report to the Surdna Foundation, May 2001, pp. 24–33, *www.surdna.org* for other ways to think about IT staff and IT proposals.
34. Jacqueline Dugery and Caroline Hammer, *Coming of Age in the Information Age*, The Pew Partnership For Civic Change, 2000.

RESOURCES

"The Knowledge Bank." *Knowledge Management*, June 2001, 24–26.

"High Tech Hopes Meet Reality" *The Chronicle of Philanthropy* (June 14, 2001): 1, 8–23.

Bell, Daniel. *The Coming of the Post-Industrial Society: A venture in social forecasting*. New York: Basic Books, Inc., 1973.

Blau, Andrew. "More Than Bit Players: How Information Technology Will Change the Ways Nonprofits and Foundations Work and Thrive in the Information Age." A report to the Surdna Foundation, May 2001. *www.surdna.org*

Bukowitz, Wendi R. and Ruth L. Williams. *The Knowledge Management Fieldbook*. Edinburgh: Pearson Education Limited, 1999.

Brown, John Seely and Paul Duguid. *The Social Life of Information*. Boston: Harvard Business School Press, 2000.

Cortada, James W. *Best Practices in Information Technology*. Upper Saddle River, NJ: Prentice-Hall, Inc., 1998.

Davenport, Thomas and Laurence Prusak. *Working Knowledge: How Organizations Manage What they Know*. Boston: Harvard Business School Press, 1998.

Dugery, Jacqueline and Caroline Hammer. *Coming of Age in the Information Age*. The Pew Partnership For Civic Change. Richmond, VA: The University of Richmond, 2000.

Gadeish, Orit and Scott Olivet. "Designing for Implementability." In Frances Hesselbein, Marshall Goldsmith and Richard Beckhard, eds., *The Organization of the Future* (New York: The Peter F. Drucker Foundation for Nonprofit Management, 1997): 53–64.

Garvin, David A. *Learning in Action: A Guide to Putting the Learning Organization to Work*. Boston: Harvard Business School Press, 2000

Geisler, Eliezer. "Harnessing the Value of Experience in the Knowledge-Driven Firm." *Business Horizon* (May–June 1999): 18–25.

German, Kent. "Charity Beat: Newspapers are devoting more attention to covering philanthropies." *American Journalism Review* (September 2000). *www.ajr.newslink.org/ajrkentsept00.html*.

Gladwell, Malcolm. *The Tipping Point: How Little Things Can Make a Big Difference*. New York: Little Brown and Co., 2000.

Hansen, Morten T., Nitin Nohria and Thomas Tierney. "What's Your Strategy for Managing Knowledge?" *Harvard Business Review* (March–April 1999): 106–116.

Harreld, J. Bruce. "Building Smarter, Faster Organizations." In Don Tapscott, *Blueprint to the Digital Economy: Creating Wealth in the Era of New Business* (New York: McGraw-Hill, 1998): 60–76.

Hesselbein, Frances, Marshall Goldsmith and Richard Beckhard, eds. *The Organization of the Future*. New York: The Peter F. Drucker Foundation for Nonprofit Management, 1997.

Huang, Kuan-Tsae, Yang W. Lee and Richard Y Wang. *Quality Information and Knowledge*. Upper Saddle River, NJ: Prentice-Hall, Inc., 1999.

Jarboe, Kenan P. *Knowledge Management as an Economic Development Strategy*. Washington, DC: U.S. Economic Development Alliance, 2001. Available at *www.athenaalliance.org*

Litman, Jessica. *Digital Copyright*. Amherst, NY: Prometheus Books, 2001.

O'Dell, Carla and C. Jackson Grayson, Jr. *If Only We Knew What We Know*. New York: The Free Press, 1998.

Pfeffer, Jeffrey. "Will the Organization of the Future Make the Mistakes of the Past?" In Frances Hesselbein, Marshall Goldsmith and Richard Beckhard, eds., *The Organization of the Future* (New York: The Peter F. Drucker Foundation for Nonprofit Management, 1997): 43–51.

Porter, Michael and Mark Kramer. "Philanthropy's New Agenda: Creating Value." *Harvard Business Review* (November 1999).

Prahalad, C.K. and Venkratam Ramaswamy. "Co-opting Customer Competence." *Harvard Business Review* (January–February 2000): 79–87.

Stauber, Karl. "Mission-driven Philanthropy: What Do We Want to Accomplish and How Do We Do It?" *Nonprofit and Voluntary Sector Quarterly* 30, no. 2 (June 2001): 393–399.

Tapscott, Don. *Blueprint to the Digital Economy: Creating Wealth in the Era of New Business*. New York: McGraw-Hill, 1998.

Teece, David J. "Capturing Value from Knowledge Assets: The New Economy, Markets for Know-How, and Intangible Assets." *California Management Review* (Spring 1998): 55–79.

Wagner, Etienne and William Snyder. *Communities of Practice: The Organizational Frontier*. Boston: *Harvard Business Review* (January–February 2000): 139–145.

ACKNOWLEDGMENTS

This paper is part of the Project on Foundations in the Knowledge Economy. Project leaders are Lucy Bernholz, Blueprint Research & Design, Inc., Laura Breeden, Laura Breeden and Associates, Inc., and Rochelle Lefkowitz, ProMedia Communications, Inc.

The Project is made possible through the financial and intellectual support of the David and Lucile Packard Foundation. Barbara Kibbe and Gabriel Kasper have been instrumental advisers to this work. The Project is guided by an advisory committee, without which this paper would not exist. Paul Duguid, Katherine Fulton, Robert Horn, Nancy Kranich, Larry Lessig, Laurence Prusak, Tom Reis, and Hal Varian advised and revised the paper both individually and as a group. Finally, the staff of Blueprint Research & Design, Inc. patiently edited many versions of the paper and managed all of the project logistics. My colleagues at Blueprint also do the consulting work that feeds these concepts on a daily basis. My thanks to all. I alone am responsible for misrepresentations and mistakes.

Lucy Bernholz, *San Francisco, California, October 2001*

Index

Index

Index